Excel® Data Analysis

for
dummies®
A Wiley Brand

Excel Data Analysis

Analysis

5th Edition

by Paul McFedries

Excel® Data Analysis For Dummies®, 5th Edition

Published by: **John Wiley & Sons, Inc.**, 111 River Street, Hoboken, NJ 07030-5774, www.wiley.com

Copyright © 2022 by John Wiley & Sons, Inc., Hoboken, New Jersey

Media and software compilation copyright © 2022 by John Wiley & Sons, Inc. All rights reserved.

Published simultaneously in Canada

For general information on our other products and services, please contact our Customer Care Department within the U.S. at 877-762-2974, outside the U.S. at 317-572-3993, or fax 317-572-4002. For technical support, please visit https://hub.wiley.com/community/support/dummies.

Wiley publishes in a variety of print and electronic formats and by print-on-demand. Some material included with standard print versions of this book may not be included in e-books or in print-on-demand. If this book refers to media such as a CD or DVD that is not included in the version you purchased, you may download this material at http://booksupport.wiley.com. For more information about Wiley products, visit www.wiley.com.

Library of Congress Control Number is available from the publisher.

ISBN 978-1-119-84442-6 (pbk); ISBN 978-1-119-84446-4 (ebk); ISBN 978-1-119-84447-1 (ebk)

SKY10032303_010322

Contents at a Glance

Table of Contents

Introduction

The world is bursting at the seams with data. It's on our computers, it's in our networks, it's on the web. Some days, it seems to be in the very air itself, borne on the wind. But here's the thing: No one actually cares about data. A collection of data — whether it resides on your PC or some giant server somewhere — is really just a bunch of numbers and text, dates and times. No one cares about data because data doesn't *mean* anything. Data isn't cool. You know what's cool? *Knowledge* is cool. *Insight* is cool.

So how do you turn data into knowledge? How do you tweak data to generate insight? You need to organize that data, and then you need to sort it, filter it, run calculations on it, and summarize it. In a word, you need to *analyze* the data.

Now for the good news: If you have (or can get) that data into Excel, you have a giant basket of data-analysis tools at your disposal. Excel really seems to have been made with data analysis in mind, because it offers such a wide variety of features and techniques for organizing, manipulating, and summarizing just about anything that resides in a worksheet. If you can get your data into Excel, it will help you turn that data into knowledge and insight.

This book takes you on a tour of Excel's data-analysis tools. You learn everything you need to know to make your data spill its secrets and to uncover your data's hidden-in-plain-sight wisdom. Best of all, if you already know how to perform the basic Excel chores, you don't need to learn any other fancy-schmancy Excel techniques to get started in data analysis. Sweet? You bet.

About This Book

This book contains 16 chapters (and a bonus appendix), but that doesn't mean that you have to, as the King says gravely in *Alice's Adventures in Wonderland*, "Begin at the beginning and go on till you come to the end: Then stop." If you've done a bit of data-analysis work in the past, please feel free to dip into the book wherever it strikes your fancy. The chapters all present their data-analysis info and techniques in readily digestible, bite-sized chunks, so you can certainly graze your way through this book.

However, if you're brand spanking new to data analysis — particularly if you're not even sure what data analysis even *is* — no problem: I'm here to help. To get your data-analysis education off to a solid start, I highly recommend reading the book's first three chapters to get some of the basics down cold. From there, you can travel to more advanced territory, safe in the knowledge that you've got some survival skills to fall back on.

What You Can Safely Ignore

This book consists of several hundred pages. Do I expect you to read every word on every page? Yes, I do. Just kidding! No, of course I don't. Entire sections — heck, maybe even entire *chapters* — might contain information that's not relevant to what you do. That's fine and my feelings won't be hurt if you skim through (or — who's kidding whom? — skip over) those parts of the book.

If time (or attention) is short, what else might you want to ignore? Okay, in many places throughout the book I provide step-by-step instructions to complete some task. Each of those steps includes some bold type that gives you the basic instruction. In many cases, however, below that bold text I offer supplementary information to flesh out or extend or explain the bold instruction. Am I just showing off how much I know about all this stuff? Yes, sometimes. Do you have to read these extended instructions? Nope. Read the bold stuff, for sure, but feel free to skip the details if they seem unnecessary or unimportant.

Foolish Assumptions

This book is for people who are new (or relatively new) to Excel data analysis. That doesn't mean, however, that the book is suitable to people who have never used a PC, Microsoft Windows, or even Excel. So first I assume not only that you have a PC running Microsoft Windows but also that you've had some experience with both. (For the purposes of this book, that just means you know how to start and switch between programs.) I also assume that your PC has a recent version of Excel installed. What does "recent" mean? Well, this book is based on Excel 2021, but you should be fine if you're running Excel 365, Excel 2019, Excel 2016, or even Excel 2013.

As I said before, I do *not* assume that you're an Excel expert, but I do assume that you know at least the following Excel basics:

- » Creating, saving, opening, and switching between workbooks

- » Creating and switching between worksheets

- » Finding and running commands on the Ribbon

- » Entering numbers, text, dates, times, and formulas into worksheet cells

- » Working with Excel's basic worksheet functions

Icons Used in This Book

Like other books in the *For Dummies* series, this book uses icons, or little margin pictures, to flag things that don't quite fit into the flow of the chapter discussion. Here are the icons that I use:

REMEMBER

This icon marks text that contains some things that are useful or important enough that you'd do well to store the text somewhere safe in your memory for later recall.

TECHNICAL STUFF

This icon marks text that contains some for-nerds-only technical details or explanations that you're free to skip.

TIP

This icon marks text that contains a shortcut or an easier way to do things, which I hope will make your life — or, at least, the data-analysis portion of your life — more efficient.

WARNING

This icon marks text that contains a friendly but unusually insistent reminder to avoid doing something. You have been warned.

Beyond the Book

- » **Examples:** This book's sample Excel workbooks can be found by going to www.dummies.com/go/exceldataanalysisfd5e or at my website: www.paulmcfedries.com.

- » **Cheat Sheet:** To locate this book's cheat sheet, go to www.dummies.com and search for *Excel Data Analysis For Dummies*. See the cheat sheet for info on

Excel database functions, Boolean expressions, and important statistical terms.

>> **Updates:** If this book has any updates after printing, they will be posted to this book's page at www.dummies.com.

Where to Go from Here

If you're just getting your feet wet with Excel data analysis, flip the page and start perusing the first chapter.

If you have some experience with Excel data analysis or you have a special problem or question, use the Table of Contents or the index to find out where I cover that topic and then turn to that page.

Either way, happy analyzing!

1
Getting Started with Data Analysis

Understand data analysis and get to know basic analysis features such as conditional formatting and subtotals.

Discover Excel's built-in tools for analyzing data.

Learn how to build Excel tables that hold and store the data you need to analyze.

Find quick and easy ways to begin your analysis using simple statistics, sorting, and filtering.

Get practical stratagems and common-sense tactics for grabbing data from extra sources.

Chapter **1**

Learning Basic Data-Analysis Techniques

You are awash in data. Information multiplies around you so fast that you wonder how to make sense of it all. You think, "I know what to do. I'll paste the data into Excel. That way, at least the data will be nicely arranged in the worksheet cells, and I can add a little formatting to make things somewhat palatable." That's a fine start, but you're often called upon to do more with your data than make it merely presentable. Your boss, your customer, or perhaps just your curiosity requires you to divine some inner meaning from the jumble of numbers and text that litter your workbooks. In other words, you need to *analyze* your data to see what nuggets of understanding you can unearth.

This chapter gets you started down that data-analysis path by exploring a few straightforward but useful analytic techniques. After discovering what data analysis entails, you investigate a number of Excel data-analysis techniques, including conditional formatting, data bars, color scales, and icon sets. From there, you dive into some useful methods for summarizing your data, including subtotals, grouping, and consolidation. Before you know it, that untamed wilderness of a worksheet will be nicely groomed and landscaped.

What Is Data Analysis, Anyway?

Are you wondering, "What is data analysis, anyway?" That's an excellent question! Here's an answer that I unpack for you as I go along: *Data analysis* is the application of tools and techniques to organize, study, reach conclusions, and sometimes make predictions about a specific collection of information.

For example, a sales manager might use data analysis to study the sales history of a product, determine the overall trend, and produce a forecast of future sales. A scientist might use data analysis to study experimental findings and determine the statistical significance of the results. A family might use data analysis to find the maximum mortgage it can afford or how much it must put aside each month to finance retirement or the kids' education.

Cooking raw data

The point of data analysis is to understand information on some deeper, more meaningful level. By definition, *raw data* is a mere collection of facts that by themselves tell you little or nothing of any importance. To gain some understanding of the data, you must manipulate the data in some meaningful way. The purpose of manipulating data can be something as simple as finding the sum or average of a column of numbers or as complex as employing a full-scale regression analysis to determine the underlying trend of a range of values. Both are examples of data analysis, and Excel offers a number of tools — from the straightforward to the sophisticated — to meet even the most demanding needs.

Dealing with data

The *data* part of *data analysis* is a collection of numbers, dates, and text that represents the raw information you have to work with. In Excel, this data resides inside a worksheet, which makes the data available for you to apply Excel's satisfyingly large array of data-analysis tools.

Most data-analysis projects involve large amounts of data, and the fastest and most accurate way to get that data onto a worksheet is to import it from a non-Excel data source. In the simplest scenario, you can copy the data from a text file, a Word table, or an Access datasheet and then paste it into a worksheet. However, most business and scientific data is stored in large databases, so Excel offers tools to import the data you need into your worksheet. I talk about all this in more detail later in the book.

After you have your data in the worksheet, you can use the data as is to apply many data-analysis techniques. However, if you convert the range into a *table*, Excel treats the data as a simple database and enables you to apply a number of database-specific analysis techniques to the table.

Building data models

In many cases, you perform data analysis on worksheet values by organizing those values into a *data model*, a collection of cells designed as a worksheet version of some real-world concept or scenario. The model includes not only the raw data but also one or more cells that represent some analysis of the data. For example, a mortgage amortization model would have the mortgage data — interest rate, principal, and term — and cells that calculate the payment, principal, and interest over the term. For such calculations, you use formulas and Excel's built-in worksheet functions.

Performing what-if analysis

One of the most common data-analysis techniques is *what-if analysis,* for which you set up worksheet models to analyze hypothetical situations. The "what-if" part means that these situations usually come in the form of a question: "What happens to the monthly payment if the interest rate goes up by 2 percent?" "What will the sales be if you increase the advertising budget by 10 percent?" Excel offers four what-if analysis tools: data tables, Goal Seek, Solver, and scenarios, all of which I cover in this book.

Analyzing Data with Conditional Formatting

Many Excel worksheets contain hundreds of data values. You could try to make sense of such largish sets of data by creating complex formulas and wielding Excel's powerful data-analysis tools. However, just as you wouldn't use a steamroller to crush a tin can, sometimes these sophisticated techniques are too much tool for the job. For example, what if all you want are answers to simple questions such as the following:

>> Which cell values are less than 0?

>> What are the top 10 values?

>> Which cell values are above average, and which are below average?

These simple questions aren't easy to answer just by glancing at the worksheet, and the more numbers you're dealing with, the harder it gets. To help you eyeball your worksheets and answer these and similar questions, Excel lets you apply conditional formatting to the cells. Excel applies this special format only to cells that satisfy some condition, which Excel calls a *rule*. For example, you could apply formatting to display all negative values in a red font, or you could apply a filter to show only the top 10 values.

Highlighting cells that meet some criteria

A *conditional format* is formatting that Excel applies only to cells that meet the criteria you specify. For example, you can tell Excel to apply the formatting only if a cell's value is greater or less than some specified amount, between two specified values, or equal to some value. You can also look for cells that contain specified text, dates that occur during a specified time frame, and more.

When you set up your conditional format, you can specify the font, border, and background pattern. This formatting helps to ensure that the cells that meet your criteria stand out from the other cells in the range. Here are the steps to follow:

1. **Select the range you want to work with.**

Select just the data values you want to format. Don't select any surrounding data.

2. **Choose Home ⇨ Conditional Formatting.**

3. **Choose Highlight Cells Rules and then select the rule you want to use for the condition.**

You have six rules to play around with:

- **Greater Than:** Applies the conditional format to cells that have a value larger than a value that you specify.

- **Less Than:** Applies the conditional format to cells that have a value smaller than a value that you specify.

- **Between:** Applies the conditional format to cells that have a value that is greater than or equal to a minimum value that you specify and less than or equal to a maximum value that you specify.

- **Equal To:** Applies the conditional format to cells that have a value that is the same as a value that you specify.

- **Text that Contains:** Applies the conditional format to cells that include the text that you specify.

- **A Date Occurring:** Applies the conditional format to cells that have a date value that meets the condition that you specify (such as Yesterday, Last Week, or Next Month).

(I cover a seventh rule — Duplicate Values — later in this chapter.) A dialog box appears, the name of which depends on the rule you click in Step 3. For example, Figure 1-1 shows the dialog box for the Greater Than rule.

	A	B	C	D	E	F	G	H	I	J	K
2	Country Name	2007	2008	2009	2010	2011	2012	2013	2014	2015	2016
3	Afghanistan	13.7	3.6	21.0	8.4	6.1	14.4	3.9	2.7	1.3	2.4
4	Albania	5.9	3.8	3.4	3.7	2.6	1.4	1.0	1.8	2.2	3.4
5	Algeria	3.4	2.4	1.6	3.6	2.9	3.4	2.8	3.8	3.8	3.3
6	American Samoa	2.0	-2.6	-4.2	0.4	0.3	-4.4	-2.8	0.9	1.2	-2.6
7	Andorra	0.0	-8.6	-3.7	-5.4	-4.6	-1.6	0.4	2.3	0.8	1.2
8	Angola	22.6	13.8	2.4	3.4	3.9	5.2	6.8	4.8	3.0	-0.7
9	Antigua and Barbuda	9.3	0.0							4.1	5.3
10	Arab World	4.6	5.8							3.4	3.2
11	Argentina	9.0	4.1							2.6	-2.2
12	Armenia	13.7	6.9							3.2	0.2
13	Australia	3.7	3.7							2.4	2.8
14	Austria	3.6	1.5	-3.8	1.9	2.9	0.7	0.0	0.8	1.1	1.5
15	Azerbaijan	25.0	10.8	9.4	4.9	0.1	2.2	5.8	2.0	1.1	-3.1
16	Bahamas, The	1.4	-2.3	-4.2	1.5	0.6	3.1	-0.6	-1.2	-3.1	0.2
17	Bangladesh	7.1	6.0	5.0	5.6	6.5	6.5	6.0	6.1	6.6	7.1
18	Barbados	1.8	0.4	-4.0	0.3	0.5	0.3	0.0	0.0	0.9	2.0
19	Belarus	8.6	10.2	0.2	7.8	5.5	1.7	1.0	1.7	-3.8	-2.6

Dialog box overlay:
Greater Than
Format cells that are GREATER THAN:
5   with   Light Red Fill with Dark Red Text
OK   Cancel

FIGURE 1-1: The Greater Than dialog box and some highlighted values.

4. **Type the value to use for the condition.**

   You can also click the up arrow button that appears to the right of the text box and select a worksheet cell that contains the value. Also, depending on the operator, you might need to specify two values.

5. **Use the right drop-down list to select the formatting to apply to cells that match your condition.**

   If you're feeling creative, you can make up your own format by selecting the Custom Format command.

6. **Click OK.**

   Excel applies the formatting to cells that meet the condition you specified.

TIP

Excel enables you to specify multiple conditional formats for the same range. For example, you can set up one condition for cells that are greater than some value and a separate condition for cells that are less than some other value. You can apply unique formats to each condition. Keep the range selected and follow Steps 2 through 6 to configure the new condition.

Showing pesky duplicate values

You use conditional formatting mostly to highlight numbers greater than or less than some value, or dates occurring within some range. However, you can use conditional formatting also to look for duplicate values in a range. Why would you want to do that? The main reason is that many range or table columns require unique values. For example, a column of student IDs or part numbers shouldn't have duplicates.

Unfortunately, scanning such numbers and picking out the repeat values is hard. Not to worry! With conditional formatting, you can specify a font, border, and background pattern that ensures that any duplicate cells in a range or table stand out from the other cells. Here's what you do:

1. **Select the range that you want to check for duplicates.**

2. **Choose Home ⇨ Conditional Formatting.**

3. **Choose Highlight Cells Rules ⇨ Duplicate Values.**

   The Duplicate Values dialog box appears. The left drop-down list has Duplicate selected by default, as shown in Figure 1-2. However, if you want to highlight all the unique values instead of the duplicates, select Unique from this list.

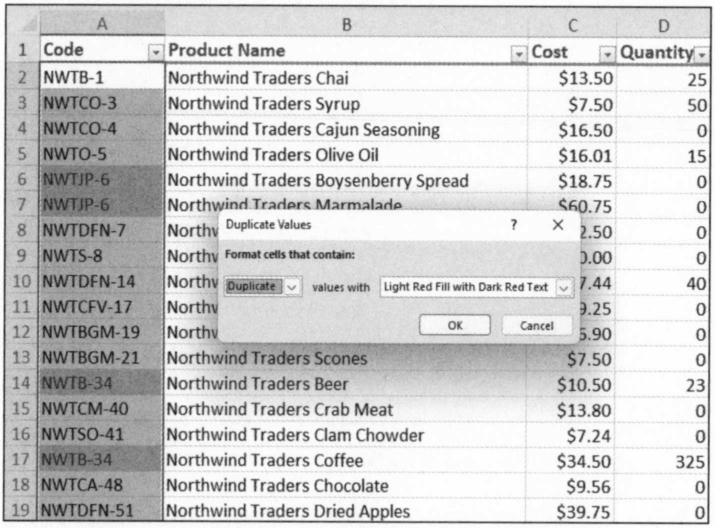

FIGURE 1-2:
Use the Duplicate Values rule to highlight worksheet duplicates.

4. **In the right drop-down list, select the formatting to apply to the cells with duplicate values.**

   You can create your own format by choosing the Custom Format command. In the Format Cells dialog box, use the Font, Border, and Fill tabs to specify the formatting you want to apply, and then click OK.

5. **Click OK.**

   Excel applies the formatting to any cells that have duplicate values in the range.

Highlighting the top or bottom values in a range

When analyzing worksheet data, looking for items that stand out from the norm is often useful. For example, you might want to know which sales reps sold the most last year, or which departments had the lowest gross margins. To quickly and easily view the extreme values in a range, you can apply a conditional format to the top or bottom values of that range.

You can apply such a format by setting up a *top/bottom rule*, in which Excel applies a conditional format to those items that are at the top or bottom of a range of values. For the top or bottom values, you can specify a number, such as the top 5 or 10, or a percentage, such as the bottom 20 percent. Here's how it works:

1. **Select the range you want to work with.**

2. **Choose Home ⇨ Conditional Formatting.**

3. **Choose Top/Bottom Rules and then select the type of rule you want to create.**

   You have six rules to mess with:

   - **Top 10 Items:** Applies the conditional format to cells that rank in the top X, where X is a number that you specify (the default is 10).

   - **Top 10 %:** Applies the conditional format to cells that rank in the top X %, where X is a number that you specify (the default is 10).

   - **Bottom 10 Items:** Applies the conditional format to cells that rank in the bottom X, where X is a number that you specify (the default is 10).

   - **Bottom 10 %:** Applies the conditional format to cells that rank in the bottom X %, where X is a number that you specify (the default is 10).

   - **Above Average:** Applies the conditional format to cells that rank above the average value of the range.

   - **Below Average:** Applies the conditional format to cells that rank below the average value of the range.

   A dialog box appears, the name of which depends on the rule you selected in Step 3. For example, Figure 1-3 shows the dialog box for the Top Ten Items rule.

4. **Type the value to use for the condition.**

   You can also click the spin buttons that appear to the right of the text box. Note that you don't need to enter a value for the Above Average and Below Average rules.

	A	B	C	D
1		Sales Rep	2017 Sales	2018 Sales
2		Nancy Freehafer	$996,336	$960,492
3		Andrew Cencini	$606,731	$577,983
4		Jan Kotas	$622,781	$967,580
5		Mariya Sergienko	$765,327	$771,399
6		Steven Thorpe	$863,589	$827,213
7		Michael Neipper	$795,518	$669,394
8			740	$626,945
9			059	$574,472
10			380	$827,932
11			623	$569,609
12			777	$558,601
13		Paul Durbin	$685,091	$692,182
14		Andrea Granek	$540,484	$693,762
15		Charles Aster	$650,733	$823,034
16		Karen Reilly	$509,863	$511,569
17		Karen Munson	$503,699	$975,455
18		Vince Voyatzis	$630,263	$599,514
19		Paul Sellars	$779,722	$596,353

Top 10 Items

Format cells that rank in the TOP:

5 with Light Red Fill with Dark Red Text

OK   Cancel

FIGURE 1-3:
The Top 10 Items
dialog box with
the top 5 values
highlighted.

5. **In the right drop-down list, select the formatting to apply to cells that match your condition.**

REMEMBER

When you set up your top/bottom rule, select a format that ensures that the cells that meet your criteria will stand out from the other cells in the range. If none of the predefined formats suits your needs, you can always choose Custom Format and then use the Format Cells dialog box to create a suitable formatting combination. Use the Font, Border, and Fill tabs to specify the formatting you want to apply, and then click OK.

6. **Click OK.**

Excel applies the formatting to cells that meet the condition you specified.

Analyzing cell values with data bars

In some data-analysis scenarios, you might be interested more in the relative values within a range than the absolute values. For example, if you have a table of products that includes a column showing unit sales, you might want to compare the relative sales of all products.

Comparing relative values is often easiest if you visualize the values, and one of the easiest ways to visualize data in Excel is to use *data bars*, a data visualization feature that applies colored horizontal bars to each cell in a range of values; these bars appear "behind" (that is, in the background of) the values in the range. The length of the data bar in each cell depends on the value in that cell: the larger the value, the longer the data bar.

Follow these steps to apply data bars to a range:

1. **Select the range you want to work with.**

2. **Choose Home ⇨ Conditional Formatting.**

3. **Choose Data Bars and then select the fill type of data bars you want to create.**

   You can apply two type of data bars:

   - **Gradient fill:** The data bars begin with a solid color and then gradually fade to a lighter color.

   - **Solid fill:** The data bars are a solid color.

   Excel applies the data bars to each cell in the range. Figure 1-4 shows an example in the Units column.

	A	B	C
1	Product Name	Units	$ Total
2	Northwind Traders Almonds	20	$ 200
3	Northwind Traders Beer	487	$ 6,818
4	Northwind Traders Boysenberry Spread	100	$ 2,500
5	Northwind Traders Cajun Seasoning	40	$ 880
6	Northwind Traders Chai	40	$ 720
7	Northwind Traders Chocolate	200	$ 2,550
8	Northwind Traders Chocolate Biscuits Mix	85	$ 782
9	Northwind Traders Clam Chowder	290	$ 2,799
10	Northwind Traders Coffee	650	$ 29,900
11	Northwind Traders Crab Meat	120	$ 2,208
12	Northwind Traders Curry Sauce	65	$ 2,600
13	Northwind Traders Dried Apples	40	$ 2,120
14	Northwind Traders Dried Pears	40	$ 1,200
15	Northwind Traders Dried Plums	75	$ 263
16	Northwind Traders Fruit Cocktail	40	$ 1,560
17	Northwind Traders Gnocchi	10	$ 380
18	Northwind Traders Green Tea	275	$ 822
19	Northwind Traders Long Grain Rice	40	$ 280
20	Northwind Traders Marmalade	40	$ 3,240
21	Northwind Traders Mozzarella	90	$ 3,132
22	Northwind Traders Olive Oil	25	$ 534

FIGURE 1-4: The higher the value, the longer the data bar.

TIP

If your range includes right-aligned values, gradient-fill data bars are a better choice than solid-fill data bars. Why? Because even the longest gradient-fill bars fade to white toward the right edge of the cell, so your range values will mostly appear on a white background, making them easier to read.

Analyzing cell values with color scales

Getting some idea about the overall distribution of values in a range is often useful. For example, you might want to know whether a range has many low values and just a few high values. Color scales can help you analyze your data in this way. A *color scale* compares the relative values in a range by applying shading to each cell, where the color reflects each cell's value.

Color scales can also tell you whether your data includes *outliers:* values that are much higher or lower than the others. Similarly, color scales can help you make value judgments about your data. For example, high sales and low numbers of product defects are good, whereas low margins and high employee turnover rates are bad.

To apply a color scale to a range of values, do the following:

1. **Select the range you want to format.**

2. **Choose Home ⇨ Conditional Formatting.**

3. **Choose Color Scales and then select the color scale that has the color scheme you want to apply.**

   Color scales come in two varieties: three-color scales and two-color scales.

TIP

If your goal is to look for outliers, go with a three-color scale because it helps the outliers stand out more. A three-color scale is also useful if you want to make value judgments about your data, because you can assign your own values to the colors (such as positive, neutral, and negative). Use a two-color scale when you want to look for patterns in the data, because a two-color scale offers less contrast.

Excel applies the color scale to each cell in your selected range.

Analyzing cell values with icon sets

Symbols that have common or well-known associations are often useful for analyzing large amounts of data. For example, a check mark usually means that something is good or finished or acceptable, whereas an X means that something is bad or unfinished or unacceptable. Similarly, a green circle is positive, whereas a red circle is negative (think traffic lights). Excel puts these and other symbolic associations to good use with the *icon sets* feature. You use icon sets to visualize the relative values of cells in a range.

REMEMBER

With icon sets, Excel adds a particular icon to each cell in the range, and that icon tells you something about the cell's value relative to the rest of the range. For example, the highest values might be assigned an upward-pointing arrow, the lowest values a downward-pointing arrow, and the values in between a horizontal arrow.

Here's how you apply an icon set to a range:

1. **Select the range you want to format with an icon set.**

2. **Choose Home ⇨ Conditional Formatting.**

3. **Choose Icon Sets and then select the type of icon set you want to apply.**

   Icon sets come in four categories:

   - **Directional:** Indicates trends and data movement

   - **Shapes:** Points out the high (green) and low (red) values in the range

   - **Indicators:** Adds value judgments

   - **Ratings:** Shows where each cell resides in the overall range of data values

   Excel applies the icons to each cell in the range, as shown in Figure 1-5.

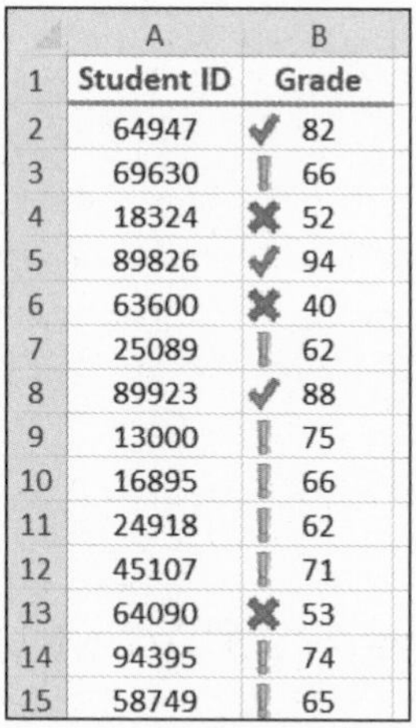

	A	B
1	Student ID	Grade
2	64947	✔ 82
3	69630	66
4	18324	✖ 52
5	89826	✔ 94
6	63600	✖ 40
7	25089	62
8	89923	✔ 88
9	13000	75
10	16895	66
11	24918	62
12	45107	71
13	64090	✖ 53
14	94395	74
15	58749	65

FIGURE 1-5: Excel applies an icon based on each cell's value.

Creating a custom conditional-formatting rule

The conditional-formatting rules in Excel — highlight cells rules, top/bottom rules, data bars, color scales, and icon sets — offer an easy way to analyze data through visualization. However, you can tailor your formatting-based data analysis also by creating a custom conditional-formatting rule that suits how you want to analyze and present the data.

REMEMBER

Custom conditional-formatting rules are ideal for situations in which normal value judgments — that is, that higher values are good and lower values are bad — don't apply. In a database of product defects, for example, lower values are better than higher ones. Similarly, data bars are based on the relative numeric values in a range, but you might prefer to base them on the relative percentages or on percentile rankings.

To get the type of data analysis you prefer, follow these steps to create a custom conditional-formatting rule and apply it to your range:

1. **Select the range you want to analyze with a custom conditional-formatting rule.**

2. **Choose Home ⇨ Conditional Formatting ⇨ New Rule.**

The New Formatting Rule dialog box appears.

3. **In the Select a Rule Type box, select the type of rule you want to create.**

4. **Use the controls in the Edit the Rule Description box to edit the rule's style and formatting.**

The controls you see depend on the rule type you selected in Step 3. For example, if you select Icon Sets, you see the controls shown in Figure 1-6.

TIP

With Icon Sets, select Reverse Icon Order (as shown in the figure) if you want to reverse the normal icon assignments.

5. **Click OK.**

Excel applies the conditional formatting to each cell in the range.

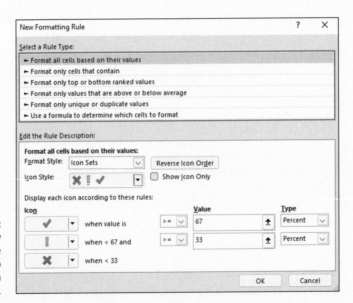

FIGURE 1-6:
Use the New Formatting Rule dialog box to create a custom rule.

TECHNICAL STUFF

HIGHLIGHT CELLS BASED ON A FORMULA

You can apply conditional formatting based on the results of a formula. That is, you set up a logical formula as the conditional-formatting criteria. For each cell in which that formula returns TRUE, Excel applies the formatting you specify; for all the other cells, Excel doesn't apply the formatting.

In most cases, you use a comparison formula, or you use an IF function, often combined with another logical function such as AND or OR. In each case, your formula's comparison value must reference only the first value in the range. For example, if the range you are working with is a set of dates in A2:A100, the comparison formula =WEEKDAY(A2)=6 would apply conditional formatting to every cell in the range that occurs on a Friday.

The following steps show you how to apply conditional formatting based on the results of a formula:

1. **Select the range you want to work with.**

2. **Choose Home ⇨ Conditional Formatting ⇨ New Rule.**

   The New Formatting Rule dialog box appears.

3. **Select Use a Formula to Determine Which Cells to Format.**

4. **In the Format Values Where this Formula Is True text box, type the logical formula.**

   The figure shows an example of using a formula to apply conditional formatting.

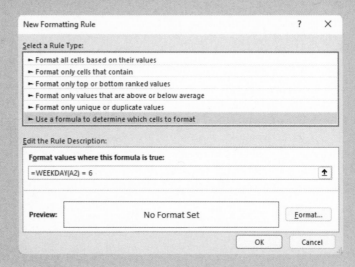

(continued)

(continued)

5. Choose Format, use the Format Cells dialog box to define the rule's style and formatting, and then click OK.

6. Click OK.

Excel applies the conditional formatting to each cell in the range in which the logical formula returns TRUE.

When you're messing around with formula-based rules, one useful technique is to apply a conditional format based on a formula that compares all the cells in a range to one value in that range. The simplest case is a formula that applies conditional formatting to those range cells that are equal to a cell value in the range. Here's the logical formula to use for such a comparison:

=range=cell

Here, *range* is an absolute reference to the range of cells you want to work with, and *cell* is a relative reference to the comparison cell. For example, to apply a conditional format to those cells in the range A1:A50 that are equal to the value in cell A1, you would use the following logical formula:

=$A$1 : $A$50=A1

Editing a conditional-formatting rule

Conditional-formatting rules are excellent data-visualization tools that can make analyzing your data easier and faster. Whether you're highlighting cells based on criteria, showing cells in the top or bottom of a range, or using features such as data bars, color scales, and icon sets, conditional formatting enables you to interpret your data quickly.

But it doesn't follow that all your conditional-formatting experiments will be successful ones. For example, you might find that the conditional formatting you used isn't working out because it doesn't let you visualize your data the way you'd hoped. Similarly, a change in data might require a change in the condition you used. Whatever the reason, you can edit your conditional-formatting rules to ensure that you get the best visualization for your data. Here's how:

1. Select a cell in the range that includes the conditional-formatting rule you want to edit.

You can select a single cell, multiple cells, or the entire range.

2. Choose Home ➪ Conditional Formatting ➪ Manage Rules.

The Conditional Formatting Rules Manager dialog box appears, as shown in Figure 1-7.

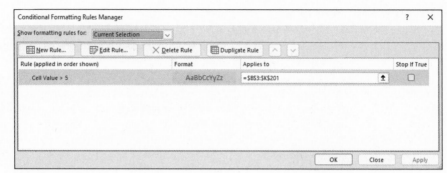

FIGURE 1-7:
Use the
Conditional
Formatting Rules
Manager to edit
your rules.

3. **Select the rule you want to modify.**

   If you don't see the rule, click the Show Formatting Rules For drop-down list
   and then select This Worksheet. The list that appears displays every
   conditional-formatting rule that you've applied in the current worksheet.

4. **Choose Edit Rule.**

   The Edit Formatting Rule dialog box appears.

5. **Make your changes to the rule.**

6. **Click OK.**

   Excel returns you to the Conditional Formatting Rules Manager dialog box.

7. **Select OK.**

   Excel updates the conditional formatting.

WARNING

If you have multiple conditional-formatting rules applied to a range, the visualization
is affected by the order in which Excel applies the rules. Specifically, if a cell already
has a conditional format applied, Excel does not overwrite that format with a new
one. For example, suppose that you have two conditional-formatting rules applied to
a list of student grades: one for grades over 90 and one for grades over 80. If you apply
the over-80 conditional format first, Excel will never apply the over-90 format
because those values are already covered by the over-80 format. The solution is to
change the order of the rule. In the Conditional Formatting Rules Manager dialog box,
select the rule that you want to modify and then click the Move Up and Move Down
button to set the order you want. If you want Excel to stop processing the rest of the
rules after it has applied a particular rule, select that rule's Stop If True check box.

Removing conditional-formatting rules

Conditional-formatting rules are useful critters, but they don't work in all scenarios. For example, if your data is essentially random, conditional-formatting
rules won't magically produce patterns in that data. You might also find that

conditional formatting isn't helpful for certain collections of data or certain types of data. Or you might find conditional formatting useful for getting a handle on your data set but then prefer to remove the formatting.

Similarly, although the data-visualization aspect of conditional-formatting rules is part of the appeal of this Excel feature, as with all things visual, you can overdo it. That is, you might end up with a worksheet that has multiple conditional-formatting rules and therefore some unattractive and confusing combinations of highlighted cells, data bars, color scales, and icon sets.

If, for whatever reason, you find that a range's conditional formatting isn't helpful or is no longer required, you can remove the conditional formatting from that range by following these steps:

1. **Select a cell in the range that includes the conditional-formatting rule you want to trash.**

   You can select a single cell, multiple cells, or the entire range.

2. **Choose Home ⇨ Conditional Formatting ⇨ Manage Rules.**

   The Conditional Formatting Rules Manager dialog box appears.

3. **Select the rule you want to remove.**

   If you don't see the rule, use the Show Formatting Rules For list to select This Worksheet, which tells Excel to display every conditional-formatting rule that you've applied in the current worksheet.

4. **Choose Delete Rule.**

   Excel removes the rule from the range.

5. **Click OK.**

TIP

If you have multiple rules defined and want to remove them all, click the Home tab, choose Conditional Formatting, choose Clear Rules, and then select either Clear Rules from Selected Cells or Clear Rules from Entire Sheet.

Summarizing Data with Subtotals

Although you can use formulas and worksheet functions to summarize your data in various ways — including sums, averages, counts, maximums, and minimums — if you're in a hurry, or if you just need a quick summary of your data, you can get Excel to do the work for you. The secret here is a feature called *automatic subtotals*, which are formulas that Excel adds to a worksheet automatically.

REMEMBER

Excel sets up automatic subtotals based on data groupings in a selected field. For example, if you ask for subtotals based on the Customer field, Excel runs down the Customer column and creates a new subtotal each time the name changes. To get useful summaries, you should sort the range on the field containing the data groupings you're interested in.

Follow these steps to summarize your data with subtotals:

1. Select a cell within the range you want to subtotal.

2. Choose Data ⇨ Subtotal.

If you don't see the Subtotal command, choose Outline ⇨ Subtotal. The Subtotal dialog box appears.

3. In the At Each Change In list, select the column you want to use to group the subtotals.

4. In the Use Function list, select Sum.

5. In the Add Subtotal To list, select the check box for the column you want to summarize.

In Figure 1-8, for example, each change in the Customer field displays the sum of that customer's Total cells.

6. Click OK.

Excel calculates the subtotals and adds them into the range. Note, too, that Excel also adds outline symbols to the range. I talk about outlining in a bit more detail in the next section.

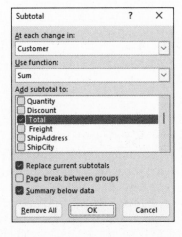

FIGURE 1-8:
Use the Subtotal dialog box to apply subtotals to a range.

Figure 1-9 shows some subtotals applied to a range.

H7			f_x =SUBTOTAL(9,H2:H6)					
	A	B	C	E	F	G	H	I
1	Customer	Country	Region	Unit Price	Quantity	Discount	Total	Freight
2	Cactus Comidas para llevar	Argentina		$ 46.00	7	0%	$ 322.00	$ 19.76
3	Cactus Comidas para llevar	Argentina		$ 7.75	20	0%	$ 155.00	$ 19.76
4	Cactus Comidas para llevar	Argentina		$ 15.00	10	0%	$ 150.00	$ 2.84
5	Cactus Comidas para llevar	Argentina		$ 45.60	8	0%	$ 364.80	$ 31.51
6	Cactus Comidas para llevar	Argentina		$ 14.00	20	0%	$ 280.00	$ 31.51
7	**Cactus Comidas para llevar Total**						$ 1,271.80	
8	Océano Atlántico Ltda.	Argentina		$ 6.00	5	0%	$ 30.00	$ 1.27
9	Océano Atlántico Ltda.	Argentina		$ 21.35	20	0%	$ 427.00	$ 49.56
10	Océano Atlántico Ltda.	Argentina		$ 30.00	6	0%	$ 180.00	$ 49.56
11	Océano Atlántico Ltda.	Argentina		$ 34.80	5	0%	$ 174.00	$ 49.56
12	Océano Atlántico Ltda.	Argentina		$ 21.00	30	0%	$ 630.00	$217.86
13	Océano Atlántico Ltda.	Argentina		$ 81.00	15	0%	$ 1,215.00	$217.86
14	Océano Atlántico Ltda.	Argentina		$ 18.00	10	0%	$ 180.00	$217.86
15	Océano Atlántico Ltda.	Argentina		$ 13.00	15	0%	$ 195.00	$217.86
16	**Océano Atlántico Ltda. Total**						$ 3,031.00	
17	Rancho grande	Argentina		$ 81.00	5	0%	$ 405.00	$ 90.85
18	Rancho grande	Argentina		$263.50	2	0%	$ 527.00	$ 90.85
19	Rancho grande	Argentina		$ 17.45	6	0%	$ 104.70	$ 63.77
20	Rancho grande	Argentina		$ 32.00	6	0%	$ 192.00	$ 63.77
21	Rancho grande	Argentina		$ 19.50	20	0%	$ 390.00	$ 63.77
22	**Rancho grande Total**						$ 1,618.70	

FIGURE 1-9:
Some subtotals applied to the Total column for each customer.

REMEMBER

Note that in the phrase, *automatic subtotals,* the word *subtotals* is misleading because it implies that you can summarize your data only with totals. Not even close! Using "subtotals," you can also count the values (all the values or just the numeric values), calculate the average of the values, determine the maximum or minimum value, and calculate the product of the values. For statistical analysis, you can also calculate the standard deviation and variance, both of a sample and of a population. To change the summary calculation, follow Steps 1 to 3, open the Use Function drop-down list, and then select the function you want to use for the summary.

Grouping Related Data

To help you analyze a worksheet, you might be able to control what parts of the worksheet are displayed by grouping the data based on the worksheet formulas and data. Grouping the data creates a worksheet outline, which works similarly to the outline feature in Microsoft Word. In a worksheet outline, you can *collapse* sections of the sheet to display only summary cells (such as quarterly or regional totals), or *expand* hidden sections to show the underlying detail. Note that when you add subtotals to a range, as I describe in the preceding section, Excel automatically groups the data and displays the outline tools.

REMEMBER

Not all worksheets can be grouped, so you need to make sure that your worksheet is a candidate for outlining:

>> The worksheet must contain formulas that reference cells or ranges directly adjacent to the formula cell. Worksheets with SUM functions that subtotal cells above or to the left are particularly good candidates for outlining.

>> There must be a consistent pattern to the direction of the formula references. For example, a worksheet with formulas that always reference cells above or to the left can be outlined. Excel won't outline a worksheet with, say, SUM functions where some of the range references are above the formula cell and some are below.

Here are the steps to follow group-related data:

1. **Display the worksheet you want to outline.**

2. **Choose Data ⇨ Group ⇨ Auto Outline.**

If you don't see the Group command, choose Outline ⇨ Group. Excel outlines the worksheet data.

As shown in Figure 1-10, Excel uses *level bars* to indicate the grouped ranges and *level numbers* to indicate the various levels of the underlying data available in the outline.

Level bar

Level numbers   Collapse button   Expand button

	A	B	C	D	E	I	M	Q	R
1		Jan	Feb	Mar	1st Quarter	2nd Quarter	3rd Quarter	4th Quarter	TOTAL
2	*Sales*								
3	Division I	23,500	23,000	24,000	70,500	75,500	74,000	74,000	294,000
4	Division II	28,750	27,800	29,500	86,050	91,500	90,000	91,000	358,550
5	Division III	24,400	24,000	25,250	73,650	80,350	77,500	78,500	310,000
6	SALES TOTAL	76,650	74,800	78,750	230,200	247,350	241,500	243,500	962,550
7	*Expenses*								
8	Cost of Goods	6,132	5,984	6,700	18,816	19,788	19,320	19,480	77,404
9	Advertising	4,600	4,200	5,200	14,000	15,750	15,900	14,900	60,550
10	Rent	2,100	2,100	2,100	6,300	6,300	6,300	6,300	25,200
11	Supplies	1,300	1,200	1,400	3,900	3,950	4,100	4,000	15,950
12	Salaries	16,000	16,000	16,500	48,500	50,000	51,000	52,000	201,500
13	Shipping	14,250	13,750	14,500	42,500	44,250	44,000	46,500	177,250
14	Utilities	500	600	600	1,700	1,800	1,850	1,925	7,275
15	EXPENSES TOTAL	44,882	43,834	47,000	135,716	141,838	142,470	145,105	565,129
16	GROSS PROFIT	31,768	30,966	31,750	94,484	105,512	99,030	98,395	397,421

FIGURE 1-10:
When you group a range, Excel displays its outlining tools.

Here are some ways you can use the outline to control the range display:

>> Click the – (collapse) button to hide the range indicated by the level bar.

>> Click the + button (expand) for a collapsed range to view it again.

>> Click a level number to collapse multiple ranges on the same outline level.

>> Click a level number to display multiple collapsed ranges on the same outline level.

Consolidating Data from Multiple Worksheets

Companies often distribute similar worksheets to multiple departments to capture budget numbers, inventory values, survey data, and so on. Those worksheets must then be combined into a summary report showing company-wide totals. Combining multiple worksheets into a summary report is called *consolidating* the data.

Sounds like a lot of work, right? It sure is, if you do it manually, so forget that. Instead, Excel can consolidate your data automatically. You can use the consolidate feature to consolidate the data in either of two ways:

>> **By position:** Excel consolidates the data from two or more worksheets, using the same range coordinates on each sheet. Use this method if the worksheets you're consolidating have an identical layout.

>> **By category:** Excel consolidates the data from two or more worksheets by looking for identical row and column labels in each sheet. Reach for this method if the worksheets you're consolidating have different layouts but common labels.

In both cases, you specify one or more *source ranges* (the ranges that contain the data you want to consolidate) and a *destination range* (the range where the consolidated data will appear).

Consolidating by position

Here are the steps to trudge through if you want to consolidate multiple worksheets by position:

1. **Create a new worksheet that uses the same layout — including row and column labels — as the sheets you want to consolidate.**

   The identical layout in this new worksheet is your destination range.

2. **If necessary, open the workbooks that contain the worksheets you want to consolidate.**

   If the worksheets you want to consolidate are in the current workbook, you can skip this step.

3. **In the new worksheet from Step 1, select the upper-left corner of the destination range.**

4. **Choose Data ⇨ Consolidate.**

   The Consolidate dialog box appears.

5. **In the Function list, select the summary function you want to use.**

6. **In the Reference text box, select one of the ranges you want to consolidate.**

7. **Click Add.**

   Excel adds the range to the All References list, as shown in Figure 1-11.

8. **Repeat Steps 6 and 7 to add all the consolidation ranges.**

9. **Click OK.**

   Excel consolidates the data from the source ranges and displays the summary in the destination range.

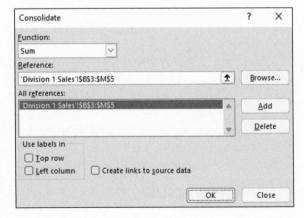

FIGURE 1-11: Consolidate multiple worksheets by adding a range from each one.

TIP

If the source data changes, you probably want to reflect those changes in the consolidation worksheet. Rather than run the entire consolidation over again, a much easier solution is to select the Create Links to Source Data check box in the Consolidate dialog box. You can then update the consolidation worksheet by choosing Data ⇨ Refresh All.

Consolidating by category

Here are the steps to follow to consolidate multiple worksheets by category:

1. **Create a new worksheet for the consolidation.**

   You use this worksheet to specify your destination range.

2. **If necessary, open the workbooks that contain the worksheets you want to consolidate.**

   If the worksheets you want to consolidate are in the current workbook, you can skip this step.

3. **In the new worksheet from Step 1, select the upper-left corner of the destination range.**

4. **Choose Data ⇨ Consolidate.**

   The Consolidate dialog box appears.

5. **In the Function list, select the summary function you want to use.**

6. **In the Reference text box, select one of the ranges you want to consolidate.**

   When you're selecting the range, be sure to include the row and column labels in the range.

7. **Click Add.**

   Excel adds the range to the All References list.

8. **Repeat Steps 6 and 7 to add all the consolidation ranges.**

9. **If you have labels in the top row of each range, select the Top Row check box.**

10. **If you have labels in the left-column row of each range, select the Left Column check box.**

    Figure 1-12 shows a completed version of the Consolidate dialog box.

11. **Click OK.**

    Excel consolidates the data from the source ranges and displays the summary in the destination range.

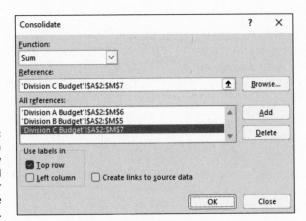

FIGURE 1-12:
When consolidating by category, tell Excel where your labels are located.

Chapter **2**

Working with Data-Analysis Tools

When it comes to data analysis, you're best off getting Excel to perform most — or, ideally, all — of the work. After all, Excel is a complex, powerful, and expensive piece of software, so why shouldn't it take on the lion's share of the data-analysis chores? Sure, you still have to get your data into the worksheet (although a bit later in the book, I talk about ways to get Excel to help with that chore, too), but after you've done that, it's time for Excel to get busy.

In this chapter, you investigate some built-in Excel tools that will handle most of the data-analysis dirty work. I show you how to build two different types of data tables; give you the details on using the very cool Goal Seek tool; delve into scenarios and how to use them for fun and profit; and take you on a tour of the powerful Solver add-in.

Working with Data Tables

If you want to study the effect that different input values have on a formula, one solution is to set up the worksheet model and then manually change the formula's input cells. For example, if you're calculating a loan payment, you can enter different interest rate values to see what effect changing the value has on the payment.

The problem with modifying the values of a formula input is that you see only a single result at one time. A better solution is to set up a *data table*, which is a range that consists of the formula you're using and multiple input values for that formula. Excel automatically creates a solution to the formula for each different input value.

Data tables are an example of *what-if analysis*, which is perhaps the most basic method for analyzing worksheet data. With what-if analysis, you first calculate a formula D, based on the input from variables A, B, and C. You then say, "What happens to the result if I change the value of variable A?" "What happens if I change B or C?" and so on.

Don't confuse data tables with the Excel tables that I talk about in Chapter 3. Remember that a data table is a special range that Excel uses to calculate multiple solutions to a formula.

Creating a basic data table

The most basic type of data table is one that varies only one of the formula's input cells. Not even remotely surprisingly, this basic version is known far and wide as a *one-input data table*. Here are the steps to follow to create a one-input data table:

1. **Type the input values.**

    - To enter the values in a column, start the column one cell down and one cell to the left of the cell containing the formula, as shown in Figure 2-1.

    - To enter the values in a row, start the row one cell up and one cell to the right of the cell containing the formula.

2. **Select the range that includes the input values and the formula.**

    In the example shown in Figure 2-1, you'd select the range B7:C15.

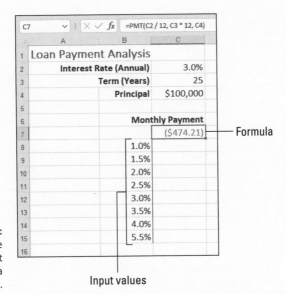

FIGURE 2-1:
This data table has the input values in a column.

Input values

3. **Choose Data ⇨ What-If Analysis ⇨ Data Table to open the Data Table dialog box.**

4. **Enter the address of the *input cell*, which is the cell referenced by the formula that you want the data table to vary.**

   That is, for whatever cell you specify, the data table will substitute each of its input values into that cell and calculate the formula result. You have two choices:

   - If you entered the input values in a row, enter the input cell's address in the Row Input Cell text box.

   - If the input values are in a column, enter the input cell's address in the Column Input Cell text box. In the example shown in Figure 2-1, the data table's input values are annual interest rates, so the column input cell is C2, as shown in Figure 2-2.

5. **Click OK.**

   Excel fills the input table with the results. Figure 2-3 shows the results of the example data table.

WARNING

When you see the data table results, you might find that all the calculated values are identical. What gives? The problem most likely is Excel's current calculation mode. Choose Formulas ⇨ Calculation Options ⇨ Automatic, and the data table results should recalculate to the correct values.

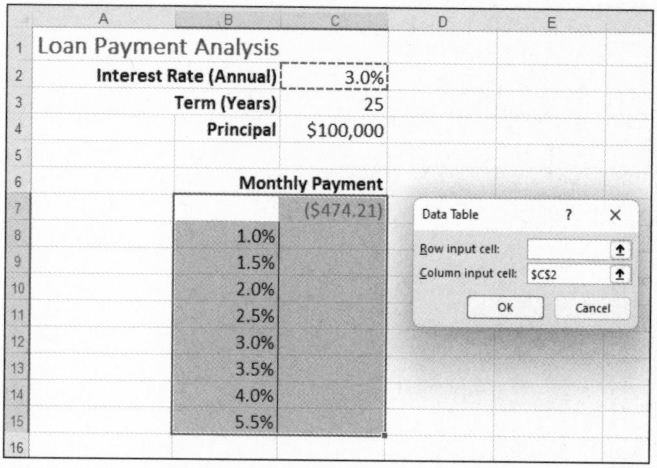

FIGURE 2-2:
Enter the address
of the input cell.

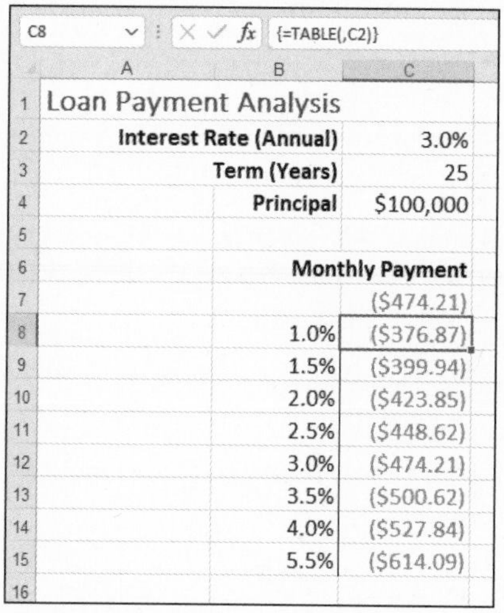

FIGURE 2-3:
The data table
results.

Creating a two-input data table

Rather than vary a single formula input at a time — as in the one-input data table I discuss in the preceding section — Excel also lets you kick things up a notch by enabling you to set up a *two-input* data table. As you might have guessed, a two-input data table is one that varies two formula inputs at the same time. For example, in a loan payment worksheet, you could set up a two-input data table that varies both the interest rate and the term.

To set up a two-input data table, you must set up two ranges of input cells. One range must appear in a column directly below the formula, and the other range must appear in a row directly to the right of the formula. Here are the steps to follow:

1. Type the input values:

- To enter the column values, start the column one cell down and one cell to the left of the cell containing the formula.

- To enter the row values, start the row one cell up and one cell to the right of the cell containing the formula.

Figure 2-4 shows an example.

B7		✕ ✓ *fx*	=PMT(C2 / 12, C3 * 12, C4)			
	A	B	C	D	E	F
1	Loan Payment Analysis					
2		Interest Rate (Annual)	3.0%			
3		Term (Years)	25			
4		Principal	$100,000			
5						
6		Monthly Payment		Term		
7		($474.21)	15	20	25	30
8		1.0%				
9		1.5%				
10		2.0%				
11	Interest Rate	2.5%				
12		3.0%				
13		3.5%				
14		4.0%				
15		5.5%				
16						

FIGURE 2-4: For a two-input data table, enter one set of values in a column and the other in a row.

2. Select the range that includes the input values and the formula.

In the example shown in Figure 2-4, you'd select the range B7:F15.

3. Choose Data ⇨ What-If Analysis ⇨ Data Table to open the Data Table dialog box.

4. In the Row Input Cell text box, enter the cell address of the input cell that corresponds to the row values you entered.

In the example shown in Figure 2-4, the row values are term inputs, so the input cell is C3 (see Figure 2-5).

5. In the Column Input Cell text box, enter the cell address of the input cell you want to use for the column values.

In the example shown in Figure 2-4, the column values are interest rate inputs, so the input cell is C2 (refer to Figure 2-5).

6. Click OK.

Excel displays the results. Figure 2-6 shows the results of the example two-input data table.

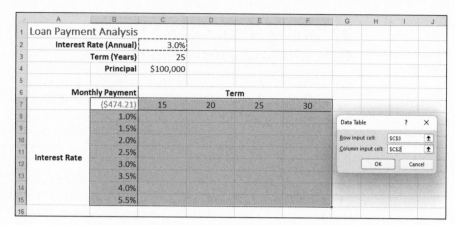

FIGURE 2-5:
Enter the addresses of the input cells.

FIGURE 2-6:
The two-input data table results.

When you run the Data Table command, Excel enters an array formula in the interior of the data table. The formula is a TABLE function (a special function available only by using the Data Table command) with the following syntax:

```
{=TABLE(row_input_ref, column_input_ref)}
```

Here, `row_input_ref` and `column_input_ref` are the cell references you entered in the Data Table dialog box. The braces ({ }) indicate an array, which means you can't change or delete individual elements in the results. If you want to change the results, you need to select the entire data table and then run the Data Table command again. If you want to delete the results, you must select the entire array and then delete it.

Skipping data tables when calculating workbooks

Because a data table is an array, Excel treats it as a unit, so a worksheet recalculation means that the entire data table is always recalculated. Such a recalculation is not a big problem for a small data table that has just a few dozen formulas. However, it's not uncommon to have data tables with hundreds or even thousands of formulas, and these larger data tables can slow down worksheet recalculation.

If you're working with a large data table, you can reduce the time it takes for Excel to recalculate the workbook if you configure Excel to bypass data tables when it's running the recalculation. Here are the two methods you can use:

>> Choose Formulas ⇨ Calculation Options ⇨ Automatic Except for Data Tables.

>> Choose File ⇨ Options to open the Excel Options dialog box, choose Formulas, select the Automatic Except for Data Tables option, and then click OK.

Now every time you calculate a workbook, Excel bypasses the data tables.

TIP

When you want to recalculate a data table, you can repeat either of the preceding procedures and then choose the Automatic option. On the other hand, if you prefer to leave the Automatic Except for Data Tables option selected, you can still recalculate the data table by selecting any cell in the data table and either choosing Formulas ⇨ Calculate Now or pressing F9.

Analyzing Data with Goal Seek

What if you already know the formula result you need and you want to produce that result by tweaking one of the formula's input values? For example, suppose that you know that you need to have $100,000 saved for your children's college education. In other words, you want to start an investment now that will be worth $100,000 at some point in the future.

This is called a *future value* calculation, and it requires three parameters:

>> The term of the investment

>> The interest rate you earn on the investment

>> The amount of money you invest each year

Assume that you need that money 18 years from now and that you can make a 4 percent annual return on your investment. Here's the question that remains: How much should you invest each year to make your goal?

Sure, you could waste large chunks of your life guessing the answer. Fortunately, you don't have to, because you can put Excel's Goal Seek tool to work. Goal Seek works by trying dozens of possibilities — called *iterations* — that enable it to get closer and closer to a solution. When Goal Seek finds a solution (or finds a solution that's as close as it can get), it stops and shows you the result.

You must do three things to set up your worksheet for Goal Seek:

>> Set up one cell as the *changing cell,* which is the formula input cell value that Goal Seek will manipulate to reach the goal. In the college fund example, the formula cell that holds the annual deposit is the changing cell.

>> Set up the other input values for the formula and give them proper initial values. In the college fund example, you enter 4 percent for the interest rate and 18 years for the term.

>> Create a formula for Goal Seek to use to reach the goal. In the college fund example, you use the FV() function, which calculates the future value of an investment given an interest rate, term, and regular deposit.

When your worksheet is ready for action, here are the steps to follow to get Goal Seek on the job:

1. **Select Data ⇨ What-If Analysis ⇨ Goal Seek.**

   The Goal Seek dialog box appears.

2. **In the Set Cell box, enter the address of the cell that contains the formula you want Goal Seek to work with.**

3. **In the To Value text box, enter the value that you want Goal Seek to find.**

4. **In the By Changing Cell box, enter the address of the cell that you want Goal Seek to modify.**

   Figure 2-7 shows an example model for the college fund calculation as well as the completed Goal Seek dialog box.

5. **Click OK.**

   Goal Seek adjusts the changing cell value until it reaches a solution. When it's done, the formula shows the value you entered in Step 3, as shown in Figure 2-8.

6. **Click OK to accept the solution.**

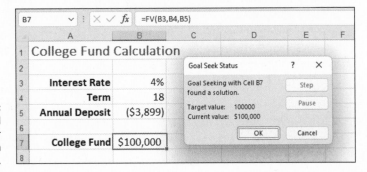

FIGURE 2-7:
Using Goal Seek to calculate the annual deposit required to end up with $100,000 in a college fund.

FIGURE 2-8:
Goal Seek took all of a second or two to find a solution.

TECHNICAL STUFF

In some cases, Goal Seek might not find an exact solution to your model. Goal Seek stops either after 100 iterations or if the current result is within 0.001 of the desired result.

You can get a more accurate solution by increasing the number of iterations that Goal Seek can use, by reducing the value that Goal Seek uses to mark a solution as close enough, or both. Choose File ➪ Options and then choose Formulas. Increase the value of the Maximum Iterations spin button, decrease the value in the Maximum Change text box, or both, and then click OK.

Analyzing Data with Scenarios

Many formulas require a number of input values to produce a result. Previously in this chapter, in the "Working with Data Tables" section, I talk about using data tables to quickly see the results of varying one or two of those input values. Handy stuff, for sure, but when you're analyzing a formula's results, manipulating three or more input values at a time and performing this manipulation in some systematic way often help. For example, one set of values might represent a best-case approach, whereas another might represent a worst-case approach.

In Excel, each of these coherent sets of input values — known as *changing cells* — is called a *scenario.* By creating multiple scenarios, you can quickly apply these different value sets to analyze how the result of a formula changes under different conditions.

Excel scenarios are a powerful data-analysis tool for a number of reasons. First, Excel enables you to enter up to 32 changing cells in a single scenario, so you can create models that are as elaborate as you need. Second, no matter how many changing cells you have in a scenario, Excel enables you to show the scenario's result with just a few taps or clicks. Third, because the number of scenarios you can define is limited only by the available memory on your computer, you can effectively use as many scenarios as you need to analyze your data model.

REMEMBER

When building a worksheet model, you can use a couple of techniques to make the model more suited to scenarios:

>> Group all your changing cells in one place and label them.

>> Make sure that each changing cell is a constant value. If you use a formula for a changing cell, another cell could change the formula result and throw off your scenarios.

Create a scenario

If scenarios sound like your kind of data-analysis tool, follow these steps to create a scenario for a worksheet model that you've set up:

1. Choose Data ➪ What-If Analysis ➪ Scenario Manager.

The Scenario Manager dialog box appears.

2. Click Add.

The Add Scenario dialog box appears.

3. In the Scenario Name box, type a name for the scenario.

4. In the Changing Cells box, enter the cells you want to change in the scenario.

You can type the address of each cell or range, separating each by a comma, or you can select the changing cells directly in the worksheet.

TIP

5. In the Comment box, enter a description for the scenario.

Your scenarios appear in the Scenario Manager dialog box, and for each scenario, you see its changing cells and its description. The description is often very useful, particularly if you have several scenarios defined, so be sure to write a detailed description to help you differentiate your scenarios later on.

Figure 2-9 shows a worksheet model for a mortgage analysis and a filled-in Add Scenario dialog box.

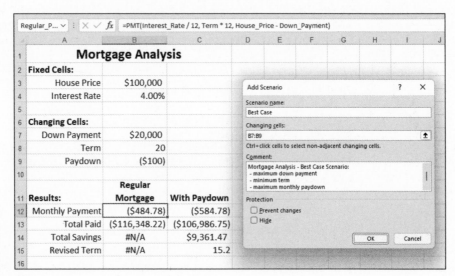

FIGURE 2-9: Creating a scenario for a mortgage analysis.

6. Click OK.

The Scenario Values dialog box appears.

7. In the text boxes, enter a value for each changing cell.

Figure 2-10 shows some example values for a scenario.

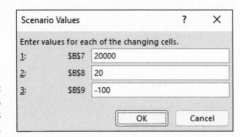

FIGURE 2-10: Example values for a scenario's changing cells.

8. To add more scenarios, click Add and then repeat Steps 3 through 7.

9. Click OK.

The Scenario Values dialog box closes and then the Scenario Manager dialog box returns, showing the scenarios you've added.

10. Click Close.

Apply a scenario

The real value of a scenario is that no matter how many changing cells you've defined or how complicated the formula is, you can apply any scenario with just a few straightforward steps. Don't believe me? Here, I'll prove it:

1. Choose Data ⇨ What-If Analysis ⇨ Scenario Manager.

The Scenario Manager dialog box appears.

2. Select the scenario you want to display.

3. Click Show.

Without even a moment's hesitation, Excel enters the scenario values into the changing cells and displays the formula result.

4. Feel free to repeat Steps 2 and 3 to display other scenarios. When it's this easy, why not?

5. When you've completed your analysis, click Close.

Edit a scenario

If you need to make changes to a scenario, you can edit the name, the changing cells, the description, and the scenario's input values. Here are the steps to follow:

1. Choose Data ⇨ What-If Analysis ⇨ Scenario Manager.

The Scenario Manager dialog box appears.

2. Select the scenario you want to modify.

3. Click Edit.

The Edit Scenario dialog box appears.

4. Modify the scenario name, changing cells, and comment, as needed.

5. Click OK.

The Scenario Values dialog box appears.

6. Modify the scenario values, as needed.

7. Click OK.

Excel returns you to the Scenario Manager dialog box.

8. Click Close.

Delete a scenario

If you have a scenario that has worn out its welcome, you should delete it to reduce clutter in the Scenario Manager dialog box. Here are the steps required:

1. Choose Data ➪ What-If Analysis ➪ Scenario Manager.

The Scenario Manager dialog box appears.

2. Select the scenario you want to remove.

Excel does not ask you to confirm the deletion, so double- (perhaps even triple-) check that you've selected the correct scenario.

WARNING

3. Click Delete.

Scenario Manager gets rids of the scenario.

4. Click Close.

Optimizing Data with Solver

Spreadsheet tools such as Goal Seek that change a single variable are useful, but unfortunately most problems in business are not so simple. You'll usually face formulas with at least two and sometimes dozens of variables. Often, a problem will have more than one solution, and your challenge will be to find the *optimal* solution (that is, the one that maximizes profit, minimizes costs, or matches other criteria). For these bigger challenges, you need a more muscular tool. Excel has just the answer: Solver, a sophisticated optimization program that enables you to find the solutions to complex problems that would otherwise require high–level mathematical analysis.

Understanding Solver

Solver, like Goal Seek, uses an iterative method to perform its calculations. Using iteration means that Solver tries a solution, analyzes the results, tries another solution, and so on. However, this cyclic iteration isn't just guesswork on Solver's part. That would be silly. No, Solver examines how the results change with each new iteration and, through some sophisticated mathematical processes (which, thankfully, happen way in the background and can be ignored), can usually tell in what direction it should head for the solution.

The advantages of Solver

Yes, Goal Seek and Solver are both iterative, but that doesn't make them equal. In fact, Solver brings a number of advantages to the table:

>> **Solver enables you to specify multiple adjustable cells.** You can use up to 200 adjustable cells in all.

>> **Solver enables you to set up constraints on the adjustable cells.** For example, you can tell Solver to find a solution that not only maximizes profit but also satisfies certain conditions, such as achieving a gross margin between 20 and 30 percent or keeping expenses less than $100,000. These conditions are said to be *constraints* on the solution.

>> **Solver seeks not only a desired result (the "goal" in Goal Seek) but also the optimal one.** For example, looking for an optimal result might mean that you can find a solution that's the maximum or minimum possible.

>> **For complex problems, Solver can generate multiple solutions.** You can then save these different solutions under different scenarios.

When should you use Solver?

Okay, I'll be straight with you: Solver is a powerful tool that most Excel users don't need. It would be overkill, for example, to use Solver to compute net profit given fixed revenue and cost figures. Some problems, however, require nothing less than the Solver approach. These problems cover many different fields and situations, but they all have the following characteristics in common:

>> **They have a single *objective cell* (also called the *target cell*) that contains a formula you want to maximize, minimize, or set to a specific value.** This formula could be a calculation such as total transportation expenses or net profit.

>> **The objective cell formula contains references to one or more *variable cells* (also called *unknowns* or *changing cells*).** Solver adjusts these cells to find the optimal solution for the objective cell formula. These variable cells might include items such as units sold, shipping costs, or advertising expenses.

» **Optionally, there are one or more *constraint cells* that must satisfy certain criteria.** For example, you might require that advertising be less than 10 percent of total expenses, or that the discount to customers be an amount between 40 and 60 percent.

For example, Figure 2-11 shows a worksheet data model that's all set up for Solver. The model shows revenue (price times units sold) and costs for two products, the profit produced by each product, and the total profit. The question to be answered here is this: How many units of each product must be sold to get a total profit of $0? This is known in business as a *break-even analysis.*

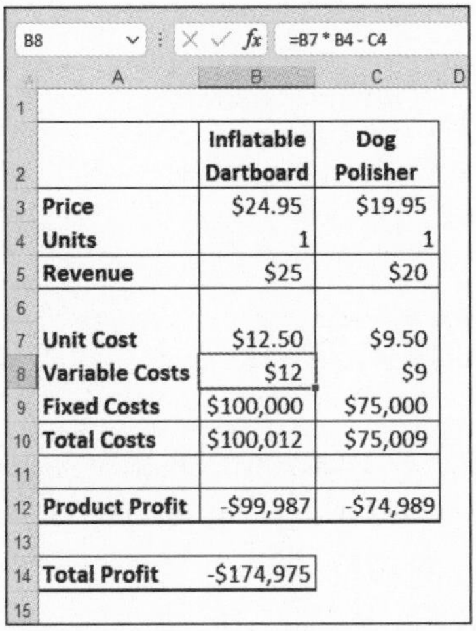

	A	B	C
1			
2		Inflatable Dartboard	Dog Polisher
3	Price	$24.95	$19.95
4	Units	1	1
5	Revenue	$25	$20
6			
7	Unit Cost	$12.50	$9.50
8	Variable Costs	$12	$9
9	Fixed Costs	$100,000	$75,000
10	Total Costs	$100,012	$75,009
11			
12	Product Profit	-$99,987	-$74,989
13			
14	Total Profit	-$174,975	
15			

FIGURE 2-11: The goal for this data model is to find the break-even point (where total profit is $0).

That sounds like a straightforward Goal Seek task, but this model has a tricky aspect: the variable costs. Normally, the variable costs of a product are its unit cost times the number of units sold. If it costs $10 to produce product A and you sell 10,000 units, the variable costs for that product are $100,000. However, in the real world, such costs are often mixed up among multiple products. For example, if you run a joint advertising campaign for two products, the costs are borne by both products. Therefore, this model assumes that the costs of one product are related to the units sold of the other.

Here, for example, is the formula used to calculate the costs of the Inflatable Dartboard (cell B8):

```
=B7 * B4 - C4
```

In other words, the variable costs for the Inflatable Dartboard are reduced by one dollar for every unit sold of the Dog Polisher. The latter's variable costs use a similar formula (in cell C8):

```
=C7 * C4 - B4
```

Having the variable costs related to multiple products puts this data model outside of what Goal Seek can do, but Solver is up to the challenge. Here are the special cells in the model that Solver will use:

>> The objective cell is C14; the total profit and the target solution for this formula is 0 (that is, the break-even point).

>> The changing cells are B4 and C4, which hold the number of units sold for each product.

>> For constraints, you might want to add that both the product profit cells (B12 and C12) should also be 0.

Loading the Solver add-in

An *add-in* is software that adds one or more features to Excel. Installing add-ins gives you additional Excel features that aren't available on the Ribbon by default. Bundled add-in software is included with Excel but isn't automatically installed when you install Excel. Several add-ins come standard with Excel, including Solver.

You install bundled add-ins by using the Excel Options dialog box; you can find them in the Add-Ins section. After they're installed, add-ins are available right away. They usually appear on a tab related to their function. For example, Solver appears on the Data tab.

Here are the steps to follow to load the Solver add-in:

1. **Choose File ➪ Options.**

   The Excel Options dialog box appears.

2. **Choose Add-Ins.**

3. **In the Manage list, select Excel Add-Ins and then select Go.**

   Excel displays the Add-Ins dialog box.

4. Select the Solver Add-In check box.

5. Click OK.

Excel adds a Solver button to the Data tab's Analysis group.

Optimizing a result with Solver

You set up your Solver model by using the Solver Parameters dialog box. In the Set Objective field, you specify the objective cell. You use the options in the To group to tell Solver what you want from the objective cell: the maximum possible value, the minimum possible value, or a specific value. Finally, you use the By Changing Variable Cells box to specify the cells that Solver can use to plug in values to optimize the result.

WARNING

When Solver finds a solution, you can choose either Keep Solver Solution or Restore Original Values. If you choose Keep Solver Solution, Excel permanently changes the worksheet. You can't undo the changes.

With your Solver-ready worksheet model prepared, here are the steps to follow to find an optimal result for your model using Solver:

1. Choose Data ➪ Solver.

Excel opens the Solver Parameters dialog box.

2. In the Set Objective box, enter the address of your model's objective cell.

In the example in the "When should you use Solver?" section, previously in the chapter (refer to Figure 2-11), the objective cell is B14. Note that if you click the cell to enter it, Solver automatically enters an absolute cell address (for example, $B$14 instead of B14). Solver works fine either way.

3. In the To group, select an option:

● **Max:** Returns the maximum possible value.

● **Min:** Returns the minimum possible value.

● **Value Of:** Enter a number to set the objective cell to that number.

For the example model, I selected Value Of and entered **0** in the text box.

4. In the By Changing Variable Cells box, enter the addresses of the cells you want Solver to change while it looks for a solution.

In the example, the changing cells are B4 and C4. Figure 2-12 shows the completed Solver Parameters dialog box. (What about constraints? I talk about those in the next section.)

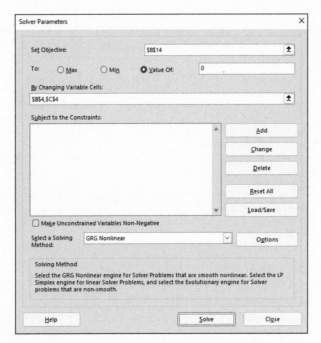

FIGURE 2-12:
The completed
Solver Parameters
dialog box.

5. **Click Solve.**

   Solver gets down to business. As Solver works on the problem, the Show Trial Solution dialog boxes might show up one or more times.

6. **In any Show Trial Solution dialog box that appears, click Continue to move things along.**

   When the optimization is complete, Excel displays the Solver Results dialog box, shown in Figure 2-13.

7. **Select the Keep Solver Solution option.**

   If you don't want to accept the result, select the Restore Original Values option instead.

8. **Click OK.**

TECHNICAL STUFF

You can ask Solver to display one or more reports that give you extra information about the results. In the Solver Results dialog box, use the Reports list to select each report you want to view:

>> **Answer:** Displays information about the model's objective cell, variable cells, and constraints. For the objective cell and variable cells, Solver shows the original and final values.

>> **Sensitivity:** Attempts to show how sensitive a solution is to changes in the model's formulas. The layout of the Sensitivity report depends on the type of model you're using.

>> **Limits:** Displays the objective cell and its value, as well as the variable cells and their addresses, names, and values.

TECHNICAL STUFF

Solver can use one of several solving methods. In the Solver Parameters dialog box, use the Select a Solving Method list to select one of the following:

>> **Simplex LP:** Use if your worksheet model is linear. In the simplest possible terms, a *linear model* is one in which the variables are not raised to any powers and none of the so-called transcendent functions — such as SIN and COS — are used.

>> **GRG Nonlinear:** Use if your worksheet model is nonlinear and smooth. In general terms, a *smooth model* is one in which a graph of the equation doesn't show sharp edges or breaks.

>> **Evolutionary:** Use if your worksheet model is nonlinear and nonsmooth.

Do you have to worry about any of this? Almost certainly not. Solver defaults to using GRG Nonlinear, and that should work for almost anything you do with Solver.

FIGURE 2-13:
The Solver Results dialog box and the solution to the break-even problem.

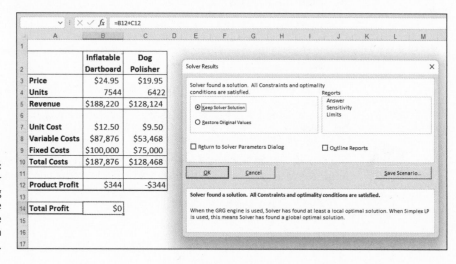

Adding constraints to Solver

The real world puts restrictions and conditions on formulas. A factory might have a maximum capacity of 10,000 units a day, the number of employees in a company can't be a negative number, and your advertising costs might be restricted to 10 percent of total expenses.

Similarly, suppose that you're running a break-even analysis on two products, as I discuss in the preceding section. If you run the optimization without any restrictions, Solver might reach a total profit of 0 by setting one product at a slight loss and the other at a slight profit, where the loss and profit cancel each other out. In fact, if you take a close look at Figure 2-13, this is exactly what Solver did. To get a true break-even solution, you might prefer to see both product profit values as 0.

Such restrictions and conditions are examples of what Solver calls *constraints*. Adding constraints tells Solver to find a solution so that these conditions are not violated.

Here's how to run Solver with constraints added to the optimization:

1. **Choose Data ⇨ Solver.**

   Excel opens the Solver Parameters dialog box.

2. **Use the Set Objective box, the To group, and the By Changing Variable Cells box to set up Solver as I describe in the preceding section, "Optimizing a result with Solver."**

3. **Click Add.**

   Excel displays the Add Constraint dialog box.

4. **In the Cell Reference box, enter the address of the cell you want to constrain.**

   You can type the address or select the cell on the worksheet.

5. **In the drop-down list, select the operator you want to use.**

   Most of the time, you use a comparison operator, such as equal to (=) or greater than (>). Use the int (integer) operator when you need a constraint, such as total employees, to be an integer value instead of a real number (that is, a number with a decimal component; you can't have 10.5 employees!). Use the bin (binary) operator when you have a constraint that must be either TRUE or FALSE (or 1 or 0).

6. **If you chose a comparison operator in Step 5, in the Constraint box, enter the value by which you want to restrict the cell.**

Figure 2-14 shows an example of a completed Add Constraint dialog box. In the example model, this constraint tells Solver to find a solution such that the product profit of the Inflatable Dartboard (cell B12) is equal to 0.

FIGURE 2-14:
The completed
Add Constraint
dialog box.

7. **To specify more constraints, click Add and repeat Steps 4 through 6, as needed.**

For the example, you add a constraint that asks for the Dog Polisher product profit (cell C12) to be 0.

8. **Click OK.**

Excel returns to the Solver Parameters dialog box and displays your constraints in the Subject to the Constraints list box.

9. **Click Solve.**

10. **In any Show Trial Solution dialog box that appears, click Continue to move things along.**

Figure 2-15 shows the example break-even solution with the constraints added. Note that not only is the Total Profit cell (B14) set to 0, but so are the two Product Profit cells (B12 And C12).

11. **Select the Keep Solver Solution option.**

If you don't want to accept the result, select the Restore Original Values option instead.

12. **Click OK.**

REMEMBER

You can add a maximum of 100 constraints. Also, if you need to make a change to a constraint before you begin solving, select the constraint in the Subject to the Constraints list box, click Change, and then make your adjustments in the Change Constraint dialog box that appears. If you want to delete a constraint that you no longer need, select the constraint and then click Delete.

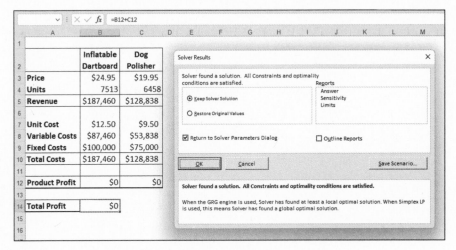

FIGURE 2-15:
The Solver Results dialog box and the final solution to the break-even problem.

Save a Solver solution as a scenario

Whenever you have a spreadsheet model that uses a coherent set of input values — known as changing cells — you have what Excel calls a scenario. With Solver, these changing cells are its variable cells, so a Solver solution amounts to a kind of scenario. However, Solver does not give you an easy way to save and rerun a particular solution. To work around this problem, you can save a solution as a scenario that you can then later recall using Excel's scenario manager feature.

Follow these steps to save a Solver solution as a scenario:

1. **Choose Data ⇨ Solver.**

Excel opens the Solver Parameters dialog box.

2. **Use the Set Objective box, the To group, the By Changing Variable Cells box, and the Subject to the Constraints list to set up Solver as I describe in the "Optimizing a result with Solver" section, previously in this chapter.**

3. **Click Solve.**

4. **Anytime the Show Trial Solution dialog box appears, choose Continue.**

When the optimization is complete, Excel displays the Solver Results dialog box.

5. **Click Save Scenario.**

Excel displays the Save Scenario dialog box.

6. **In the Scenario Name dialog box, type a name for the scenario and then click OK.**

Excel returns you to the Solver Results dialog box.

7. **Select the Keep Solver Solution option.**

If you don't want to accept the result, select the Restore Original Values option instead.

8. **Click OK.**

» Building tables

» Analyzing tables with simple statistics

» Sorting tables

» Discovering the difference between using AutoFilter and filtering

Chapter **3**

Introducing Excel Tables

One of the secrets of data-analysis success is being organized. I'm talking about not your desk or your office (insert sigh of relief here) but your data. If you have a worksheet with numbers and text inserted haphazardly, analyzing that data will be next to impossible. Why? Because Excel is the neat freak of the software world. If data is strewn around the worksheet any old way, Excel throws up its hands and says, "I can't work under these conditions!"

Fortunately, Excel understands that the rest of us aren't so orderly, so it offers the table — a powerful tool designed not only to get your data lined up like soldiers on parade but also to help you analyze that data and extract useful information. In this chapter, you discover what tables are and why they're so darned useful in the data-analysis world. You also dive in to building, analyzing, sorting, and filtering a table.

What Is a Table and Why Should I Care?

In Excel, a *table* is a rectangular range of cells used to store data; it includes special tools for entering, editing, and analyzing that data. A table is designed to store a collection of related information. For example, one table might store business data such as customers, invoices, or inventory, whereas another might store personal data such as contacts, movies, or household items. You can use Excel tables to create, retrieve, and manage large or small collections of information.

To get the most out of Excel tables, you need to understand a few basic concepts:

>> **A table is a kind of database.** Microsoft Access is a powerful database-management tool that lets you work with large, complex databases. If your needs are simpler, however, you can use an Excel table as a database in which the data is organized into columns and rows. In this case, each column is the equivalent of a database field, which contains a single type of information, such as a name, an address, or a phone number; and each row serves as the equivalent of a database record, which holds a set of associated field values, such as the information for a specific contact.

>> **A table has its advantages.** Because a table is a collection of rows and columns in a worksheet, it looks very much like a regular Excel range. However, a table is actually a special type of range because Excel provides some tools that help you work more easily with the data in the table. These tools enable you to convert existing worksheet data into a table, select the rows and fields you want to work with, add new records and fields to the table, delete existing records and fields, and insert rows to display totals.

>> **A table makes data analysis easier.** Tables are also useful tools for analyzing your data. For example, you can sort the table data, both on a single field and on multiple fields. You can also make the table data easier to manage by filtering the data to show only the subset of records you want to work with. In addition, you can use a table as the basis of a PivotTable, which is a powerful tool for summarizing and analyzing data that I discuss in Part 2.

Before creating your tables, you should spend some time deciding what type of data each table should contain. This process involves thinking about what purpose your tables will serve, which fields you'll need in each table, and how you'll differentiate between each record in the table. Each table should have a single, well-defined purpose. For example, a table might store customer contact information, product inventory, or personnel records. Combining multiple purposes in a single table results in needless duplication and increases the chance of data-entry errors. If you think you might need to sort or filter the data by a certain type of information, put that information in a separate field. Finally, having at least one field that is unique to each record to differentiate between records is usually a good idea.

To help you work with Excel tables, here's a list of table terms, all of which are pointed out in Figure 3-1:

>> **Table column:** A single type of information, such as names, addresses, or phone numbers. In an Excel table, each column is the equivalent of a database field.

>> **Table row:** A set of associated table cells, such as the data for a single contact. In an Excel table, each row is the equivalent of a database record.

>> **Table cell:** An item in a table column that represents a single instance of that column's data, such as a name, an address, or a phone number. In an Excel table, each cell is equivalent to a database field value.

>> **Table headers:** The unique names you assign to every table column that serve to label the data in each column. These names are always found in the first row of the table.

>> **Sort & filter button:** An Excel feature that gives you access to a set of commands that perform various actions on a column, such as sorting or filtering the column data.

FIGURE 3-1:
Some table terminology you should know.

Column headers   Table column   Sort and filter button

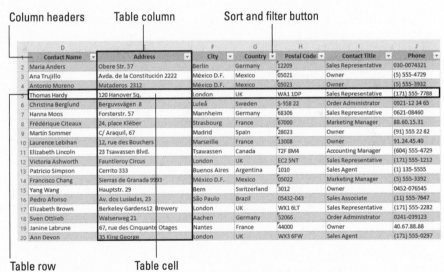

Contact Name	Address	City	Country	Postal Code	Contact Title	Phone
Maria Anders	Obere Str. 57	Berlin	Germany	12209	Sales Representative	030-0074321
Ana Trujillo	Avda. de la Constitución 2222	México D.F.	Mexico	05021	Owner	(5) 555-4729
Antonio Moreno	Mataderos 2312	México D.F.	Mexico	05023	Owner	(5) 555-3932
Thomas Hardy	120 Hanover Sq.	London	UK	WA1 1DP	Sales Representative	(171) 555-7788
Christina Berglund	Berguvsvägen 8	Luleå	Sweden	S-958 22	Order Administrator	0921-12 34 65
Hanna Moos	Forsterstr. 57	Mannheim	Germany	68306	Sales Representative	0621-08460
Frédérique Citeaux	24, place Kléber	Strasbourg	France	67000	Marketing Manager	88.60.15.31
Martín Sommer	C/ Araquil, 67	Madrid	Spain	28023	Owner	(91) 555 22 82
Laurence Lebihan	12, rue des Bouchers	Marseille	France	13008	Owner	91.24.45.40
Elizabeth Lincoln	23 Tsawassen Blvd.	Tsawassen	Canada	T2F 8M4	Accounting Manager	(604) 555-4729
Victoria Ashworth	Fauntleroy Circus	London	UK	EC2 5NT	Sales Representative	(171) 555-1212
Patricio Simpson	Cerrito 333	Buenos Aires	Argentina	1010	Sales Agent	(1) 135-5555
Francisco Chang	Sierras de Granada 9993	México D.F.	Mexico	05022	Marketing Manager	(5) 555-3392
Yang Wang	Hauptstr. 29	Bern	Switzerland	3012	Owner	0452-076545
Pedro Afonso	Av. dos Lusíadas, 23	São Paulo	Brazil	05432-043	Sales Associate	(11) 555-7647
Elizabeth Brown	Berkeley Gardens12 Brewery	London	UK	WX1 6LT	Sales Representative	(171) 555-2282
Sven Ottlieb	Walserweg 21	Aachen	Germany	52066	Order Administrator	0241-039123
Janine Labrune	67, rue des Cinquante Otages	Nantes	France	44000	Owner	40.67.88.88
Ann Devon	35 King George	London	UK	WX3 6FW	Sales Agent	(171) 555-0297

Table row   Table cell

Building a Table

You build an Excel table in one of two ways:

>> Get the data from an external source, such as a database.

>> Convert an existing range to a table.

Getting the data from an external source

The usual way to create an Excel table is to import the information from an external source, such as another workbook, an Access database, a text file, or even a web page. Importing data is such an important — and time-saving — method of getting data into Excel that I devote all of Chapter 4 to it. There, I describe the process of getting the external data into a format that Excel can use and then importing the data into Excel so you can analyze it. Hop over to that chapter for more on creating a table by importing its data.

TIP

Even if you plan on creating your tables by importing data from an external source, read through the next few paragraphs of this chapter anyway. Why? Because they give you a better understanding of the nuts and bolts of building a table, and having that know-how in your brain makes understanding and working with external data easier when you're ready to go down that road.

Converting a range to a table

If the data you want to use already exists on your worksheet, you might be able to convince Excel to convert that range into an honest-to-goodness table. I say "convince" here because not all ranges are candidates for table-hood. Fortunately, getting your data ready doesn't require elaborate planning or modifications, but you should follow a few guidelines for best results. Here are some pointers:

>> Decide whether you want column headers in your table. This is an excellent idea because it makes your table much easier to read and to analyze, but the headers are optional.

>> If you do use column headers, always place them in the top row of the range.

>> Column headers must be unique and must be text or text formulas. If you need to use numbers, format them as text. (That is, select the headers, select the Home tab, and choose Text in the Number Format list.)

>> Excel can often automatically identify the size and shape of the range that contains your data. To avoid confusing Excel, make sure that your range has no blank rows or columns.

>> If the worksheet contains data that you don't want to appear in your table, leave at least one blank row or column between the data and the range. The blank row or column helps Excel identify the correct table range without also including the nontable data.

Excel has a command that enables you to filter your table data to show only records that match certain criteria. This command works by hiding rows of data. Therefore, if the same worksheet contains nontable data that you need to see or work with, don't place this data to the left or right of the table because some or all of the rows in that data might be hidden when you filter the table.

Note that you don't need to enter all your data before converting the range to a table. After you have the table, you can add rows and columns as needed. Okay, I think you're ready to find out how to convert a range to a table:

1. **Select a cell in the range that you want to convert to a table.**

2. **Choose Insert ⇨ Tables ⇨ Table or press Ctrl+T.**

   The Create Table dialog box appears. As shown in Figure 3-2, Excel makes its best guess about the extent of the range that it will convert to a table.

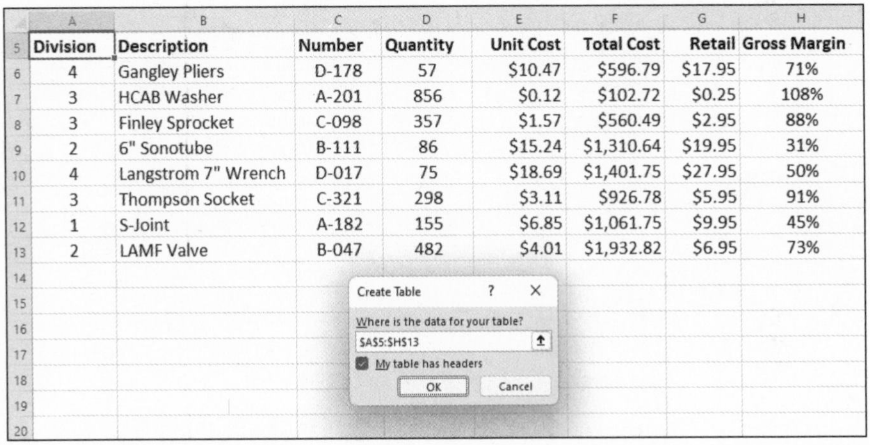

	A	B	C	D	E	F	G	H
5	Division	Description	Number	Quantity	Unit Cost	Total Cost	Retail	Gross Margin
6	4	Gangley Pliers	D-178	57	$10.47	$596.79	$17.95	71%
7	3	HCAB Washer	A-201	856	$0.12	$102.72	$0.25	108%
8	3	Finley Sprocket	C-098	357	$1.57	$560.49	$2.95	88%
9	2	6" Sonotube	B-111	86	$15.24	$1,310.64	$19.95	31%
10	4	Langstrom 7" Wrench	D-017	75	$18.69	$1,401.75	$27.95	50%
11	3	Thompson Socket	C-321	298	$3.11	$926.78	$5.95	91%
12	1	S-Joint	A-182	155	$6.85	$1,061.75	$9.95	45%
13	2	LAMF Valve	B-047	482	$4.01	$1,932.82	$6.95	73%

Create Table　　?　✕

Where is the data for your table?

$A$5:$H$13

☑ My table has headers

OK　　Cancel

FIGURE 3-2:
Excel takes a stab at the full range you want to convert.

3. **If Excel got it wrong, drag over the correct range.**

4. **If your range has labels that you want to use as column headers, make sure that the My Table Has Headers check box is selected.**

5. **Click OK.**

Excel converts the range to a table, which, as you can eyeball in Figure 3-3, also means that Excel does the following:

>> Applies a table format to the range.

>> Shoehorns a Sort & Filter button into each column header.

>> Displays the Table Design contextual tab whenever you select a cell in the table. The Table Design tab is chock-full of useful table tools.

Division	Description	Number	Quantity	Unit Co	Total Co	Reta	Gross Margin
4	Gangley Pliers	D-178	57	$10.47	$596.79	$17.95	71%
3	HCAB Washer	A-201	856	$0.12	$102.72	$0.25	108%
3	Finley Sprocket	C-098	357	$1.57	$560.49	$2.95	88%
2	6" Sonotube	B-111	86	$15.24	$1,310.64	$19.95	31%
4	Langstrom 7" Wrench	D-017	75	$18.69	$1,401.75	$27.95	50%
3	Thompson Socket	C-321	298	$3.11	$926.78	$5.95	91%
1	S-Joint	A-182	155	$6.85	$1,061.75	$9.95	45%
2	LAMF Valve	B-047	482	$4.01	$1,932.82	$6.95	73%

FIGURE 3-3: The range is now a full-fledged table, just like that.

Basic table maintenance

After you've converted your range to a table, the data isn't set in stone. You can perform all kinds of actions to keep your table up-to-date. Here's a quick summary:

>> **Select a row.** Right-click any cell in the row and then choose Select ⇨ Table Row.

>> **Select a column.** Right-click any cell in the column and then choose Select ⇨ Table Column Data. If you want the selection to also include the column header, choose Select ⇨ Entire Table Column instead.

>> **Insert a row.** Right-click the row above which you want the new row to appear and then choose Insert ⇨ Table Rows Above. If you select cells in two or more rows, Excel inserts the same number of new rows.

- » **Inserting a column:** Right-click the column to the left of which you want the new column to appear and then choose Insert ➪ Table Columns to the Left. If you select cells in two or more columns, Excel inserts the same number of new columns.

- » **Delete a row.** Right-click the row you want to delete and then choose Delete ➪ Table Rows. If you select cells in two or more rows, Excel deletes those rows.

- » **Delete a column.** Right-click the column you want to delete and then choose Delete ➪ Table Columns. If you select cells in two or more columns, Excel deletes those columns.

- » **Resize the table.** Select any cell in the table and then choose Table Design ➪ Resize Table to open the Resize Table dialog box. Drag over the new range and then click OK.

- » **Convert the table back to a range.** Select any cell in the table and then choose Table Design ➪ Convert to Range. When Excel asks you to confirm, click Yes.

Analyzing Table Information

Now that your data is nicely arranged in a table, a whole new world of data analysis opens right before your eyes. That's because Excel offers quite a few useful data-analysis tools designed with tables in mind. In the rest of this chapter, I introduce you to these handy table tools.

Displaying simple statistics

If your table includes a column that contains numeric values or prices, you might want to perform a quick analysis on that column by generating some basic statistics, such as the column's sum or average. One of Excel's slickest and quickest tools enables you to effortlessly calculate not only the sum or average for a column but also other stats, such as the count, the minimum value, and the maximum value.

To get these stats, you take advantage of the fact that a table is still a range, and Excel automatically displays statistics in the status bar when you select a range. For example, if you select the range D5:D13 in Figure 3-4 (that is, all the items in the table's Quantity column), Excel calculates the column's average, count, and sum, and then displays this useful information in the status bar:

```
Average: 295.75 Count: 8 Sum: 2366
```

FIGURE 3-4:
Select a column's
cells, and Excel
displays a few
stats in the
status bar.

	A	B	C	D	E	F	G	H
5	Division	Description	Number	Quantity	Unit Co	Total Co	Reta	Gross Margin
6	4	Gangley Pliers	D-178	57	$10.47	$596.79	$17.95	71%
7	3	HCAB Washer	A-201	856	$0.12	$102.72	$0.25	108%
8	3	Finley Sprocket	C-098	357	$1.57	$560.49	$2.95	88%
9	2	6" Sonotube	B-111	86	$15.24	$1,310.64	$19.95	31%
10	4	Langstrom 7" Wrench	D-017	75	$18.69	$1,401.75	$27.95	50%
11	3	Thompson Socket	C-321	298	$3.11	$926.78	$5.95	91%
12	1	S-Joint	A-182	155	$6.85	$1,061.75	$9.95	45%
13	2	LAMF Valve	B-047	482	$4.01	$1,932.82	$6.95	73%
14								

Customers   Parts (Range)   **Parts (Table)**   +

Ready   Average: 295.75   Count: 8   Sum: 2366

TIP

If the column you want to analyze contains many items, you might not want to select them all by dragging. An easier way to select the entire column is to right-click any item in the column and then choose Select ⇨ Table Column Data. Alternatively, select the first item in the column and then press Ctrl+Shift+down arrow.

To display some other statistical calculations for the selected table column, right-click the status bar to show the Customize Status Bar menu. Near the bottom of that menu, Excel provides six statistical measures that you can add to or remove from the status bar: Average, Count, Numerical Count, Minimum, Maximum, and Sum. In Table 3-1, I describe each of these statistical measures briefly, but you can probably guess what they do. Note that if a statistical measure is displayed on the status bar, Excel places a check mark in front of the measure on the Customize Status Bar menu. To remove the statistical measure from the status bar, click the measure to remove its check mark.

TABLE 3-1

Quick Statistical Measures Available on the Status Bar

Measure	What It Displays
Average	The average of the cells in the selected range
Count	The number of cells that contain labels, values, or formulas (that is, the number of cells that are not empty)
Numerical Count	The number of cells in a selected range that hold values or formulas
Minimum	The smallest value in the selected range
Maximum	The largest value in the selected range
Sum	The total of the values in the selected range

These basic statistical measures are often all you need to gain useful insights into data that you collect and store in an Excel table. True, by using an example parts table that contains just nine items, the power of these quick statistical measures doesn't seem all that earthshaking. But with real data, these measures often produce interesting and useful insights.

Adding a column subtotal

The quick statistical measures that I talk about in the preceding section are handy because Excel displays the status bar statistics when you select any range. So, you can get those stats without bothering to convert a range to a table. That's great, but the stats appear in the status bar only when you've selected the data. If you select another cell or range, the stats disappear or change. Bummer.

Because you've gone to the trouble of converting a regular range to a table, you can take advantage of the data's "table-ness" by summarizing a column with a subtotal that appears at the bottom of the column and doesn't disappear when you select another cell or range.

Although the word *subtotal* implies that you're summing the numeric values in a column, Excel uses the term more broadly. That is, a subtotal can be not only a numeric sum but also an average, a maximum or minimum, or a count of the values in the field. You can also choose more advanced subtotals such as the standard deviation or the variance.

Follow these steps to add a subtotal to a table column:

1. **Select the data in the column you want to total.**

2. **Click the Quick Analysis smart tag or press Ctrl+Q.**

   The Quick Analysis smart tag is the icon that appears slightly below and to the right of your selected range. A *smart tag* gives you access to a set of commands and features related to what you've selected (such as a range, in this case).

   The Quick Analysis options appear.

3. **Click the Totals tab.**

4. **Select the type of calculation you want to use.**

   Excel adds a Total row to the bottom of the table and inserts the result of the calculation you selected. In Figure 3-5, you can see that I've added a calculation for the average of the Quantity column. Note that when you select the result, its cell displays a drop-down arrow to the right. You can click the drop-down arrow to choose a different calculation.

	A	B	C	D	E	F	G	H
5	Division ▾	Description ▾	Number ▾	Quantity ▾	Unit Co ▾	Total Co ▾	Reta ▾	Gross Margin ▾
6	4	Gangley Pliers	D-178	57	$10.47	$596.79	$17.95	71%
7	3	HCAB Washer	A-201	856	$0.12	$102.72	$0.25	108%
8	3	Finley Sprocket	C-098	357	$1.57	$560.49	$2.95	88%
9	2	6" Sonotube	B-111	86	$15.24	$1,310.64	$19.95	31%
10	4	Langstrom 7" Wrench	D-017	75	$18.69	$1,401.75	$27.95	50%
11	3	Thompson Socket	C-321	298	$3.11	$926.78	$5.95	91%
12	1	S-Joint	A-182	155	$6.85	$1,061.75	$9.95	45%
13	2	LAMF Valve	B-047	482	$4.01	$1,932.82	$6.95	73%
14				295.75				

D14   fx   =SUBTOTAL(101,[Quantity])

None
Average
Count
Count Numbers
Max
Min
Sum
StdDev
Var
More Functions...

FIGURE 3-5:
Excel adds a Total row to the bottom of the table and displays the result of the calculation.

TIP

If the column you want to total is the last column in the table, Excel offers a short-cut method to add the Total row and display a subtotal for that column. Select any cell in the table and then, on the Table Design tab, select the Total Row check box. Excel automatically inserts a row named Total at the bottom of the table. Excel also adds a Sum subtotal below the last column. Select the subtotal, click the cell's drop-down arrow, and then choose the type of subtotal you want to use.

Sorting table records

Another way to analyze your table data is to sort the data based on the values in a column, which means arranging that column's numeric values from highest to lowest or from lowest to highest. (You can also sort text values alphabetically and date values from oldest to newest or newest to oldest, but these techniques are less useful for data analysis.) How does sorting help you analyze your data? Here are some ideas:

REMEMBER

>> Sorting enables you to get a feel for how your data is distributed overall. For example, you might notice that most of the values cluster around the low end of the range of values.

>> Sorting enables you to identify certain types of trends. For example, you might notice that records (that is, rows) with low values in the sorted column all come from the same geographic area, or that high values in another table all come from the same division of the company.

>> Sorting enables you to identify *outliers,* which are data points that are significantly outside the norm for your data. For example, if your sort shows that most of your column values lie between 1 and 100, but one row contains the value 250, you'll want to investigate why that value is so much greater than the others.

To sort a table based on the values in a column, follow these steps:

1. **Click the Sort & Filter button for the column you want to sort.**

   Excel displays the Sort & Filter menu. Figure 3-6 shows the top part of the Sort & Filter menu that appears when selecting the Sort & Filter button for the Quantity column.

2. **Select the sort option you want:**

   - **Sort Smallest to Largest:** Sorts the column values in ascending numeric order
   - **Sort Largest to Smallest:** Sorts the column values in descending numeric order

When you can't sort table information exactly the way you want by using the Sort Smallest to Largest and Sort Largest to Smallest commands, use the Custom Sort command.

FIGURE 3-6:
Selecting the Quantity column's Sort & Filter button displays this menu.

To use the Custom Sort command, follow these steps:

1. **Click any Sort & Filter button in the table.**

   Excel displays the Sort & Filter menu.

2. **Choose Sort by Color ⇨ Custom Sort.**

   Excel displays the Sort dialog box.

3. **In the Sort By drop-down list, select the field that you want to use for sorting.**

4. **In the Sort On list, select Cell Values.**

   If you're using conditional formatting, as described in Chapter 1, you can also choose to sort on Cell Color, Font Color, or Conditional Formatting Icon.

5. **In the Order list, select a sort order.**

   For numeric data, select either Smallest to Largest or Largest to Smallest. If you sort by color or icons, you need to tell Excel how it should sort the colors by using the options that the Order list provides.

TIP

Typically, you want the sort to work in ascending or descending order. However, you might want to sort records by using a chronological sequence, such as Sunday, Monday, Tuesday, and so on, or January, February, March, and so forth. To use one of these other sort options, choose the Order list's Custom List command and then choose one of these other ordering methods in the Custom Lists dialog box that Excel displays. You can also create your own custom lists if, say, you need to sort your data by department or job title.

6. **(Optional) Specify one or more secondary sort levels by clicking Add Level and then repeating Steps 3 to 5 for the new sort level that appears.**

   A secondary sort level means that Excel first sorts the table based on the data in the primary sort level, and then further sorts the table based on the data in the secondary sort level. For example, in the parts table, you can first sort the table based on the Division column, and then sort based on the Quantity column. Figure 3-7 shows the Sort dialog box set up for such a two-level sort.

   If you add a level that you later decide you don't want or need, select the sort level and then click the Delete Level button. You can also duplicate the selected level by clicking Copy Level. Finally, if you create multiple sort levels, you can move the selected sort up or down a level by clicking the Move Up or Move Down button.

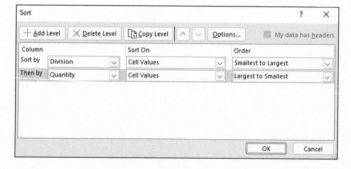

FIGURE 3-7:
The Sort dialog box set up for a two-level sort.

Note: The Sort dialog box also provides a My Data Has Headers check box that enables you to indicate whether the worksheet range selection includes the row and field names. If you've already told Excel that a worksheet range is a table, however, this check box is disabled.

7. **Click OK.**

   Excel sorts your list.

Filtering table records

When you're generating statistics, adding subtotals, and sorting data, you'll most often want to work with all the table data. However, working with just a subset of the table data can sometimes be beneficial. In the parts database, for example, you might want to see only records from Division 3 or only items whose Retail price is greater than $10.

To help you work with subsets of your table data, Excel provides a pretty cool AutoFilter command. When you use AutoFilter, you produce a new view of your table that includes only the records that match the criteria you specify, such as the Division value equal to 3 or the Retail value greater than 10.

To apply an AutoFilter to a table, follow these steps:

1. **Click the Sort & Filter button for the column you want to filter.**

   Excel displays the column's Sort & Filter menu. Above the OK and Cancel buttons, you see a list of check boxes, where the name of each check box is a unique value from the column.

2. **Deselect the Select All check box to deselect all the check boxes.**

3. **Select the check box for each column value you want to see in the filtered table.**

   Figure 3-8 shows the Sort & Filter menu for the Division column, with only the 3 check box selected.

4. **Click OK.**

   Excel filters the table to show only those values you selected in Step 3. Figure 3-9 shows the filtered parts table, which now displays only the records from Division 3. The Sort & Filter button of the Division column header now sports a tiny funnel icon, which gives you a visual heads-up that the column is filtered.

FIGURE 3-8:
Select the check box beside each column value that you want to include in your filtered table.

Filtered icon

FIGURE 3-9:
The Parts table filtered to show only the records from Division 3.

	A	B	C	D	E	F	G	H
5	Division	Description	Number	Quantity	Unit Co	Total Co	Reta	Gross Margin
7	3	HCAB Washer	A-201	856	$0.12	$102.72	$0.25	108%
8	3	Finley Sprocket	C-098	357	$1.57	$560.49	$2.95	88%
11	3	Thompson Socket	C-321	298	$3.11	$926.78	$5.95	91%
14								

Clearing a filter

To remove an AutoFilter, you have a couple ways to go:

» To clear a filter from a single column, select the column's Sort & Filter button and then select the Clear Filter From "*Column*" command from the menu (where *Column* is the name of the filtered column).

» If you have multiple filters applied to the table, you can clear all the filters in one fell swoop by choosing Data ⇨ Clear (look for it in the Sort & Filter group).

Turning off AutoFilter

If you find that you don't use AutoFilter and so those Sort & Filter buttons just cramp your style, no problem: The AutoFilter command is actually a toggle switch. When AutoFilter is turned on, Excel adds the Sort & Filter buttons to each cell in the table's header row; when you turn off AutoFilter, Excel removes the Sort & Filter buttons.

To turn off AutoFilter and remove the Sort & Filter buttons, select any cell in the table and then choose Data ➪ Filter (or press Ctrl+Shift+L). If you change your mind and decide to reinstate AutoFilter, choose Data ➪ Filter again (or do the Ctrl+Shift+L thing again).

Applying a predefined AutoFilter

A basic AutoFilter creates a subset of the table by showing only rows in which the filtered column contains the value or values you selected using the check boxes in the Sort & Filter menu. That's pretty useful, but what if your filtering needs (I bet you didn't even know you had filtering needs) are more complex? For example, you might want to see only records in which the Quantity column is greater than or equal to 100, or in which the Gross Margin column is above the average for that column.

These more complex filters sound like more work, and I won't lie to you: They do take a few extra steps. Ah, but only a few, I promise, because Excel comes with quite a few predefined filter operators, including Greater Than Or Equal To and Above Average. Here are the steps to follow to apply one of these predefined filters to a column in your table:

1. **Click the Sort & Filter button for the column you want to filter.**

   Excel displays the column's Sort & Filter menu.

2. **Choose the *X* Filters command, where *X* refers to the type of data in the column.**

   You have three possible commands:

   - **Number Filters:** Appears when the column contains numeric data
   - **Date Filters:** Appears when the column contains date values, time values, or both
   - **Text Filters:** Appears when the column contains text data

3. **Select the filter operator you want to apply.**

   Excel displays a menu of predefined filter operators. The contents of the menu depend on the data type of your column. For example, if your column contains numeric data, you see the following operators:

   - **Equals:** Filters the column to show only those rows whose column value equals a number you specify.
   - **Does Not Equal:** Filters the column to show only those rows whose column value does not equal a number you specify.
   - **Greater Than:** Filters the column to show only those rows whose column value is greater than a number you specify.

- **Greater Than or Equal To:** Filters the column to show only those rows whose column value is greater than or equal to a number you specify.

- **Less Than:** Filters the column to show only those rows whose column value is less than a number you specify.

- **Less Than or Equal To:** Filters the column to show only those rows whose column value is less than or equal to a number you specify.

- **Between:** Filters the column to show only those rows whose column value lies between (and including) two numbers you specify.

- **Top 10:** Filters the column to show only those rows whose column value is in the top 10 of all the values in the column. Note that this filter is slightly misnamed because you can pick a number other than 10 (such as 5 or 25), you can show the bottom 10 (or 20 or 30 or whatever), and you can filter based on the percentage (for example, the top 10 percent) instead of the values.

- **Above Average:** Filters the column to show only those rows whose column value is greater than the average value of the column.

- **Below Average:** Filters the column to show only those rows whose column value is less than the average value of the column.

- **Custom Filter:** Displays the Custom AutoFilter dialog box, which enables you to create your own filter condition. In particular, you can specify two separate filter conditions, and you can then select the And option to have Excel filter the table to show only those rows with column values that match both filter conditions, or you can select the Or option to have Excel filter the table to show only those rows with column values that match one or both filter conditions.

In most cases, you see the Custom AutoFilter dialog box with the operator you selected already filled in in the drop-down list. For example, Figure 3-10 shows the Custom AutoFilter dialog box that appears when you select the Greater Than Or Equal operator. Note that some operators — such as Above Average and Below Average — don't require more information from you, so Excel applies the filter right away.

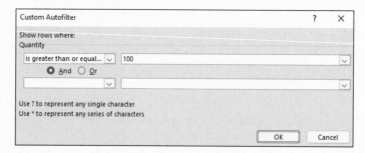

FIGURE 3-10: The Custom AutoFilter dialog box.

4. **Complete the AutoFilter condition.**

How you complete the condition depends on the operator you chose. For most numeric filters, you specify a number. For example, in Figure 3-11, I entered the number 100 in the text box, which means that this filter will show the subset of the table when the Quantity column value is 100 or more.

5. **Click OK.**

Excel filters your table according to your custom AutoFilter. Figure 3-11 shows the filter from Figure 3-10 applied to the Parts table.

	A	B	C	D	E	F	G	H
5	Division	Description	Number	Quantity	Unit Co	Total Co	Reta	Gross Margin
7	3	HCAB Washer	A-201	856	$0.12	$102.72	$0.25	108%
8	3	Finley Sprocket	C-098	357	$1.57	$560.49	$2.95	88%
11	3	Thompson Socket	C-321	298	$3.11	$926.78	$5.95	91%
12	1	S-Joint	A-182	155	$6.85	$1,061.75	$9.95	45%
13	2	LAMF Valve	B-047	482	$4.01	$1,932.82	$6.95	73%
14								

FIGURE 3-11:
The filter shown in Figure 3-10 applied to the Parts table.

Applying multiple filters

The predefined AutoFilter operators described in the preceding section enable you to filter your table based on a condition applied to a single column. What if your filtering needs (there are those needs again) are such that you want to filter the table by using multiple columns? In the Parts table, for example, you might want to filter the table to show only rows where the Quantity field is greater than or equal to 100, and you might want the resulting rows to themselves be filtered to show only those where the Gross Margin column is less than 75%.

The good news is that Excel doesn't mind in the least if you apply an AutoFilter to one column and then apply another AutoFilter to a second column. In fact, you can apply AutoFilters to as many columns as you need. In each case, just follow the same steps as those outlined in the preceding section.

REMEMBER

The idea of applying multiple filters might seem unnecessary. Okay, granted, it's most likely an over-the-top technique for small tables. However, when you start dealing with massive tables containing hundreds, nay, thousands, of rows, you'll almost certainly find that applying several sets of filters can reduce a very large and nearly incomprehensible table to a smaller subset of data that provides just the information you need.

Applying advanced filters

Most of the time, you'll be able to filter table records by using the Sort & Filter menu's check boxes or the Filter command. However, in some cases, you might want to gain more control over your filters, and that requires applying Excel's advanced filters.

Before you can create advanced filters in Excel, you need to know how to construct *comparison* expressions, through which you compare the items in a column with a value you specify. To construct a comparison expression, you enter a comparison operator from Table 3-2 and then a value used in the comparison.

TABLE 3-2 ## Excel's Comparison Operators

Operator	Name
=	Equals
<>	Not equal to
>	Greater than
>=	Greater than or equal to
<	Less than
<=	Less than or equal to

For example, if you want to filter the parts table so that it shows only items where the Unit Cost is less than $10, you use the following comparison expression:

```
< 10
```

Hmm, okay, I hear you musing, but where does the expression appear?

Surprisingly, it goes on the worksheet itself. To get this set up, first insert three or four blank rows above the table headers. Now copy your table headers and then paste them into the first of the blank rows above your table.

With that done, enter your comparison expression in the cell immediately below the copied header of the column you want to work with. In my example, I want to filter based on the Unit Cost column, so I enter **< 10** in the cell below the copied Unit Cost header. In Figure 3-12, you can see the expression in cell E2.

	A	B	C	D	E	F	G	H
1	Division	Description	Number	Quantity	Unit Cost	Total Cost	Retail	Gross Margin
2					< 10			
3								
4								
5	Division	Description	Number	Quantity	Unit Co	Total Co	Reta	Gross Margin
6	4	Gangley Pliers	D-178	57	$10.47	$596.79	$17.95	71%
7	3	HCAB Washer	A-201	856	$0.12	$102.72	$0.25	108%
8	3	Finley Sprocket	C-098	357	$1.57	$560.49	$2.95	88%
9	2	6" Sonotube	B-111	86	$15.24	$1,310.64	$19.95	31%
10	4	Langstrom 7" Wrench	D-017	75	$18.69	$1,401.75	$27.95	50%
11	3	Thompson Socket	C-321	298	$3.11	$926.78	$5.95	91%
12	1	S-Joint	A-182	155	$6.85	$1,061.75	$9.95	45%
13	2	LAMF Valve	B-047	482	$4.01	$1,932.82	$6.95	73%
14								

FIGURE 3-12: A table set up for an advanced filter.

So far, this "advanced" filtering doesn't seem all that different than using one of Excel's predefined operators. True! But the real power of advanced filters is that you're free to enter as many comparison expressions as you need. There are three ways to go about this:

>> **Enter the comparison expressions on the same row.** This tells Excel to filter the table to show only rows that match all the comparison expressions you enter. In Figure 3-13, for example, I'm asking Excel to filter the Parts table to show only rows in which the Unit Cost is less than 10 (cell E2), the Quantity is greater than 300 (cell D2), and the Division equals 3 (cell A2; note that you don't need to use = when you want to match a value exactly).

>> **Enter the comparison expression on separate rows.** This tells Excel to filter the table to show only rows that match at least one of the comparison expressions you enter. In Figure 3-14, for example, I'm asking Excel to filter the Parts table to show only rows in which either the Total Cost is greater than 1000 (cell F2) or the Quantity is greater than 400 (cell D3).

	A	B	C	D	E	F	G	H
1	Division	Description	Number	Quantity	Unit Cost	Total Cost	Retail	Gross Margin
2	3			> 300	< 10			
3								
4								
5	Division	Description	Number	Quantity	Unit Co	Total Co	Reta	Gross Margin
6	4	Gangley Pliers	D-178	57	$10.47	$596.79	$17.95	71%
7	3	HCAB Washer	A-201	856	$0.12	$102.72	$0.25	108%
8	3	Finley Sprocket	C-098	357	$1.57	$560.49	$2.95	88%
9	2	6" Sonotube	B-111	86	$15.24	$1,310.64	$19.95	31%
10	4	Langstrom 7" Wrench	D-017	75	$18.69	$1,401.75	$27.95	50%
11	3	Thompson Socket	C-321	298	$3.11	$926.78	$5.95	91%
12	1	S-Joint	A-182	155	$6.85	$1,061.75	$9.95	45%
13	2	LAMF Valve	B-047	482	$4.01	$1,932.82	$6.95	73%
14								

FIGURE 3-13: Put the comparison expressions on one row to match them all.

>> **Mix and match the preceding as needed.** Feel free to add as many comparison expressions as you need, and don't be shy about using multiple columns and multiple rows. Hey, it's your filter!

	A	B	C	D	E	F	G	H
1	Division	Description	Number	Quantity	Unit Cost	Total Cost	Retail	Gross Margin
2						>1000		
3				>400				
4								
5	Division▼	Description	Number▼	Quantity▼	Unit Co▼	Total Co▼	Reta▼	Gross Margin▼
6	4	Gangley Pliers	D-178	57	$10.47	$596.79	$17.95	71%
7	3	HCAB Washer	A-201	856	$0.12	$102.72	$0.25	108%
8	3	Finley Sprocket	C-098	357	$1.57	$560.49	$2.95	88%
9	2	6" Sonotube	B-111	86	$15.24	$1,310.64	$19.95	31%
10	4	Langstrom 7" Wrench	D-017	75	$18.69	$1,401.75	$27.95	50%
11	3	Thompson Socket	C-321	298	$3.11	$926.78	$5.95	91%
12	1	S-Joint	A-182	155	$6.85	$1,061.75	$9.95	45%
13	2	LAMF Valve	B-047	482	$4.01	$1,932.82	$6.95	73%
14								

FIGURE 3-14:
Put the comparison expressions on separate rows to match one or more.

The extra column headers that you copied and the rows below where you enter your comparison expressions are known as the *criteria range*. Note, however, that just setting up the criteria range doesn't do any filtering. Only after you've set up your criteria range — as was done in Figures 3-13 and 3-14 — are you ready to run the advanced filter operation. Here's how it works:

1. **Select any cell in the table.**

2. **Choose Data ⇨ Advanced.**

Excel displays the Advanced Filter dialog box.

3. **Tell Excel where to place the filtered table.**

Use the Action radio buttons to specify where you want the filtered records to appear:

- **Filter the list, in-place:** Excel hides the records in the table that don't meet the filtering criteria. (Note that *list* is just another word for *table*.) This is the most common way to go because you can work with the filtered data and whatever changes you make will remain when you remove the filter.

- **Copy to another location:** Excel copies the records that meet the filtering criteria to a new location. Take this route if you want to include the filtered data as part of a report, or you want to manipulate the filtered data and don't want those changes to appear in the original table.

4. **In the List Range box, verify the table range.**

Because you selected a cell in the table in Step 1, Excel should correctly identify the table and display its range coordinates in the List Range box. If the text box doesn't show the proper worksheet range for your table, enter or select the correct range.

5. **In the Criteria Range box, select the criteria range.**

The criteria range consists of the copied headers plus the row or rows below the copied headers that you're using to enter the comparison expressions. In Figure 3-14, for example, the criteria range is $A$1:$H$3.

6. **(Optional) If you're copying the filtered records, use the Copy To box to specify the destination.**

Because you don't know in advance how many records will be in the results, you don't need to specify a range in the Copy To box. Instead, enter or select the address of the cell that you want to be the top-left cell of the destination.

Figure 3-15 shows the completed Advanced Filter dialog box, which I used to apply the advanced filter (refer to Figure 3-14).

7. **Click OK.**

Excel filters your table. Figure 3-16 shows what the filtered list looks like. Note that the table now shows only those parts where the Total Cost is greater than $1,000 or the Quantity is greater than 400.

FIGURE 3-15:
An advanced filter all set to go.

If you filtered your table in-place, you can remove the advanced filter and restore the Sort & Filter buttons by selecting any cell in the filtered results and then choosing Data ⇨ Filter in the Sort & Filter group.

	A	B	C	D	E	F	G	H
1	Division	Description	Number	Quantity	Unit Cost	Total Cost	Retail	Gross Margin
2						>1000		
3				>400				
4								
5	Division	Description	Number	Quantity	Unit Cost	Total Cost	Retail	Gross Margin
7	3	HCAB Washer	A-201	856	$0.12	$102.72	$0.25	108%
9	2	6" Sonotube	B-111	86	$15.24	$1,310.64	$19.95	31%
10	4	Langstrom 7" Wrench	D-017	75	$18.69	$1,401.75	$27.95	50%
12	1	S-Joint	A-182	155	$6.85	$1,061.75	$9.95	45%
13	2	LAMF Valve	B-047	482	$4.01	$1,932.82	$6.95	73%
14								

FIGURE 3-16:
The results of the advanced filter in Figure 3-15.

Yep, advanced filters take a bit of work to set up, but after your criteria range is in place, you can entertain yourself for hours by adding comparison expressions to different columns and different rows. Before you know it, that once ornery table data will be like putty in your hands.

» **Exporting data from other programs**

» **Importing data into Excel**

» **Grabbing data from the web**

» **Querying an external database**

Chapter **4**

Grabbing Data from External Sources

In many cases, the data that you want to analyze resides outside Excel. That data could be in a text file or a Word document, on a web page, in a database file, in a database program, such as a corporate accounting system, or on a special database server. Alas, you can't analyze anything that's hunkered down "out there" in a file, a program, or a server. Instead, you have to figure out a way to get the data "in here," by which I mean that you import the data into an Excel workbook and in the form of an Excel table. Importing can be a challenge, but fortunately, Excel offers many powerful tools for importing outside data.

You can use two basic approaches to grabbing external data that you want to analyze. You can export data from another program and then import that data into Excel, or you can query a database directly from Excel. I describe both approaches in this chapter.

What's All This about External Data?

A vast amount of data exists in the world, and most of it resides in some kind of non-workbook format. Some data exists in simple text files, perhaps as comma-separated lists of items. Other data resides in tables, either in Word documents or, more likely, Access databases. Also, an increasing amount of data is available on web pages. *External data* is data that resides outside Excel in a file, database, server, or website.

By definition, external data is not directly available to you via Excel. However, Excel offers a number of tools that enable you to import external data into the program, and from there you can break out Excel's data-analysis tools to extract useful information from that data.

The world's data exists in a seemingly endless variety of files and formats. Here are some of the external data types you're most likely to come across:

- » **Access table:** Microsoft Access is the Office suite's relational database management system. It's often used to store and manage the bulk of the data used by a person, team, department, or company. You can connect to Access tables either via Excel's Query Wizard or by importing table data directly into Excel.

- » **Word table:** Simple collections of data are often stored in a table embedded in a Word document. You can perform only so much analysis on that data in Word, so importing the data from the Word table into an Excel worksheet is often useful.

- » **Text file:** Text files often contain useful data. If the data is formatted properly — for example, each line has the same number of items, all separated by spaces, commas, or tabs — you can import the data into Excel for further analysis.

- » **Web page:** People and companies often make useful data available on web pages that reside either on the internet or on company networks. This data is often a combination of text and tables, but you can't analyze web-based data in any meaningful way in your web browser. Fortunately, Excel enables you to create a web query that lets you import text and tables from a web page.

- » **XML file:** XML (Extensible Markup Language) is a special text format for storing data in a machine-readable format.

- » **External programs and services:** Many programs store data, such as accounting and finance systems, contact management programs, and inventory control software. The bad news is that for the vast majority of such programs, Excel has no way to import the program's data directly. The good news is that Excel is so popular that many programs that store data include a feature that lets you export the data as an Excel workbook. Even programs that don't offer a way to save data as a workbook offer techniques for exporting the data to other formats that Excel can work with, such as text or XML files.

Exporting Data from Other Programs

Before getting to the techniques for importing data into Excel, take a minute to consider how you might export data from an external program into a format that Excel can use. Fortunately, most programs that store data also offer a (usually) straightforward way to export data. Even better, because Excel is the dominant data-analysis tool available to business, you can almost always tweak a program's export routine to produce data in an Excel-friendly format.

For exported data to be Excel friendly, the data must be in one of the following two formats:

>> **Excel workbook:** This format is the gold standard of exporting because you don't even need to import the data into Excel. Instead, you just open the workbook and start analyzing the data (although you might need to convert the data into a table as a first step).

>> **External file that Excel can import:** In most cases, this format is a text file or an XML file.

Therefore, when exporting data from some other program, your first step is to do a little bit of digging to see whether you have a way to easily and automatically export the data to Excel. This fact-finding shouldn't take much time if you use the program's Help system. Next, you need to find the program's Export feature. You can usually find the Export command on the File menu, although you might first need to open a submenu with a name such as Import/Export, Save As, or Utilities. After you've launched the export process, look for an option to save the data directly to an Excel workbook. If you don't see an Excel option, say "Aw, too bad!" and look for a way to export the data as a text file or an XML file. If you go the text file route, be sure to export the data using one of the following two formats:

>> **Delimited text file:** Uses a structure in which each item on a line of text is separated by a character called a *delimiter*. The most common text delimiter is the comma (,) and such a file is known as a *comma-separated values* (*CSV*) file. When Excel imports a delimited text file, it treats each line of text as a record and each delimited item as a field.

>> **Fixed-width text file:** Uses a structure in which all the items use a set amount of space — for example, one item might always use 10 characters, whereas another might always use 20 characters, with the widths padded with blanks as needed — and these fixed widths are the same on every line of text. Excel imports a fixed-width text file by treating each line of text as a record and each fixed-width item as a field.

With your external data in a format that Excel can work with, you're ready to get that data imported into Excel.

Importing External Data into Excel

After you have access to the data, your next step is to import it into an Excel worksheet for analysis and manipulation. Depending on the amount of data, this process can make your worksheet quite large. However, having direct access to the data gives you maximum flexibility when it comes to analyzing it. You can not only use Excel's main data-analysis tools — tables, scenarios, and what-if analysis — but also create a PivotTable from the imported data. I talk about powerful PivotTables in Part 2.

The next few sections take you through the specifics of importing various data types into Excel.

Importing data from an Access table

If you want to use Excel to analyze data from a table or query in an Access database, you can import the table or query into an Excel worksheet. You can use Query Wizard (described later in this chapter) to perform this task. However, if you don't need to filter or sort the data before importing it, you can import the table or query directly from the Access database, which is usually faster. Here are the steps to follow to import a table or query directly from Access:

1. **(Optional) If you want the imported data to appear in an existing worksheet, select the cell that you want Excel to use as the upper-left corner of the destination range.**

2. **Choose Data ⇨ Get Data ⇨ From Database ⇨ From Microsoft Access Database.**

   The Import Data dialog box appears.

3. **Open the folder that contains the database, select the Access database file, and then click Import.**

   Excel analyzes the Access database and then displays the Navigator dialog box that lists the tables and queries that are available to import.

   Alternatively, you might see message similar to *The database has been placed in a state by user whoever on machine whatever that prevents it from being opened or locked.* Yikes! This means that someone else is using the database right now, so you should try again later.

4. In the Navigator dialog box, select the table or query you want to import.

A preview of the data appears, as shown in Figure 4-1.

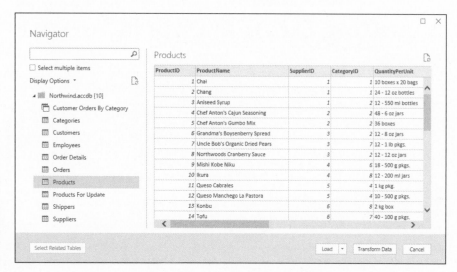

FIGURE 4-1:
Select a table or
query in the
Navigator dialog
box to see a
preview of
the data.

5. Tell Excel where you want the imported data to appear by choosing Load ⇨ Load To to open the Import Data dialog box (note that this is a different Import Data dialog box than the one that appeared after Step 2) and then selecting one of the following:

- **Existing Worksheet:** Imports the data starting at the cell you selected in Step 1. If you decide that you prefer a different cell, use the range box below this option to select where you want the imported data to begin.

- **New Worksheet:** Imports the data into a new worksheet. Note that this is the default import, so you can import the data directly to a new worksheet by selecting the Load button instead of dropping down the Load list.

6. Select OK.

Excel imports the Access data into the worksheet.

Importing data from a Word table

A Microsoft Word *table* is a collection of rows, columns, and cells, which means that it looks something like an Excel range. Moreover, you can insert fields into Word table cells to perform calculations. These fields support cell references, built-in functions, and operators. Cell references designate specific cells; for example, a reference such as B1 refers to the cell in the second column and first row of the table. You can use cell references with built-in functions, such as SUM and AVERAGE, and operators, such as addition (+), multiplication (*), and greater than (>), to build formulas that calculate results based on the table data.

However, Excel still offers far more sophisticated data-analysis tools. Therefore, to analyze your Word table data properly, you should import the table into an Excel worksheet. Here are the steps to trudge through:

1. **Launch Microsoft Word and open the document that contains the table.**

2. **Select a cell in the table you want to import.**

   Word adds the Table Design and Layout contextual tabs to the Ribbon.

3. **Choose Layout ⇨ Select ⇨ Select Table.**

   You can also select the table by clicking the table selection handle, which appears in the upper-left corner of the table.

4. **Choose Home ⇨ Copy or press Ctrl+C.**

5. **Switch to the Excel workbook into which you want to import the table.**

6. **Select the cell where you want the upper-left cell of the table to appear.**

7. **Paste the table data.**

   How you paste the table depends on whether you want Excel to create a link with the original Word table:

   - **If you don't want any connection between Excel and the original Word table:** Choose Home ⇨ Paste or press Ctrl+V. If you make changes to the Word data, those changes aren't reflected in the Excel data (and vice versa).

   - **If you want any changes made to the original Word table to be reflected in the pasted Excel range:** Choose Home ⇨ Paste ⇨ Paste Special. In the Paste Special dialog box, select the Paste Link radio button, select HTML in the As list, and then click OK. The resulting Excel range is linked to the original Word data, so any changes you make to the data in Word automatically appear in the Excel range. Sweet! However, you can't change the data in Excel.

Introducing text file importing

Nowadays, most data resides in some kind of special format: an Excel workbook, an Access database, a server database, a web page, and so on. However, finding data stored in simple text files is still relatively common because text is a universal format that users can work with on any system and in a wide variety of programs. You can analyze the data contained in certain text files by importing the data into an Excel worksheet. Note, however, that you cannot import just any text file into Excel; the file needs to use either the *delimited* or *fixed-width* format.

Importing a delimited text file

A *delimited* text file uses a structure in which each item on a line of text is separated by a character called a *delimiter*. The most common text delimiter is the comma (,), and the resulting file is called a *comma-separated values* (or CSV) file. When Excel imports a delimited text file, it treats each line of text as a row (record) and each item between the delimiter as a column (field).

Follow these steps to import a delimited text file into Excel:

1. **(Optional) To import the data to a specific location in an existing worksheet, select the cell that you want to use as the upper-left corner of the destination range.**

2. **Choose Data ⇨ From Text/CSV (or, if you want the workout, choose Data ⇨ Get Data ⇨ From File ⇨ From Text/CSV).**

   The Import Data dialog box appears.

3. **Open the folder that contains the text file, select the file, and then click Import.**

   Excel analyzes the file and then opens a window that displays a preview of the data in the file.

4. **In the Delimiter list, select the delimiter character that your text data uses.**

   How do you know which delimiter character to choose? The comma is by far the most common delimiter, so start with that. You'll know you've hit the delimiter jackpot when the previewed data appears in separate columns, as shown in Figure 4-2.

5. **Do one of the following to import the data starting at the cell you selected in Step 1:**

   - **To import the data into a new worksheet:** Choose Load.
   - **To import the data into an existing worksheet:** Choose Load ⇨ Load To to open the Import To dialog box, select the Existing Worksheet option, and then click OK.

   Excel imports the delimited text data into the worksheet.

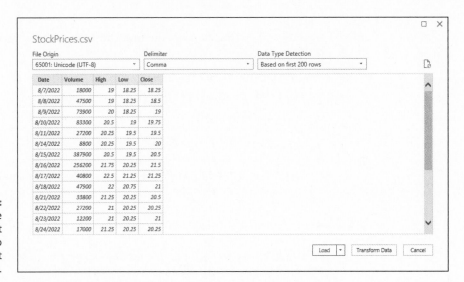

Importing a fixed-width text file

A *fixed-width* text file uses a structure in which all the items use a set amount of space. The first item might always be, say, 10 characters wide (including spaces); the second item might always be 8 characters wide; and so on. Crucially, these fixed widths are the same on every line of text, which gives the entire file a predictable and regular structure that Excel can work with. Excel imports a fixed-width text file by treating each line of text as a row (record) and each fixed-width item as a column (field).

If you're importing data that uses the fixed-width structure, you need to tell Excel where the separation between each field occurs. In a fixed-width text file, each column of data is a constant width, and Excel is usually quite good at determining these widths. So in most cases, Excel automatically sets up *column break lines,* which are vertical lines that separate one field from the next. However, titles or introductory text at the beginning of the file can impair the wizard's calculations, so you should check carefully that the proposed break lines are accurate.

Follow these steps to import a fixed-width text file into Excel:

1. **(Optional) To load the data into a specific worksheet location, select the cell that you want to use as the upper-left corner of the destination range.**

2. **Choose Data ➪ From Text/CSV (or, if you have time to kill, choose Data ➪ Get Data ➪ From File ➪ From Text/CSV).**

    The Import Data dialog box appears.

3. **Open the folder that contains the text file, select the file, and then click Import.**

   Excel analyzes the file and then opens a window that displays a preview of the data in the file.

4. **In the Delimiter list, make sure that the Fixed Width item is selected.**

   Below the Delimiter list, Excel displays a series of numbers, each of which represents the starting point of a column in the text file. The first column always starts at 0, and each subsequent value depends on the width of each column. Figure 4-3 shows these values as 0, 30, 45.

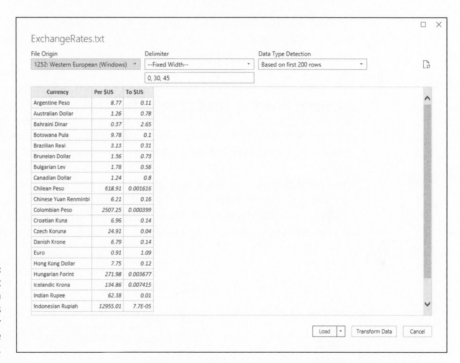

FIGURE 4-3:
If needed, edit the column starting points until your columns are correct.

5. **If your columns look incorrect — for example, one or more columns are too large or too small — edit the column starting-point values until the columns are correct, as shown in Figure 4-3.**

6. **Do one of the following to import the data starting at the cell you selected in Step 1:**

- **To import the data into a new worksheet:** Choose Load.

- **To import the data into an existing worksheet:** Choose Load ⇨ Load To to open the Import To dialog box, select the Existing Worksheet option, and then click OK.

Excel imports the fixed-width text data into the worksheet.

Importing data from a web page

You already know that the web is home to more information than you can ever use, but did you know that some of that data is available to import into Excel? I talk about a more sophisticated web-based data format in the next section, but here I want to introduce you to web data that comes in the form of a table. A *web page table* is a rectangular array of rows and columns, with data values in the cells created by the intersection of the rows and columns. Why, that sounds just like an Excel table, doesn't it? It sure does, and that similarity means that if you know the address of the page that contains the table, you can use an Excel tool to import the data into a worksheet for more data-analysis fun.

Here are the steps to follow to import a web page table into Excel:

1. **(Optional) To load the data into a specific worksheet location, select the cell that you want to use as the upper-left corner of the destination range.**

2. **Choose Data ⇨ From Web (or, if you prefer the scenic route, choose Data ⇨ Get Data ⇨ From Other Sources ⇨ From Web).**

   The From Web window appears.

3. **Enter the address of the web page in the URL text box and then click OK.**

   Excel displays the Access Web Content dialog box.

4. **Specify how you want to access the web page and then click Connect.**

   As shown in Figure 4-4, Excel offers five methods that you can use to access the web content:

   - **Anonymous:** Accesses the content directly, without authentication (such as a username and password). Use this method for most web pages.

   - **Windows:** Accesses the content by logging in using the credentials (that is, the username and password) of your Windows account. Use this method if the content resides on your company's network.

- **Basic:** Accesses the content by logging in with a username and password that you provide. Use this method if you have an account on the website that hosts the content.

- **Web API:** Accesses the content by using a unique value — called a *key* — to authenticate your request. Use this method if content is made available through a web application programming interface (API). The instructions for using the web API tell you how to obtain a key.

- **Organizational Account:** Accesses the content by having you sign in to your organization's Office 365 or OneDrive for Business account.

Excel connects to the web content, analyzes the web page, and then opens the Navigator dialog box, which displays a list of the tables found on the page. One of these objects is always named Document, and it contains a table of data related to the entire web page (so you can safely ignore it).

FIGURE 4-4:
Choose the method you want to use to access the web data.

5. **Select the table you want to import.**

   Excel displays a preview of the table, as shown in Figure 4-5. If you want to see what the table looks like on the web page, click the Web View tab.

6. **(Optional) If you want to import multiple tables, select the Select Multiple Items check box and then select the check box beside each table you want to import.**

7. **Do one of the following to import the data starting at the cell you selected in Step 1:**

   - **To import the data into a new worksheet:** Choose Load.

   - **To import the data into an existing worksheet:** Choose Load ⇨ Load To to open the Import To dialog box, select the Existing Worksheet option, and then click OK.

   Excel imports the web table data into the worksheet.

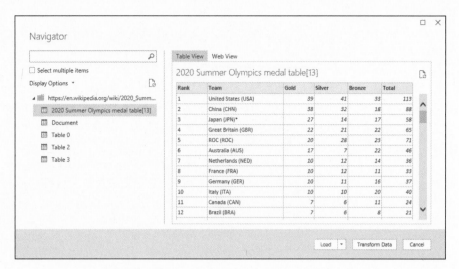

FIGURE 4-5:
Select a table to
preview its data.

Importing an XML file

XML (Extensible Markup Language) is a standard that enables the management
and sharing of structured data using simple text files. These XML files organize
data using *tags*, among other elements, that specify the equivalent of a table name
and field names. Here's an example that shows the first few records in an XML
table of book info:

```xml
<?xml version="1.0"?>
<catalog>
    <book>
        <author>Gambardella, Matthew</author>
        <title>XML Developer's Guide</title>
        <genre>Computer</genre>
        <price>44.95</price>
        <publish_date>2000-10-01</publish_date>
        <description>An in-depth look at creating applications
        with XML.</description>
    </book>
    <book>
        <author>Ralls, Kim</author>
        <title>Midnight Rain</title>
        <genre>Fantasy</genre>
        <price>5.95</price>
        <publish_date>2000-12-16</publish_date>
        <description>A former architect battles corporate zombies,
        an evil sorceress, and her own childhood to become queen
```

```
        of the world.</description>
    </book>
    <book>
        <author>Corets, Eva</author>
        <title>Maeve Ascendant</title>
        <genre>Fantasy</genre>
        <price>5.95</price>
        <publish_date>2000-11-17</publish_date>
        <description>After the collapse of a nanotechnology
        society in England, the young survivors lay the
        foundation for a new society.</description>
    </book>
    etc.
</catalog>
```

Because XML is just text, if you want to perform data analysis on the XML file, you must import the file into an Excel worksheet. Excel stores imported XML data in an Excel table.

Here are the steps to follow to import an XML file into an Excel worksheet:

1. **(Optional) To import the data to a specific location in an existing worksheet, select the cell that you want to use as the upper-left corner of the destination range.**

2. **Choose Data ⇨ Get Data ⇨ From File ⇨ From XML.**

   The Import Data dialog box appears.

3. **Open the folder that contains the XML file, select the file, and then click Import.**

   Excel analyzes the XML file and then opens the Navigator dialog box, which displays a list of the tables found in the file.

4. **Select the table you want to import.**

   Excel displays a preview of the table, as shown in Figure 4-6.

5. **(Optional) If you want to import multiple XML tables, select the Select Multiple Items check box and then select the check box beside each table you want to import.**

FIGURE 4-6:
Select an XML
table to preview
its data.

6. **Do one of the following to import the data starting at the cell you selected in Step 1:**

   - **To import the data into a new worksheet:** Choose Load.

   - **To import the data into an existing worksheet:** Choose Load ⇨ Load To to open the Import To dialog box, select the Existing Worksheet option, and then click OK.

   Excel imports the XML data into the worksheet.

Querying External Databases

If you want to analyze data using a sorted, filtered subset of an external data source, use the Query Wizard tool, which enables you to specify the sorting and filtering options and the subset of the source data that you want to work with. Why bother doing all that work? Because databases such as those used in Microsoft Access and SQL Server are often very large and contain a wide variety of data scattered over many different tables.

With data analysis, you rarely use an entire database as the source. Instead, you extract a subset of the database: a table or perhaps two or three related tables. You might also require the data to be sorted in a certain way, and perhaps need to filter the data so that you work with only certain records. The specifics of these three operations — extracting a subset, sorting, and filtering — constitute the *criteria* for the data you want to work with, and all together they make up what's known in the trade as a database *query*.

Defining a data source

All database queries require two things at the very beginning: access to a database and an *Open Database Connectivity,* or *ODBC,* data source for the database. ODBC is a database standard that enables a program to connect to and manipulate a data source. An ODBC data source contains three things: a pointer to the file or server where the database resides; a driver that enables Query Wizard to connect to, manipulate, and return data from the database; and optional login information that you require to access the database.

Before you can do any work with Query Wizard, you must select the data source that you want to use. If you have a particular database that you want to query, you can define a new data source that points to the appropriate file or server.

Most data sources point to database files. For example, the relational database management program Microsoft Access uses file-based databases. You can also create data sources based on text files and Excel workbooks. However, some data sources point to server-based databases. For example, SQL Server and Oracle run their databases on special servers. As part of the data-source definition, you need to include the software driver that Query Wizard uses to communicate with the database, as well as any information that you require to access the database.

Follow these steps to define a data source for your query:

1. **Choose Data ⇨ Get Data ⇨ From Other Sources ⇨ From Microsoft Query.**

   The Choose Data Source dialog box appears, as shown in Figure 4-7.

   Your computer probably comes with a few predefined data sources that you can use instead of creating new ones. In the Choose Data Source dialog box, any predefined data sources appear in the Databases tab. For example, Microsoft Office creates two default data sources: Excel Files and MS Access Database. These incomplete data sources don't point to a specific file. Instead, when you select one of these data sources and then click OK, Excel prompts you for the name and location of the file. These data sources are useful if you often switch the files that you're using. However, if you want a data source that always points to a specific file, you need to follow the steps in this section.

2. **Choose <New Data Source>, deselect the Use the Query Wizard to Create/ Edit Queries check box, and then click OK.**

   The Create New Data Source dialog box appears.

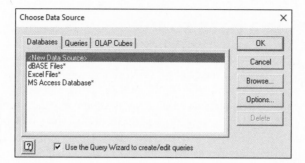

FIGURE 4-7:
The Choose Data
Source dia-
log box.

3. **In the What Name Do You Want to Give Your Data Source? text box, enter a name for your data source.**

This name appears in the Databases tab of the Choose Data Source dialog box, so enter a name that helps you remember which data source you're working with.

4. **From the Select a Driver for the Type of Database You Want to Access list, select the database driver that your data source requires.**

For example, for an Access database, select Microsoft Access Driver (*.mdb, *.accdb).

TECHNICAL STUFF

Many businesses store their data in Microsoft SQL Server databases (SQL is usually pronounced *ess-kew-ell*). This is a powerful server-based system that can handle the largest databases and thousands of users. To define an SQL Server data source, select SQL Server. Click Connect to display the SQL Server Login dialog box. Ask your SQL Server database administrator for the information you require to complete this dialog box. Type the name or remote address of the SQL Server in the Server text box, type your SQL Server login ID and password, and then click OK. Perform Steps 9 and 10 later in this section to complete the data source.

5. **Click Connect.**

The dialog box for the database driver appears. The steps that follow show you how to set up a data source for a Microsoft Access database.

6. **Click the Select button.**

The Select Database dialog box appears.

7. **Open the folder that contains the database, select the database file, and then click OK.**

Excel returns you to the database driver's dialog box.

If you use a login name and password to access the database, click Advanced to display the Set Advanced Options dialog box. Type the login name and password and then click OK.

8. **Click OK.**

Excel returns you to the Create New Data Source dialog box. Figure 4-8 shows the completed dialog box for the Northwind Access database that I'm using.

You can use the Select a Default Table for Your Data Source list to select a table from the database. When you do this, each time you start a new query based on this data source, Query Wizard automatically adds the default table to the query, thus saving you several steps.

If you specified a login name and password as part of the data source, you can select the Save My User ID and Password in the Data Source Definition check box to save the login data.

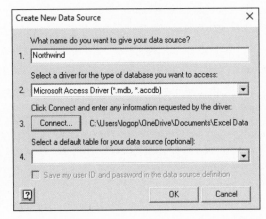

FIGURE 4-8:
The completed Create New Data Source dialog box for the Northwind database.

9. **Click OK.**

Excel returns to the Choose Data Source dialog box, which now displays your shiny, new data source.

10. **Click Cancel to bypass the steps for importing the data.**

You can now use the data source in Query Wizard, which I talk about in the next section.

Querying a data source

To run a database query and import the query results, follow these steps:

1. **Choose Data ⇨ Get Data ⇨ From Other Sources ⇨ From Microsoft Query.**

Excel displays the Choose Data Source dialog box. In Figure 4-9, you can see that the Northwind data source I created in the preceding section now appears in the Databases tab.

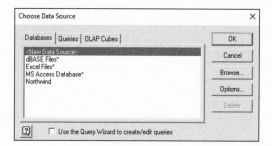

FIGURE 4-9:
Any data sources you've created appear in the Databases tab.

2. **Select the Use the Query Wizard to Create/Edit Queries check box.**

If you didn't define a new data source as described in the preceding section, this check box should already be selected for you.

3. **On the Databases tab, select the database you want to query and then click OK. If you choose a predefined database type, select the database that you want to query in the Select Database dialog box that appears, and then click OK.**

Excel displays the Query Wizard — Choose Columns dialog box.

You use the Query Wizard — Choose Columns dialog box to pick which tables and which table columns (fields) you want to appear in your query results. In the Available Tables and Columns box, Excel lists tables and columns. Initially, this list shows only tables, but you can see the columns in a table by clicking the + icon next to the table name.

4. **Populate the Columns in Your Query list with the columns you want to work with.**

You can choose from three techniques:

- **Add an entire table to the list.** Click the table name and then click the right-facing arrow button that points to the Columns in Your Query list box.

- **Add a single column from a table to the list.** Click the + icon beside the table name, select the column, and then click the right-facing arrow button that points to the Columns in Your Query list box.

- **Remove a column.** Select the column in the Columns in Your Query list box and then click the left-facing arrow button that points to the Available Tables and Columns list box.

This all sounds complicated, but it really isn't. Essentially, all you do is identify the columns of information that you want in your Excel table. Figure 4-10 shows how the Query Wizard — Choose Columns dialog box looks after adding several columns from the Products table and one column (CategoryName) from the Categories table.

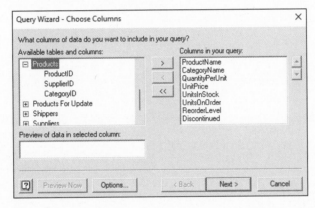

5. **After you identify which columns you want in your query, click the Next button to filter the query data.**

Excel displays the Query Wizard — Filter Data dialog box.

6. **(Optional) You can filter the data returned as part of your query by using the Only Include Rows Where text boxes. For example, to include only rows in which the CategoryName column equals Beverages, click the CategoryName column in the Column to Filter list box. Then select the Equals filtering operation from the first drop-down list and enter the value Beverages into the second drop-down list (or select it); you can see this filter in action in Figure 4-11.**

TIP

The Query Wizard — Filter Data dialog box performs the same sorts of filtering that you can perform with the AutoFilter command and the Advanced Filter command. Because I discuss these tools in Chapter 3, I don't repeat that discussion here. However, note that you can perform quite sophisticated filtering as part of your query.

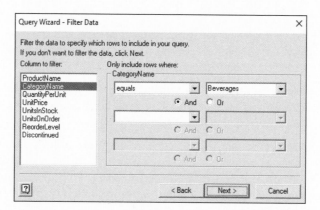

FIGURE 4-11:
The Query
Wizard – Filter
Data dialog box
with a filter
added.

7. **(Optional) Filter your data based on multiple filters by selecting the And or Or radio button.**

- **And:** A row is included in the query only if it matches all the filter conditions.

- **Or:** A row is included in the query if it matches one or more of the filter conditions.

8. **Click Next.**

Excel displays the Query Wizard — Sort Order dialog box.

9. **Choose a sort order for the query result data from the Query Wizard — Sort Order dialog box.**

Select the column that you want to use for sorting from the Sort By drop-down list and then select one of the following radio buttons (see Figure 4-12):

- **Ascending:** The column values are sorted in increasing order: A to Z if the column contains text, 0 to 9 for numbers, earlier to later for dates or times.

- **Descending:** The column values are sorted in decreasing order: Z to A for text, 9 to 0 for numbers, later to earlier for dates or times.

You can also use additional sort keys by selecting fields in one or more of the Then By drop-down lists that appear in the Query Wizard — Sort Order dialog box. The wizard displays a drop-down list for every field in your query.

TIP

You sort query results the same way that you sort rows in an Excel table. If you have more questions about how to sort rows, refer to Chapter 3. Sorting works the same whether you're dealing with query results or rows in a table.

10. **Click Next.**

Excel displays the Query Wizard — Finish dialog box.

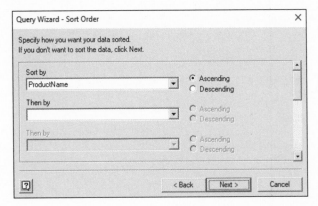

FIGURE 4-12:
The Query
Wizard — Sort
Order dialog box.

11. **In the Query Wizard — Finish dialog box, specify where Excel should place the query results.**

For most types of data, you have two choices:

- **Return Data to Microsoft Excel:** Sends the data to Excel without further review on your part.

- **View Data or Edit Query in Microsoft Query:** Opens the query in a separate Office program called Microsoft Query. This is a sophisticated database query program, the workings of which are beyond the scope of this book. If you decide to try this program, when you're finished with it, choose File ➪ Return Data to Microsoft Excel and then continue with Step 13.

12. **Click the Finish button.**

After you click the Finish button to complete Query Wizard, Excel displays the Import Data dialog box.

13. **In the Import Data dialog box, choose the worksheet location for the query result data.**

Use this dialog box to specify where query-result data should be placed.

- **To place the query-result data in an existing worksheet:** Select the Existing Worksheet radio button. Then identify the cell in the top-left corner of the worksheet range and enter its location in the Existing Worksheet text box.

- **To place the data into a new worksheet:** Select the New Worksheet radio button.

14. **Click OK.**

Excel places the data at the location you chose.

Chapter **5**

Analyzing Table Data with Functions

After you've imported your data and converted it to an Excel range, you might find yourself asking a most unmusical question: Now what? The what-do-I-do-next? conundrum is particularly relevant to tables that contain a vast sea of numbers. You're sure that those numbers must contain some important information for you to glean, but how do you get at it? You're sure that the data has something useful to say about your business, but how do you hear it?

The answer to all these questions is to put Excel to work analyzing the table. Excel handily provides a special set of functions — called *database functions* — especially for the statistical analysis of information stored in Excel tables. In this chapter, you learn about these database functions and see how to take advantage of them to get your table to spill its secrets.

The Database Functions: Some General Remarks

You might be wondering right off the bat why Excel calls these "database" functions, which seems a touch grand. However, Excel is using the word *database* as a synonym for *table*, so I follow suit and use the terms interchangeably in the pages that follow. Why not just call them table functions and avoid confusion? Because technically, these functions don't require a table: Any old range will do in a pinch.

The database functions all use the same three arguments, so I describe those arguments here to save some wear and tear on my typing fingers:

» *database*: The range of cells that make up the table you want to work with. You can use the table name or the table range address. If you go with the table name, be sure to reference the entire table by using the syntax `Table[#All]` (where `Table` is the name of your table).

» *field*: A reference to the table column on which you want to perform the operation. You can use either the column header or the column number (where the leftmost column is 1, the next column is 2, and so on). If you use the column name, enclose it in quotation marks (for example, "Unit Price").

» *criteria*: The range of cells that hold the criteria you want to work with. You can use either a range name, if one is defined, or the range address.

I talk about making a criteria range for advanced filter work in Chapter 3, and setting up a criteria range for database functions is similar. That is, you insert three or four blank rows above your table headers, copy your table headers, select the first cell of the first row of those blank rows, and then paste the copied headers there. For example, Figure 5-1 shows two ranges: the bigger range beginning in cell A7 is a table named Inventory, whereas the smaller range in A4:G5 is the criteria range.

Now you can enter your criteria, which consists of one or more comparison expressions that you enter into the cells below the copied header of each column you want to work with:

» **Enter the comparison expressions on the same row:** This tells Excel to apply the database function to the *field* rows that match all the comparison expressions you enter.

>> **Enter the comparison expressions on separate rows:** This tells Excel to apply the database function to the *field* rows that match at least one of the comparison expressions you enter.

	A	B	C	D	E	F	G
4	Product Name	Category	On Hold	On Hand	Unit Cost	List Price	Value
5							
6							
7	Product Name	Category	On Hold	On Hand	Unit Cost	List Price	Value
8	Chai	Beverages	25	25	$13.50	$18.00	$337.50
9	Syrup	Confections	0	50	$7.50	$10.00	$375.00
10	Cajun Seasoning	Confections	0	0	$16.50	$22.00	$0.00
11	Olive Oil	Condiments	0	15	$16.01	$21.35	$240.19
12	Boysenberry Spread	Condiments	0	0	$18.75	$25.00	$0.00
13	Dried Pears	Fruits	0	0	$22.50	$30.00	$0.00
14	Curry Sauce	Sauces/Soups	0	0	$30.00	$40.00	$0.00
15	Walnuts	Produce	0	40	$17.44	$23.25	$697.50
16	Fruit Cocktail	Produce	0	0	$29.25	$39.00	$0.00
17	Chocolate Biscuits Mix	Confections	0	0	$6.90	$9.20	$0.00
18	Marmalade	Condiments	0	0	$60.75	$81.00	$0.00
19	Scones	Grains/Cereals	0	0	$7.50	$10.00	$0.00
20	Beer	Beverages	23	23	$10.50	$14.00	$241.50
21	Crab Meat	Seafood	0	0	$13.80	$18.40	$0.00
22	Clam Chowder	Seafood	0	0	$7.24	$9.65	$0.00

FIGURE 5-1:
A table and its criteria range.

Retrieving a Value from a Table

As part of your data analysis, retrieving a single value from a table to use in a formula is often useful. For example, if you have a table that lists the inventory of all your products, you might want to check how much of a particular product is on hand now to decide whether now's the time to reorder that product. Similarly, you might want to calculate a product's gross margin given its list price and unit cost:

```
(List Price - Unit Cost) / List Price
```

Whenever you need a value from the table to use in a formula, use the DGET function. DGET retrieves a value from a table according to the criteria you specify. The function uses the following syntax:

```
DGET(database, field, criteria)
```

For example, consider the Inventory table shown previously in Figure 5-1. Suppose you want to know how many units are on hand of the product named Beer. To set up the criteria range, you enter Beer below the Product Name field, as shown in Figure 5-2. With that done, you can build your DGET function, which is in cell B1 in Figure 5-2:

```
DGET(Inventory[#All], "On Hand", A4:G5)
```

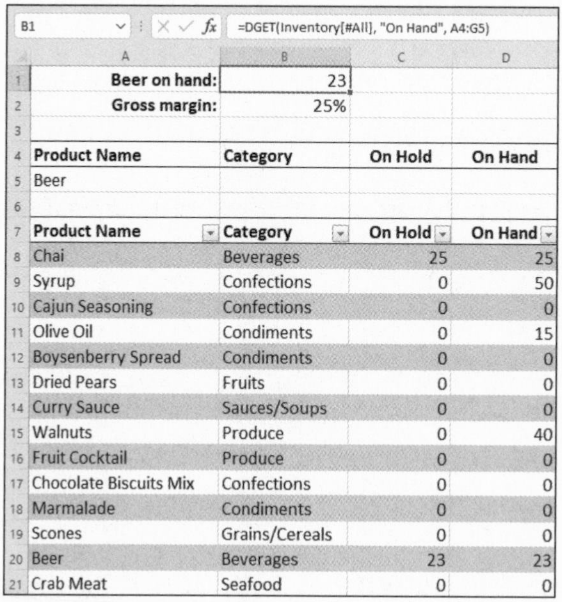

FIGURE 5-2:
Use DGET to
retrieve a value
from a table
based on your
criteria.

This DGET function is saying to Excel, in effect, "Take a look at the entire table named Inventory, locate the row that has Beer in the Product Name column, and then retrieve the value in the On Hand column. Thanks in advance." Sure enough, DGET returns the value 23 to cell B1 because that's the On Hand value of the Beer product.

TIP

By the way, if no record in your list matches your selection criteria, DGET returns the #VALUE error message. For example, if you construct selection criteria that look for Northwind Traders Lager, DGET returns #VALUE because that product doesn't exist. Also, if multiple records in your list match your selection criteria, DGET returns the #NUM error message. For example, if you enter *Chocolate* in the Product Name field of the criteria range, that string matches all the products that have Chocolate in the name. Two such products exist, so DGET returns the #NUM error message.

Summing a Column's Values

In Chapter 3, I talk about two ways to display simple table sums: by selecting some column cells and viewing the sum in Excel's status bar, and by adding subtotals to the table. Those techniques are fine if all you want to do is view the sum, but what if you want to use the sum in a formula or as part of a table summary? Yep, Excel's

SUM function would work, but what if you want the sum of only those items that meet some criteria? For example, in an inventory table, what if you want to know the total value of just the items in the Beverages category?

Ah, for that you need the DSUM function, which adds values from a table based on the criteria you specify. The function uses the standard database function syntax:

```
DSUM(database, field, criteria)
```

For example, to get the total value of just the products in the Beverages category, you set up your criteria range with the string Beverages under the Category header (see Figure 5-3). With that value in place, you build your DSUM function (as shown in cell B1 in Figure 5-3):

```
DSUM(Inventory2[#All], "Value", A3:G4)
```

B1	▼ : × ✓ fx	=DSUM(Inventory2[#All], "Value", A3:G4)					
	A	B	C	D	E	F	G
1	**Total value of Beverages:**	$12,041.50					
2							
3	**Product Name**	**Category**	**On Hold**	**On Hand**	**Unit Cost**	**List Price**	**Value**
4		Beverages					
5							
6	**Product Name** ▼	**Category** ▼	**On Hold** ▼	**On Hand** ▼	**Unit Cost** ▼	**List Price** ▼	**Value** ▼
7	Chai	Beverages	25	25	$13.50	$18.00	$337.50
8	Syrup	Confections	0	50	$7.50	$10.00	$375.00
9	Cajun Seasoning	Confections	0	0	$16.50	$22.00	$0.00
10	Olive Oil	Condiments	0	15	$16.01	$21.35	$240.19
11	Boysenberry Spread	Condiments	0	0	$18.75	$25.00	$0.00
12	Dried Pears	Fruits	0	0	$22.50	$30.00	$0.00
13	Curry Sauce	Sauces/Soups	0	0	$30.00	$40.00	$0.00
14	Walnuts	Produce	0	40	$17.44	$23.25	$697.50
15	Fruit Cocktail	Produce	0	0	$29.25	$39.00	$0.00
16	Chocolate Biscuits Mix	Confections	0	0	$6.90	$9.20	$0.00
17	Marmalade	Condiments	0	0	$60.75	$81.00	$0.00
18	Scones	Grains/Cereals	0	0	$7.50	$10.00	$0.00
19	Beer	Beverages	23	23	$10.50	$14.00	$241.50
20	Crab Meat	Seafood	0	0	$13.80	$18.40	$0.00

FIGURE 5-3:
Use DSUM to add a column's values based on your criteria.

You might be wondering why the table name changed from Inventory in the DGET example to Inventory2 in the DSUM example. That's because in my example workbook for this chapter, I use a separate worksheet for each database function, so when I copy the Inventory table to a new worksheet, I need to give the table a new name (because table names must be unique in a workbook).

TIP

DSUM isn't the only way to total stuff based on criteria. Excel also offers the SUMIF and SUMIFS functions, which I talk about in Chapter 11.

Counting a Column's Values

If you select some values in a table column, Excel's status bar will gladly display a Count item, which tells you how many cells you selected. Fine and dandy, but data analysis is usually a bit more sophisticated than that. For example, in an inventory table, suppose you want to know many products are low in stock (that is, have fewer than 10 in the On Hand column)?

That kind of calculation falls under the bailiwick of both the DCOUNT and DCOUNTA functions, which count records in a table that match criteria you specify:

```
DCOUNT(database, field, criteria)
DCOUNTA(database, field, criteria)
```

What's the diff? DCOUNT counts the numeric values in field, whereas DCOUNTA counts all the nonblank items in field.

For example, to get the count of the products that have low stock, you set up your criteria range with the expression < 10 under the On Hand header (see Figure 5-4) and then add the DCOUNT function (as shown in cell B1 in Figure 5-4):

```
DCOUNT(Inventory3[#All], "On Hand", A3:G4)
```

	B1 ⌄ ⠿ ✕ ✓ fx	=DCOUNT(Inventory3[#All], "On Hand", A3:G4)					
	A	B	C	D	E	F	G
1	Count of out of stock:	25					
2							
3	Product Name	Category	On Hold	On Hand	Unit Cost	List Price	Value
4				<10			
5							
6	Product Name ⌄	Category ⌄	On Hold ⌄	On Hand ⌄	Unit Cost ⌄	List Price ⌄	Value ⌄
7	Chai	Beverages	25	25	$13.50	$18.00	$337.50
8	Syrup	Confections	0	50	$7.50	$10.00	$375.00
9	Cajun Seasoning	Confections	0	0	$16.50	$22.00	$0.00
10	Olive Oil	Condiments	0	15	$16.01	$21.35	$240.19
11	Boysenberry Spread	Condiments	0	0	$18.75	$25.00	$0.00
12	Dried Pears	Produce	0	0	$22.50	$30.00	$0.00
13	Curry Sauce	Sauces/Soups	0	0	$30.00	$40.00	$0.00
14	Walnuts	Produce	0	40	$17.44	$23.25	$697.50
15	Fruit Cocktail	Produce	0	0	$29.25	$39.00	$0.00
16	Chocolate Biscuits Mix	Confections	0	0	$6.90	$9.20	$0.00
17	Marmalade	Condiments	0	0	$60.75	$81.00	$0.00
18	Scones	Grains/Cereals	0	0	$7.50	$10.00	$0.00
19	Beer	Beverages	23	23	$10.50	$14.00	$241.50
20	Crab Meat	Seafood	0	0	$13.80	$18.40	$0.00

FIGURE 5-4: Use DCOUNT (or DCOUNTA) to tally a column's values based on your criteria.

TIP

If you just want to count records in a list, you can omit the *field* argument from the DCOUNT and DCOUNTA functions. When you don't specify a column name or number, the function counts the records in the table that match your criteria without regard to whether some field stores a value or is nonblank. For example, both of the following functions return the value 25:

```
DCOUNT(Inventory3[#All],, A3:G4)
DCOUNTA(Inventory3[#All],, A3:G4)
```

Note: To omit an argument, leave the space between the two commas empty.

TIP

Excel has a seemingly uncountable number of ways to count things. Besides DCOUNT, you can also use COUNT, COUNTA, COUNTIF, COUNTIFS, and COUNTBLANK. Check out Chapter 11 or Excel's online help for more information about these functions.

Averaging a Column's Values

The DAVERAGE function calculates an average for values in an Excel list. The unique and truly useful feature of DAVERAGE is that you can specify that you want only table records that meet specified criteria included in your average. DAVERAGE uses the following syntax:

```
DAVERAGE(database, field, criteria)
```

As an example of how the DAVERAGE function works, I return to the Inventory table and ask a basic question: What's the average unit cost value for those products in the Beverages and Produce categories? To answer this query, you add the text Beverages under the Category header in the criteria range, and then add the text Produce below the Beverages cell, as shown in Figure 5-5. Remember that when you enter criteria using multiple rows, Excel selects those rows in the table that match at least one of the conditions. So, in the example, I'm asking Excel to look for only those products that have either Beverages or Produce in the Category column. Here's the DAVERAGE function that returns the average Unit Cost for those products (see cell B1 in Figure 5-5):

```
DAVERAGE(Inventory4[#All], "Unit Cost", A3:G5)
```

	A	B	C	D	E	F	G
B1		fx	=DAVERAGE(Inventory4[#All], "Unit Cost", A3:G5)				
1	Average unit cost:	$11.06					
2							
3	Product Name	Category	On Hold	On Hand	Unit Cost	List Price	Value
4		Beverages					
5		Produce					
6							
7	Product Name	Category	On Hold	On Hand	Unit Cost	List Price	Value
8	Chai	Beverages	25	25	$13.50	$18.00	$337.50
9	Syrup	Confections	0	50	$7.50	$10.00	$375.00
10	Cajun Seasoning	Confections	0	0	$16.50	$22.00	$0.00
11	Olive Oil	Condiments	0	15	$16.01	$21.35	$240.19
12	Boysenberry Spread	Condiments	0	0	$18.75	$25.00	$0.00
13	Dried Pears	Produce	0	0	$22.50	$30.00	$0.00
14	Curry Sauce	Sauces/Soups	0	0	$30.00	$40.00	$0.00
15	Walnuts	Produce	0	40	$17.44	$23.25	$697.50
16	Fruit Cocktail	Produce	0	0	$29.25	$39.00	$0.00
17	Chocolate Biscuits Mix	Confections	0	0	$6.90	$9.20	$0.00
18	Marmalade	Condiments	0	0	$60.75	$81.00	$0.00
19	Scones	Grains/Cereals	0	0	$7.50	$10.00	$0.00
20	Beer	Beverages	23	23	$10.50	$14.00	$241.50
21	Crab Meat	Seafood	0	0	$13.80	$18.40	$0.00

FIGURE 5-5:
Use DAVERAGE to average a column's values based on your criteria.

Note that I expanded the *criteria* range to include both rows 4 and 5.

TIP

Excel offers an above-average number of functions for calculating averages, including not only the AVERAGE function (of course) but also the MEAN, MEDIAN, and MODE functions. I talk about these functions in Chapter 11.

Determining a Column's Maximum and Minimum Values

In data analysis work, it's often useful to look for *outliers,* which are values that are either much greater or much less than the average. One way to check for such anomalous values is to find the largest and smallest values in a column. You can certainly calculate such maxima and minima using every value in the column, but if you're interested only in the values that meet some criteria, have I got two functions for you: DMAX and DMIN. These functions find the largest and smallest values, respectively, in a table column for those rows that match the criteria you specify. Both functions use the same standard-issue database function syntax, as shown here:

```
DMAX(database, field, criteria)
DMIN(database, field, criteria)
```

As an example of how the DMAX and DMIN functions work, suppose you have an inventory table with a Value column that's the product of the number of units on hand and the unit cost. (For example, a product with 100 units on hand and a $5 unit cost has a total value of $500.) Here's a question for you: What are the maximum and minimum values for those items in the Produce category that are in stock?

To answer the preceding question, you add the text Produce under the Category header in the criteria range and then add the expression >0 below the On Hand header, as shown in Figure 5-6. Remember that when you enter multiple conditions on a single row, Excel matches only those rows in the table that match all the conditions. So, in the example, I'm asking Excel to look for only those products that have Produce in the Category column and a value greater than 0 in the On Hand column.

B1		f_x	=DMAX(Inventory5[#All], "Value", A4:G5)				
	A	B	C	D	E	F	G
1	Maximum value:	$697.50					
2	Minimum value:	$5.00					
3							
4	Product Name	Category	On Hold	On Hand	Unit Cost	List Price	Value
5		Produce		>0			
6							
7	Product Name	Category	On Hold	On Hand	Unit Cost	List Price	Value
8	Chai	Beverages	25	25	$13.50	$18.00	$337.50
9	Syrup	Confections	0	50	$7.50	$10.00	$375.00
10	Cajun Seasoning	Confections	0	0	$16.50	$22.00	$0.00
11	Olive Oil	Condiments	0	15	$16.01	$21.35	$240.19
12	Boysenberry Spread	Condiments	0	0	$18.75	$25.00	$0.00
13	Dried Pears	Produce	0	0	$22.50	$30.00	$0.00
14	Curry Sauce	Sauces/Soups	0	0	$30.00	$40.00	$0.00
15	Walnuts	Produce	0	40	$17.44	$23.25	$697.50
16	Fruit Cocktail	Produce	0	0	$29.25	$39.00	$0.00
17	Chocolate Biscuits Mix	Confections	0	0	$6.90	$9.20	$0.00
18	Marmalade	Condiments	0	0	$60.75	$81.00	$0.00
19	Scones	Grains/Cereals	0	0	$7.50	$10.00	$0.00
20	Beer	Beverages	23	23	$10.50	$14.00	$241.50
21	Crab Meat	Seafood	0	0	$13.80	$18.40	$0.00

FIGURE 5-6: Use DMAX and DMIN to return a column's largest and smallest values based on your criteria.

Here are the DMAX and DMIN functions that return the maximum and minimum, respectively, for those products (see cells B1 and B2 in Figure 5-6):

```
DMAX(Inventory5[#All], "Value", A4:G5)
DMIN(Inventory5[#All], "Value", A4:G5)
```

TIP

Excel provides several other functions for finding the minimum or maximum value, including MAX, MAXA, MIN, and MINA. Turn to Chapter 11 for more information about using these related functions.

Multiplying a Column's Values

Lots of table data contains the results of surveys or polls, meaning that the table values are percentages. One way you might want to interrogate such data is to ask, given two percentages, in what percentage are both true in the surveyed population? For example, if your survey says that 50% of people like item A and 50% of people like item B, what percentage of people like both items A and B? You get the answer by multiplying the percentages, so in this case, 25% of the surveyed population like both A and B.

You can perform this kind of table multiplication using the DPRODUCT function, which uses the usual syntax:

```
DPRODUCT(database, field, criteria)
```

For example, Figure 5-7 shows the results of a survey that asked people whether they liked certain items. What percentage of people like any two of the items? To calculate this, you set up a criteria range for the Item field and then add the items in separate rows below the Item header. In Figure 5-7, for example, you can see that I added Soggy cereal in the first row and Commuting in the second row. Here's the DPRODUCT function that calculates the answer (see cell B1 in Figure 5-7):

```
DPRODUCT(A6:B11, 2, A2:A4)
```

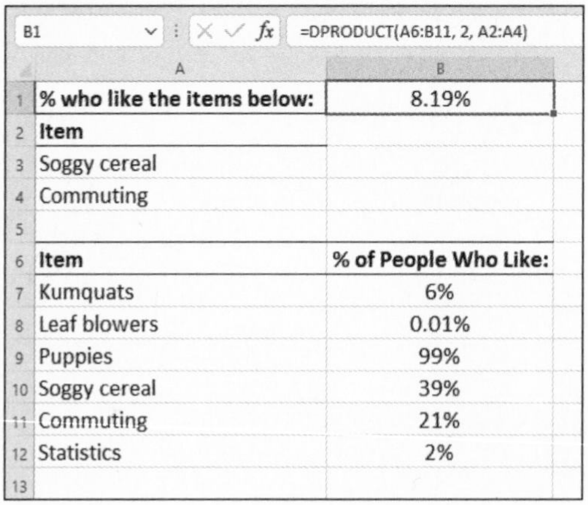

B1	▾ : × ✓ fx	=DPRODUCT(A6:B11, 2, A2:A4)
	A	B
1	% who like the items below:	8.19%
2	Item	
3	Soggy cereal	
4	Commuting	
5		
6	Item	% of People Who Like:
7	Kumquats	6%
8	Leaf blowers	0.01%
9	Puppies	99%
10	Soggy cereal	39%
11	Commuting	21%
12	Statistics	2%
13		

FIGURE 5-7:
Use DPRODUCT to multiply a column's values based on your criteria.

Deriving a Column's Standard Deviation

One of the most important statistical measures is the *standard deviation*, which tells you how much the values in a collection vary with respect to the average. I talk about this in more detail in Chapter 11, but for now I can tell you that a low standard deviation means that the data values are grouped near the average, and a high standard deviation means that the values are spread out from the average.

For your table data analysis fun, the DSTDEV and DSTDEVP functions calculate the standard deviation: DSTDEV calculates the standard deviation when you're working with a sample of the population, whereas DSTDEVP calculates the standard deviation when you're working with the entire population. As with other database statistical functions, the unique and useful feature of DSTDEV and DSTDEVP is that you can specify that you want the calculation to include only those table records that meet your specified criteria.

REMEMBER

The DSTDEV and DSTDEVP functions use the same syntax:

```
=DSTDEV(database, field, criteria)
=DSTDEVP(database, field, criteria)
```

For example, in the Inventory table, suppose you want to know the standard deviation of the Value column for products in the Condiments category and where the Value column is greater than 0. To set up this calculation, you enter the text Condiments under the criteria range's Category header and the expression > 10 under the Value header (see Figure 5-8), and then you add the DSTDEV function (as shown in cell B1 in Figure 5-8):

```
DSTDEV(Inventory6[#All], "Value", A3:G4)
```

TIP

If you want to calculate standard deviations without applying selection criteria, use one of Excel's nondatabase statistical functions, such as STDEV, STDEVA, STDEVP, or STDEVPA. In Chapter 11, I describe and illustrate these other standard deviation functions.

| B1 | | f_x | =DSTDEV(Inventory6[#All], "Value", A3:G4) | | | | |

	A	B	C	D	E	F	G
1	**Standard deviation**	$213.77					
2							
3	**Product Name**	**Category**	**On Hold**	**On Hand**	**Unit Cost**	**List Price**	**Value**
4		Condiments					>0
5							
6	**Product Name**	**Category**	**On Hold**	**On Hand**	**Unit Cost**	**List Price**	**Value**
7	Chai	Beverages	25	25	$13.50	$18.00	$337.50
8	Syrup	Confections	0	50	$7.50	$10.00	$375.00
9	Cajun Seasoning	Confections	0	0	$16.50	$22.00	$0.00
10	Olive Oil	Condiments	0	15	$16.01	$21.35	$240.19
11	Boysenberry Spread	Condiments	0	0	$18.75	$25.00	$0.00
12	Dried Pears	Produce	0	0	$22.50	$30.00	$0.00
13	Curry Sauce	Sauces/Soups	0	0	$30.00	$40.00	$0.00
14	Walnuts	Produce	0	40	$17.44	$23.25	$697.50
15	Fruit Cocktail	Produce	0	0	$29.25	$39.00	$0.00
16	Chocolate Biscuits Mix	Confections	0	0	$6.90	$9.20	$0.00
17	Marmalade	Condiments	0	0	$60.75	$81.00	$0.00
18	Scones	Grains/Cereals	0	0	$7.50	$10.00	$0.00
19	Beer	Beverages	23	23	$10.50	$14.00	$241.50
20	Crab Meat	Seafood	0	0	$13.80	$18.40	$0.00

FIGURE 5-8:
Use DSTDEV (or DSTDEVP) to derive the standard deviation of a column's values based on your criteria.

Calculating a Column's Variance

The *variance* of a set is a measure of how dispersed the data is. The variance is the square of the standard deviation, so it's rarely used because it doesn't make intuitive sense. (For example, what does it mean to say that a result is in "dollars squared" or "years squared"?)

However, for the sake of completion, I include the fact that Excel does offer the DVAR and DVARP functions to calculate the variance. DVAR calculates the variance when your data is a sample of a larger population, whereas DVARP calculates the variance when your data is the entire population. As with other database statistical functions, using DVAR and DVARP enables you to specify that you want only the table records that meet selection criteria included in your calculations.

REMEMBER

As with standard deviation calculations, don't pick one of the two variance functions based on a whim, the weather outside, or how you're feeling. If you're calculating a variance using a sample or a subset of items from the entire data set or population, you use the DVAR function. To calculate a variance when you're dealing with all the items in the population, use the DVARP function.

The DVAR and DVARP functions use the same syntax:

```
=DVAR(database, field, criteria)
=DVARP(database, field, criteria)
```

For example, in the Inventory table, suppose you want to know the variance of the Unit Cost column for products in the Confections category. To set up this calculation, you enter the text Confections under the criteria range's Category header (see Figure 5-9) and then add the DVAR function (refer to cell B1 in Figure 5-8):

```
DVAR(Inventory7[#All], "Unit Cost", A3:G4)
```

B1		✓ : f_x	=DVAR(Inventory7[#All], "Unit Cost", A3:G4)				
	A	B	C	D	E	F	G
1	Variance	26.84					
2							
3	Product Name	Category	On Hold	On Hand	Unit Cost	List Price	Value
4		Confections					
5							
6	Product Name	Category	On Hold	On Hand	Unit Cost	List Price	Value
7	Chai	Beverages	25	25	$13.50	$18.00	$337.50
8	Syrup	Confections	0	50	$7.50	$10.00	$375.00
9	Cajun Seasoning	Confections	0	0	$16.50	$22.00	$0.00
10	Olive Oil	Condiments	0	15	$16.01	$21.35	$240.19
11	Boysenberry Spread	Condiments	0	0	$18.75	$25.00	$0.00
12	Dried Pears	Produce	0	0	$22.50	$30.00	$0.00
13	Curry Sauce	Sauces/Soups	0	0	$30.00	$40.00	$0.00
14	Walnuts	Produce	0	40	$17.44	$23.25	$697.50
15	Fruit Cocktail	Produce	0	0	$29.25	$39.00	$0.00
16	Chocolate Biscuits Mix	Confections	0	0	$6.90	$9.20	$0.00
17	Marmalade	Condiments	0	0	$60.75	$81.00	$0.00
18	Scones	Grains/Cereals	0	0	$7.50	$10.00	$0.00
19	Beer	Beverages	23	23	$10.50	$14.00	$241.50
20	Crab Meat	Seafood	0	0	$13.80	$18.40	$0.00

FIGURE 5-9: Use DVAR (or DVARP) to derive the variance of a column's values based on your criteria.

TIP

If you want to calculate variances without applying selection criteria, use one of the Excel nondatabase statistical functions, such as VAR, VARA, VARP, or VARPA. I talk about these other variance functions in Chapter 11.

2

Analyzing Data Using PivotTables and PivotCharts

IN THIS PART . . .

Use PivotTables to cross-tabulate data and gain new insights into your information.

Extend the power of Excel's PivotTables by creating your own customized formulas.

Display cross-tabulated data in a chart for new perspectives on opportunities and problems.

Customize PivotCharts to make sure that your graphical information communicates the right messages.

Chapter **6**

Creating and Using PivotTables

xcel tables and external databases can contain thousands of records. Let's face it: Figuring out how to glean useful insights from that much data will either keep you awake at night or cause nightmares if you do sleep. Want to get some quality shut-eye? No need for sleeping pills when Excel offers a powerful and versatile data-analysis tool called a *PivotTable*, which enables you to take those thousands of records and summarize them in a concise tabular format. You can then manipulate the layout of — or *pivot* — the PivotTable to see different views of your data.

This chapter shows you everything you need to know to get started with what is arguably Excel's most useful data-analysis tool. You learn how to create PivotTables, refresh them, pivot them, group them, filter them, and much more.

Understanding PivotTables

In a general sense, PivotTables condense a large amount of information into a report that tells you something useful or interesting. For example, check out the table shown in Figure 6-1. This table contains well over 100 records, each of which is an order from a sales promotion. That's not a ton of data in the larger scheme of things, but trying to make sense of even this relatively small data set just by eyeballing the table's contents is futile. For example, how many earbuds were sold via social media advertising? Who knows?

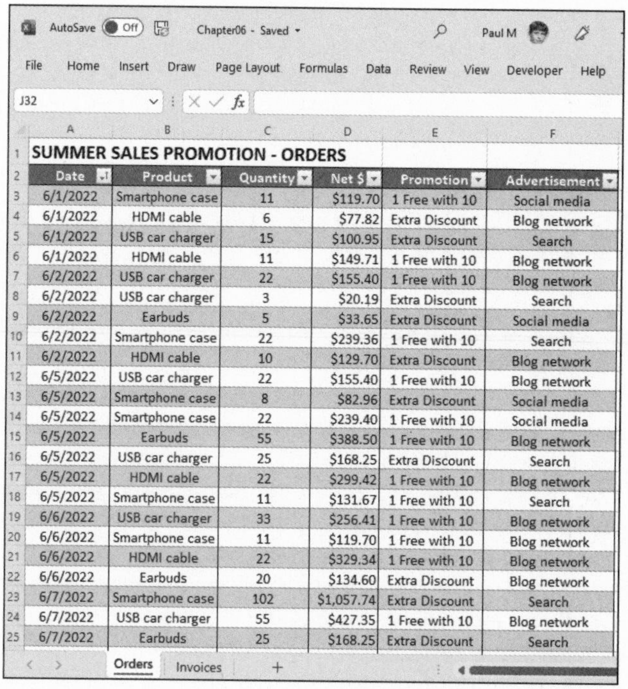

Date	Product	Quantity	Net $	Promotion	Advertisement
6/1/2022	Smartphone case	11	$119.70	1 Free with 10	Social media
6/1/2022	HDMI cable	6	$77.82	Extra Discount	Blog network
6/1/2022	USB car charger	15	$100.95	Extra Discount	Search
6/1/2022	HDMI cable	11	$149.71	1 Free with 10	Blog network
6/2/2022	USB car charger	22	$155.40	1 Free with 10	Blog network
6/2/2022	USB car charger	3	$20.19	Extra Discount	Search
6/2/2022	Earbuds	5	$33.65	Extra Discount	Social media
6/2/2022	Smartphone case	22	$239.36	1 Free with 10	Search
6/2/2022	HDMI cable	10	$129.70	Extra Discount	Blog network
6/5/2022	USB car charger	22	$155.40	1 Free with 10	Blog network
6/5/2022	Smartphone case	8	$82.96	Extra Discount	Social media
6/5/2022	Smartphone case	22	$239.40	1 Free with 10	Social media
6/5/2022	Earbuds	55	$388.50	1 Free with 10	Blog network
6/5/2022	USB car charger	25	$168.25	Extra Discount	Search
6/5/2022	HDMI cable	22	$299.42	1 Free with 10	Blog network
6/5/2022	Smartphone case	11	$131.67	1 Free with 10	Search
6/6/2022	USB car charger	33	$256.41	1 Free with 10	Blog network
6/6/2022	Smartphone case	11	$119.70	1 Free with 10	Blog network
6/6/2022	HDMI cable	22	$329.34	1 Free with 10	Blog network
6/6/2022	Earbuds	20	$134.60	Extra Discount	Blog network
6/7/2022	Smartphone case	102	$1,057.74	Extra Discount	Search
6/7/2022	USB car charger	55	$427.35	1 Free with 10	Blog network
6/7/2022	Earbuds	25	$168.25	Extra Discount	Search

FIGURE 6-1: Some great data, but how do you make sense of it?

Ah, but now look at Figure 6-2, which shows a PivotTable built from the order data. This report tabulates the number of units sold for each product based on each type of promotion. From here, you can quickly see that 322 earbuds were sold via social media advertising. *That* is what PivotTables do.

PivotTables help you analyze large amounts of data by performing three operations: grouping the data into categories, summarizing the data using calculations, and filtering the data to show just the records you want to work with:

	A	B	C	D	E
1	Promotion	(All)			
2					
3	Sum of Quantity	Column Labels			
4	Row Labels	Blog network	Search	Social media	Grand Total
5	Earbuds	555	562	322	1439
6	HDMI cable	719	587	402	1708
7	Smartphone case	546	460	338	1344
8	USB car charger	1596	1012	752	3360
9	Grand Total	3416	2621	1814	7851

FIGURE 6-2:
The PivotTable creates order out of data chaos.

» **Grouping:** A PivotTable is a powerful data-analysis tool in part because it automatically groups large amounts of data into smaller, more manageable chunks. For example, suppose you have a data source with a Region field in which each item contains one of four values: East, West, North, and South. The original data may contain thousands of records, but if you build your PivotTable using the Region field, the resulting table has just four rows — one each for the four unique Region values in your data.

You can also create your own grouping after you build your PivotTable. For example, if your data has a Country field, you can build the PivotTable to group all records that have the same Country value. Then you could further group the unique Country values into continents: North America, South America, Europe, and so on.

» **Summarizing:** In conjunction with grouping data according to the unique values in one or more fields, Excel also displays summary calculations for each group. The default calculation is Sum, which means that for each group, Excel totals all the values in some specified field. For example, if your data has a Region field and a Sales field, a PivotTable can group the unique Region values and display the total of the Sales values for each one. Excel has other summary calculations, including Count, Average, Maximum, Minimum, and Standard Deviation.

Even more powerful, a PivotTable can display summaries for one grouping broken down by another. For example, suppose your sales data also has a Product field. You can set up a PivotTable to show the total sales for each product, broken down by region.

» **Filtering:** A PivotTable also enables you to view just a subset of the data. For example, by default, the PivotTable's groupings show all unique values in the field. However, you can manipulate each grouping to hide the unique values that you don't want to view. Each PivotTable also comes with a report filter that enables you to apply a filter to the entire PivotTable. For example, suppose your sales data also includes a Customer field. By placing this field in the PivotTable's report filter, you can filter the PivotTable report to show just the results for a single Customer.

Exploring PivotTable Features

You can get up to speed with PivotTables quickly after you learn a few key concepts. You need to understand the features that make up a typical PivotTable, particularly the four areas — row, column, data, and filter — to which you add fields from your data. Figure 6-3 points out the following PivotTable features:

>> **Row area:** Displays vertically the unique values from a field in your data.

>> **Column area:** Displays horizontally the unique values from a field in your data.

>> **Value area:** Displays the results of the calculation that Excel applied to a numeric field in your data.

>> **Row field header:** Identifies the field contained in the row area. You also use the row field header to filter the field values that appear in the row area.

>> **Column field header:** Identifies the field contained in the column area. You also use the column field header to filter the field values that appear in the column area.

>> **Value field header:** Specifies both the calculation (such as Sum) and the field (such as Quantity) used in the value area.

>> **Filter area:** Displays a drop-down list that contains the unique values from a field. When you select a value (or multiple values) from the list, Excel filters the PivotTable results to include only the records that match the selected value (or values).

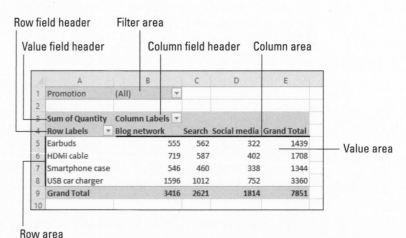

FIGURE 6-3:
The features of a typical PivotTable.

Building a PivotTable from an Excel Range or Table

If the data you want to analyze exists as an Excel range or table, you can use the Summarize with PivotTable command to quickly build a PivotTable report based on your data. You need only specify the location of your source data and then choose the location of the resulting PivotTable.

Here are the steps to follow:

1. **Select a cell in the range or table that you want to use as the source data.**

   If you're using a range, make sure each column of data has a heading.

2. **Choose Table Design ⇨ Summarize with PivotTable.**

   If your data resides in a regular Excel range instead of a table, you can still do the PivotTable thing. Select any cell in the range and then choose Insert ⇨ PivotTable.

   TIP

   While I have your attention, I should also point out the Insert tab's Recommended PivotTables command. This command displays a dialog box that shows several predefined PivotTable layouts. These might not mean anything to you now if you're new to PivotTables, but keep the Recommended PivotTables command in mind down the road; it might save you a bit of time.

   The PivotTable from Table or Range dialog box appears.

3. **Select the New Worksheet radio button.**

   Alternatively, if you want to add the PivotTable to an existing location, select the Existing Worksheet radio button and then use the Location range box to select the worksheet and cell where you want the PivotTable to appear.

4. **Click OK.**

   Excel creates a blank PivotTable and displays the PivotTable Fields task pane, as shown in Figure 6-4. This pane contains two main areas:

   - A list of the column headers from your table, each of which has a check box to its left. These are your PivotTable fields.

   - Four boxes representing the four areas of the PivotTable: Filters, Columns, Rows, and Values. To complete the PivotTable, your job is to add one or more fields to some (or even all) of these areas.

5. **Drag a field that contains text values and drop it in the Rows area.**

   For example, using the fields shown in Figure 6-4, you could drop the Product field into the Rows area.

Excel adds a button for the field to the Rows area and displays the field's unique values to the PivotTable's row area.

6. **Drag a field that contains numeric values and drop it in the Values area.**

   For example, using the fields shown in Figure 6-4, you could drop the Quantity field into the Values area.

   Excel adds a button for the field to the Values area and sums the numeric values based on the row values.

7. **If desired, drag fields and drop them in the Columns area and the Filters area.**

   For example, using the fields shown in Figure 6-4, you could drop the Advertisement field into the Columns area and the Promotion field into the Filters area.

   Excel adds a button for the field to the Columns area and displays the field's unique values to the PivotTable's column area.

Each time you drop a field in an area, Excel adds a button for the field to that area and updates the PivotTable to include the new data.

TIP

Excel offers a few shortcut techniques for building PivotTables:

» Select the check box for a text or date field to add it to the Rows area automatically.

» Select the check box for a numeric field to add it to the Values area automatically.

» Right-click a field and then select the area that you want to use.

Figure 6-5 shows a completed PivotTable, with fields in all four areas. Note, too, that when you select a cell in the PivotTable, Excel displays two contextual tabs on the Ribbon — PivotTable Analyze and Design — that offer lots of goodies for manipulating and formatting your PivotTable.

To remove a field from a PivotTable area, you have three ways to proceed:

» Drag the field from the area and out of the PivotTable Fields task pane.

» Deselect the field's check box in the PivotTable Fields task pane.

» In the PivotTable Fields task pane area where the field resides, click the field button to drop down the field menu, and then click Remove Field. For example, to remove the Advertisement field shown in Figure 6-5, click the Advertisement field button in the Columns area and then click Remove Field.

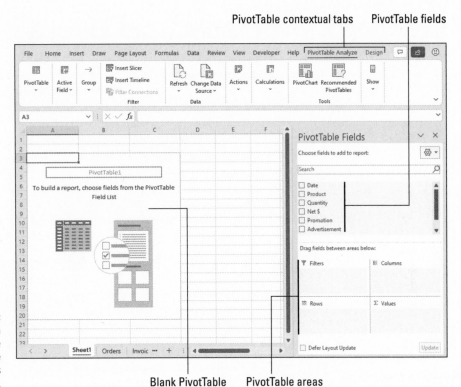

PivotTable contextual tabs   PivotTable fields

Blank PivotTable   PivotTable areas

FIGURE 6-4:
You start with a blank PivotTable and the PivotTable Fields task pane.

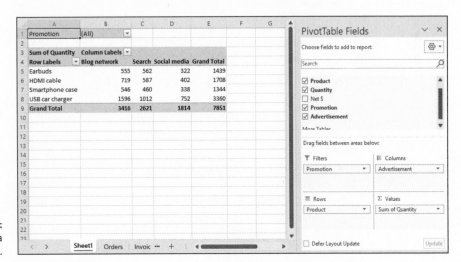

FIGURE 6-5:
The features of a typical PivotTable.

Creating a PivotTable from External Data

The data you're analyzing might not exist in an Excel range or table but rather outside Excel, in a relational database management system (RDBMS) such as Microsoft Access or SQL Server. With these programs, you can set up a table, a query, or another object that defines the data you want to work with. Then, instead of building a PivotTable from data in an Excel worksheet, you create the Pivot-Table using the external data source. This feature enables you to build reports from extremely large data sets and from relational database systems.

As I describe in the next two sections, you can specify the external data source for your new PivotTable by using Microsoft Query or by creating a new data connection.

Building a PivotTable from Microsoft Query

Here are the steps to follow to build a PivotTable based on an external data source defined using Microsoft Query's Query Wizard tool:

1. **Choose Data ⇨ Get Data ⇨ From Other Sources ⇨ From Microsoft Query.**

The Choose Data Source dialog box appears.

2. **Use Query Wizard to define the external data you want to summarize in your PivotTable.**

I talk about Query Wizard, as well as the general topics of external data and defining data sources, in the section on grabbing data from external sources in Chapter 4. The steps you follow from here repeat those from the section about querying a data source in Chapter 4, so I left them out.

3. **When you get to the Query Wizard - Finish dialog box, select the Return Data to Microsoft Excel radio button and then click Finish.**

Excel displays the Import Data dialog box, shown in Figure 6-6.

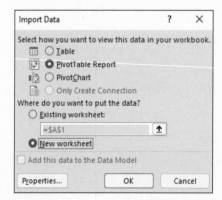

FIGURE 6-6:
Import the external data to a PivotTable Report.

4. **Select the PivotTable Report radio button, select the New Worksheet radio button, and then click OK.**

Excel creates a blank PivotTable and displays the PivotTable Fields task pane.

5. **Drag a text field and drop it in the Rows area.**

Excel adds the field's unique values to the PivotTable's row area.

6. **Drag a numeric field and drop it in the Values area.**

Excel sums the numeric values based on the row values.

7. **If desired, drag fields and drop them in the Columns area and the Filters area.**

Each time you drop a field in an area, Excel updates the PivotTable to include the new data.

REMEMBER

When you create a PivotTable from external data, you don't need the external data to be imported to Excel. Rather, the external data resides only in the new Pivot-Table; you don't see the actual data in your workbook.

The most common drawback to using external data is that you often have no control over the data source. For example, if you attempt to refresh the PivotTable, as I describe in the next section, Excel might display an error message. If you suspect that the problem is a change to the database login data, click OK to display the Login dialog box and then find out the new login name and password from the database administrator. Alternatively, the problem might be that the database file has been moved or renamed. Click OK in the error message and then click Database in the Login dialog box. Next, in the Select Database dialog box, find and select the database file.

Building a PivotTable from a new data connection

You can also summarize external data in a PivotTable by creating a connection to the source data. Here's how it works:

1. **Choose Insert ⇨ PivotTable ⇨ From External Data Source.**

When you choose Insert ⇨ PivotTable, be sure to click the PivotTable button's drop-down arrow to display its menu.

Excel displays the PivotTable from an External Source dialog box.

2. **Click Choose Connection.**

Excel opens the Existing Connections dialog box.

3. **Click Browse for More.**

Excel displays the Select Data Source dialog box.

4. **Click New Source.**

Data Connection Wizard shows up for work.

5. **Click the type of data source you want to connect to and then click Next.**

The wizard steps you follow from here depend on the data source type you selected. For example, to connect to an Access database, you follow these steps:

    a. **Select ODBC DSN and then click Next to open the Connect to ODBC Data Source dialog box.**

    b. **Select MS Access Database and then click Next to open the Select Database dialog box.**

    c. **Select the Access database file you want to connect to and then click OK to open the Select Database and Table dialog box.**

    d. **Select the table you want to use and then click Next to open the Save Data Connection File and Finish dialog box.**

6. **(Optional) Edit the file name, description, friendly name, and search keywords.**

7. **Click Finish.**

Excel saves your new data connection and returns you to the PivotTable from an External Source dialog box.

In the future, when you choose Insert ⇨ PivotTable ⇨ From External Data Source and then click Choose Connection, your saved connections appear in the Existing Connections dialog box so you can reuse them without having to run through the Data Connection Wizard.

8. **Select the New Worksheet radio button and then click OK.**

Excel creates a blank PivotTable and displays the PivotTable Fields task pane.

9. **Drag a text field and drop it in the Rows area.**

Excel adds the field's unique values to the PivotTable's row area.

10. **Drag a numeric field and drop it in the Values area.**

Excel sums the numeric values based on the row values.

11. **If desired, drag fields and drop them in the Columns area and the Filters area.**

Each time you drop a field in an area, Excel updates the PivotTable to include the new data.

Refreshing PivotTable Data

Whether your PivotTable is based on financial results, survey responses, or a database of collectibles such as rare books or cubic zirconia jewelry, the underlying data is probably not static. That is, the data changes over time as new results come in, new surveys are undertaken, and new items are added to the collection. You can ensure that the data analysis represented by the PivotTable remains up to date by refreshing the PivotTable.

Excel offers two methods for refreshing a PivotTable: manual and automatic. A manual refresh is one that you perform, usually when you know that the source data has changed, or if you just want to be sure that the latest data is reflected in your PivotTable report. An automatic refresh is one that Excel handles for you.

Refreshing PivotTable data manually

To refresh your PivotTable data manually, you have two choices:

>> **Update a single PivotTable:** Select any cell in the PivotTable and then choose PivotTable Analyze ⇨ Refresh. You can also press Alt+F5.

>> **Update every PivotTable in the workbook:** Select a cell in any PivotTable and then choose PivotTable Analyze ⇨ Refresh ⇨ Refresh All. You can also update all PivotTables by pressing Ctrl+Alt+F5.

Excel dutifully updates the PivotTable data.

Refreshing PivotTable data automatically

Here are the steps to follow to convince Excel to refresh your PivotTable data automatically:

1. **Select any cell in the PivotTable.**

2. **Choose PivotTable Analyze ⇨ PivotTable ⇨ Options.**

   You can also right-click any cell in the PivotTable and then choose PivotTable Options.

   The PivotTable Options dialog box appears.

3. **Click the Data tab.**

4. **Select the Refresh Data When Opening the File check box, as shown in Figure 6-7, and then click OK.**

From now on, Excel will automatically refresh the PivotTable data each time you open the workbook.

FIGURE 6-7:
Select Refresh Data When Opening the File to tell Excel to refresh a PivotTable automatically whenever you open its workbook.

TIP

If your PivotTable is based on external data, you can set up a schedule that automatically refreshes the PivotTable at a specified interval. Select any cell in the PivotTable and then choose PivotTable Analyze ⇨ Refresh ⇨ Connection Properties. In the Connection Properties dialog box, on the Usage tab, select the Refresh Every check box, use the spin buttons to specify the refresh interval, in minutes, and then click OK.

WARNING

Note, however, that when you set up an automatic refresh, it might be best not to have the source data updated too frequently. Depending on where the data resides and how much data you're working with, the refresh could take some time, which may slow down the rest of your work.

Adding Multiple Fields to a PivotTable Area

You can add two or more fields to any of the PivotTable areas. Having multiple fields is a powerful feature that enables you to perform further analysis of your data by viewing the data differently. For example, suppose you're analyzing the results of a sales campaign that ran different promotions in several types of advertisements (such as the partial table shown previously in Figure 6-1). A basic

PivotTable might show you the sales for each product (the row field) according to the advertisement used (the column field). You might also be interested in seeing, for each product, the breakdown in sales for each promotion. You can do that by adding the Promotion field to the row area.

REMEMBER

Excel doesn't restrict you to just two fields in any area. Depending on your data-analysis requirements, you're free to add three, four, or more fields to any PivotTable area.

Select a cell in the PivotTable and then use any of the following techniques to add another field to a PivotTable area:

>> **Add a field to the Rows area:** In the PivotTable Fields task pane, select the check box of the text or date field that you want to add.

>> **Add a field to the Value area:** In the PivotTable Fields task pane, select the check box of the numeric field that you want to add.

>> **Add a field to any area:** In the PivotTable Fields task pane, drag the field and drop it in the area where you want the field to appear.

TIP

After you add a second field to the row or column area, you can change the field positions to change the PivotTable view. In the PivotTable Fields task pane, drag the button of the field you want to move and then drop the field above or below an existing field button.

When you add a second field to the value area, Excel moves the labels, such as Sum of Quantity and Sum of Net $, into the column area for easier reference. This is also reflected in the addition of a Values button in the Columns area of the PivotTable Fields task pane. This enables you to pivot the values in the report, as I describe in the next section.

Pivoting a Field to a Different Area

A PivotTable is a powerful data-analysis tool because it can take hundreds or even thousands of records and summarize them into a compact, comprehensible report. However, unlike most of the other data-analysis features in Excel, a PivotTable is not a static collection of worksheet cells. Instead, you can move a PivotTable's fields from one area of the PivotTable to another. Moving fields to various areas enables you to view your data from different perspectives, which can greatly enhance the analysis of the data. Moving a field within a PivotTable is called *pivoting* the data.

The most common way to pivot the data is to move fields between the row and column areas. However, you can also pivot data by moving a row or column field to the filter area. Either way, you perform the pivot by dragging the field from its current box in the PivotTable Fields task pane and then dropping it in the area where you want it moved.

You can move any row, column, or filter field to the PivotTable's value area. Moving a field to this location may seem strange because row, column, and page fields are almost always text values, and the default value area calculation is Sum. How can you sum text values? You can't, of course. Instead, the default Excel Pivot-Table summary calculation for text values is Count. So, for example, if you drag the Promotion field and drop it in the value area, Excel creates a second value field named Count of Promotion.

Grouping PivotTable Values

To make a PivotTable with a large number of row or column items easier to work with, you can group the items. For example, you can group months into quarters, thus reducing the number of items from twelve to four. Similarly, a report that lists dozens of countries can group those countries by continent, thus reducing the number of items to four or five, depending on where the countries are located. Finally, if you use a numeric field in the row or column area, you may have hundreds of items, one for each numeric value. You can improve the report by creating just a few numeric ranges.

Grouping numeric values

Grouping numeric values is useful when you use a numeric field in a row or column field. Excel enables you to specify numeric ranges into which the field items are grouped. For example, suppose you have a PivotTable of invoice data that shows the extended price (the row field) and the salesperson (the column field). It would be useful to group the extended prices into ranges and then count the number of invoices each salesperson processed in each range.

Follow these steps to group numeric values in a PivotTable field:

1. Select any item in the numeric field you want to group.

2. Choose PivotTable Analyze ⇨ Group Field.

The Grouping dialog box appears, as shown in Figure 6-8.

FIGURE 6-8:
The Grouping
dialog box.

3. **In the Starting At text box, enter the starting numeric value.**

When you enter a new starting numeric value, Excel deselects the Starting At check box.

Alternatively, select the Starting At check box to have Excel extract the minimum value of the numeric items and place that value in the text box.

4. **In the Ending At text box, enter the ending numeric value.**

When you enter a new ending numeric value, Excel deselects the Ending At check box.

Alternatively, select the Ending At check box to have Excel extract the maximum value of the numeric items and place that value in the text box.

5. **In the By text box, enter the size you want to use for each grouping.**

6. **Click OK.**

Excel groups the numeric values.

Grouping date and time values

If your PivotTable includes a field with date or time data, you can use Excel's grouping feature to consolidate that data into more manageable or useful groups. Follow these steps:

1. **Select any item in the date or time field you want to group.**

2. **Choose PivotTable Analyze ⇨ Group Field.**

The Grouping dialog box appears.

3. **In the Starting At text box, enter the starting date or time.**

When you enter a new starting date or time, Excel deselects the Starting At check box.

Alternatively, select the Starting At check box to have Excel extract the earliest date or time and place that value in the text box.

4. **In the Ending At text box, enter the ending date or time.**

When you enter a new ending date or time, Excel deselects the Ending At check box.

Alternatively, select the Ending At check box to have Excel extract the latest date or time and place that value in the text box.

5. **In the By list, select the grouping you want, such as Months for dates or Hours for times.**

If you select Days, you can also use the Number of Days spin buttons to set the days you want to use for the grouping interval.

To use multiple groupings, select each type of grouping you want to use.

6. **Click OK.**

Excel groups the date or time values.

Grouping text values

One common problem that arises when you work with PivotTables is that you often need to consolidate items, but you have no corresponding field in the data. For example, the data may have a Country field, but what if you need to consolidate the PivotTable results by continent? Your source data isn't likely to include a Continent field. Similarly, your source data may include employee names, but you may need to consolidate the employees according to the people they report to. What happens if your source data doesn't include, say, a Supervisor field?

The solution in both cases is to use the grouping feature to create custom groups. For the country data, you can create custom groups named North America, South America, Europe, and so on. For the employees, you can create a custom group for each supervisor.

Here are the steps to follow to create such a custom grouping for text values:

1. **Select the items that you want to include in the group.**

2. **Choose PivotTable Analyze ➪ Group Selection.**

Excel creates a new group named Group*n* (where *n* means that this is the *n*th group you have created; the first group is Group1, the second is Group2, and so on) and restructures the PivotTable.

3. **Select the cell that contains the group label, type a new name for the group, and then press Enter.**

Excel renames the group.

4. **Repeat Steps 1 to 3 for the other items in the field until you've created all your groups.**

Filtering PivotTable Values

By default, each PivotTable report displays a summary of all the records in your source data, which is usually what you want to see. However, you may have situations in which you need to focus more closely on some aspect of the data. You can focus on a specific item (or on just a few items) from one of the source data fields by taking advantage of the PivotTable's report filter field.

Applying a report filter

Suppose you're dealing with a PivotTable that summarizes data from thousands of customer invoices over some period of time. A basic PivotTable might tell you the total amount sold for each product that you carry. That's interesting, but what if you want to see the total amount sold for each product in a specific country? If the Product field is in the PivotTable's row area, you can add the Country field to the column area. However, you may have dozens of countries, so adding the field to the column area isn't an efficient solution. Instead, you can add the Country field to the report filter and tell Excel to display the total sold for each product for the specific country that you're interested in.

Follow these steps to apply a PivotTable report filter:

1. **Select the filter field's drop-down arrow.**

Excel displays a list of the report filter field values.

2. **Select the report filter you want to view.**

In Figure 6-9, I use the report filter list to select Canada.

If you want to display data for two or more report filters, select the Select Multiple Items check box and then repeat Step 2 to select the other report filters.

To return later to showing all the items in the report field, select (All) in the filter field's drop-down list.

3. **Click OK.**

Excel filters the PivotTable to show only the data for the report filter you selected.

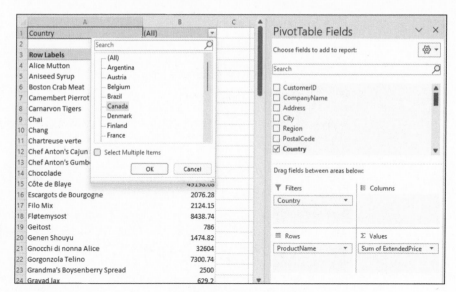

FIGURE 6-9:
From the filter field's drop-down list, select a report filter.

Filtering row or column items

By default, your PivotTable shows all the items in whatever row and column fields you added to the report layout. Seeing all the items is usually what you want because the point of a PivotTable is to summarize all the data in the original source. However, sometimes you may not want to see every item. For example, in a PivotTable report that includes items from the ProductName field in the row area, you might want to see only those products with names that begin with the letter *G* or that contain the word *tofu.*

When you modify a PivotTable report to display only a subset of the row or column items, you're applying to the report a *label filter,* which is different from a *report filter,* which filters the entire PivotTable, as described in the preceding section. Excel offers a number of label filters for text, including Equals, Does Not Equal, Begins With, Ends With, Contains, Greater Than, and Less Than.

If your PivotTable report includes a date field in the row or column area, you can apply a date filter to that field. Excel offers many different date filters, including Before, After, Between, Today, Yesterday, Last Week, Last Month, Last Quarter, This Year, and Year to Date.

Follow these steps to apply a label filter to row or column items:

1. **Click the drop-down arrow in the header of the field you want to filter.**

   The field's Sorting & Filtering menu appears.

2. **Select Label Filters and then select the filter type you want to apply, such as Begins With.**

   The Label Filter dialog box appears.

3. **Type the filter criteria and then click OK.**

   Some filters, such as Between, require you to type two criteria values.

   Excel filters the PivotTable report.

To remove a row or column label filter, click the drop-down arrow in the field's header and then select Clear Filter from *Field*, where *Field* is the name of the filtered field.

Filtering PivotTable values

Excel enables you to apply *value filters* that restrict the values you see in the value area. For example, you may want to see only those values that are larger than some amount or that fall between two specified amounts. Excel offers several value filters, including Equals, Does Not Equal, Greater Than, Greater Than or Equal To, Less Than, Less Than or Equal To, Between, and Not Between.

Similarly, you may be interested in only the highest or lowest values that appear in the PivotTable. For example, you might want to see just the top ten values. You can generate such a report by using Excel's Top 10 Filter, which filters the PivotTable to show just the top ten items based on the values in the value field.

For example, suppose you have a PivotTable report based on a database of invoices that shows the total sales for each product. The basic report shows all the products, but if you're interested in only the top performers for the year, you can activate the Top 10 Filter feature to see the ten products that sold the most. Despite its name, the Top 10 Filter can display more than just the top ten data values. You can specify any number between 1 and 2,147,483,647, and you can ask Excel to show the bottommost values instead of the topmost ones.

Follow these steps to apply a value filter to your PivotTable:

1. **Click the drop-down arrow in the header of any row or column field.**

   The field's Sorting & Filtering menu appears.

2. **Select Value Filters and then select the filter type you want to apply, such as Top 10.**

   The dialog box for that value filter appears — for example, the Top 10 Filter dialog box.

3. **Specify the filter criteria and then click OK.**

Excel filters the PivotTable report.

To remove a value filter, click the drop-down arrow in the header of the filtered field and then choose Value Filters ⇨ Clear Filter.

Filtering a PivotTable with a slicer

As mentioned previously in this chapter, you can filter a PivotTable by using the report filter, which applies to the entire PivotTable, or by using either a label filter or a value filter, which applies only to the filter field. Whether it applies to the entire PivotTable or just the filter field, the filter is usable only with the PivotTable in which it's defined. However, requiring the same filter in multiple PivotTable reports is not unusual. For example, if you're a sales manager responsible for sales in a particular set of countries, you might often need to filter a PivotTable to show data from just those countries. Similarly, if you work with a subset of your company's product line, you might often have to filter PivotTable reports to show the results from just those products.

Applying these kinds of filters to one or two PivotTables is not difficult or time consuming, but if you have to apply the same filter over and over again, the process gets old in a hurry. To combat this repetition, Excel offers a PivotTable feature called the slicer. A *slicer* is similar to a report filter, except it's independent of any PivotTable. This means you can use a single slicer to filter multiple PivotTables. Nice! Slicers also enable you to see at a glance which filters you've applied and which fields are not available.

First, here are the steps to follow to create a slicer to filter a PivotTable:

1. **Select a cell in your PivotTable.**

2. **Choose PivotTable Analyze ⇨ Insert Slicer.**

The Insert Slicers dialog box appears and displays a check box for every field in your PivotTable report.

3. **Select the check box beside each field for which you want to create a slicer, and then click OK.**

Excel displays one slicer for each field you selected. Each slicer is a box that contains a list of the items from its associated field. By default, all items in the slicer are selected, so no filtering has yet been applied to the PivotTable. Your mission is to use the slicer to select just the field items you want to see in the PivotTable.

Also, the Slicer contextual tab appears when a slicer has the focus, and you can use the controls in this tab to customize each slicer.

4. **Select a field item that you want to include in your filter.**

If you want to include multiple items in your filter, click the first item, hold down Ctrl, click the other items, and then release Ctrl. Alternatively, click the Multi-Select icon (labeled in Figure 6-10; you can also toggle Multi-Select by pressing Alt+S).

Excel filters the PivotTable based on the field items you selected in each slicer. Figure 6-10 shows an example.

TIP

If a field contains lots of items, you may have to scroll a long way in the slicer to locate the item you want. In this case, configuring the slicer to display its items in multiple columns is often easier. Select the title of the slicer to select it, click the Options tab, and then click the Column spin buttons to set the number of columns.

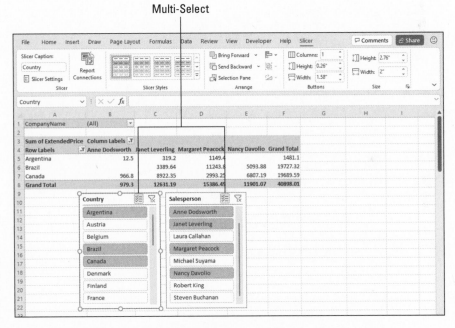

FIGURE 6-10:
Excel filters the
PivotTable to
show just the
selected items in
each slicer.

If you find that you no longer need to use a slicer, you should remove it to avoid cluttering the PivotTable window. Either select the slicer and press Delete, or right-click the slicer and then select Remove *Slicer*, where *Slicer* is the name of the slicer (which is usually the field name). If you want to temporarily hide the slicer, select any slicer, choose Slicer ⇨ Selection Pane to display the Selection task pane, and then click the eye icon beside the slicer to hide it.

Chapter **7**

Performing PivotTable Calculations

The near-ridiculous power and flexibility of a PivotTable is in contrast with the relative simplicity of what a PivotTable does, which is to take a mountain of data and turn it into a molehill of a report. With that report in place, the fun part begins when you pivot fields, group items, and filter the report (all of which I describe in painstaking detail in Chapter 6). Pivoting, grouping, and filtering represent the most visible aspects of a PivotTable's power, but lots of impressive things happen behind the PivotTable scene as well. These "hidden" features include the massive number of calculations that Excel performs to summarize all that data so succinctly. And you can harness that raw calculation horsepower for your own ends.

In this chapter, you open the PivotTable's hood to check out its calculation engine. You explore how the calculations work, swap out some parts to try different calculations, and even learn how to soup things up with your own custom calculations. Vroom vroom!

Messing around with PivotTable Summary Calculations

The calculation that Excel uses to populate the PivotTable data area is called the *summary calculation*. Most of the time, the default Sum calculation will get the job done, but Excel offers lots of options for taking the summary calculation to a higher analytical level. The next few sections fill you in on those options.

Changing the PivotTable summary calculation

The default summary calculation depends on the type of field you add to the data area:

>> If you add a numeric field to the data area, Excel uses Sum as the default summary calculation.

>> If you use a text field in the data area, Excel uses Count as the default summary calculation.

Sum and Count aren't the only calculation choices, however. If your data analysis requires a different calculation, you can configure the data field to use any one of Excel's 11 built-in summary calculations. Here's the complete list:

>> **Average:** Calculates the mean value in a numeric field

>> **Count:** Displays the total number of cells in the source field

>> **Count Numbers:** Displays the total number of numeric values in the source field

>> **Max:** Displays the largest value in a numeric field

>> **Min:** Displays the smallest value in a numeric field

>> **Product:** Multiplies the values in a numeric field

>> **StdDev:** Calculates the standard deviation of a population sample, which tells you how much the values in the source field vary with respect to the average

>> **StdDevp:** Calculates the standard deviation when the values in the data field represent the entire population

>> **Sum:** Adds the values in a numeric field

>> **Var:** Calculates the variance of a population sample, which is the square of the standard deviation

>> **Varp:** Calculates the variance when the values in the data field represent the entire population

Here are the steps to follow to try a different summary calculation:

1. **Select any cell in the data field.**

2. **Choose PivotTable Analyze ⇨ Field Settings.**

The Value Field Settings dialog box appears with the Summarize Values By tab displayed, as shown in Figure 7-1.

3. **In the Summarize Value Field By list, select the summary calculation you want to use.**

4. **Click OK.**

Excel recalculates the PivotTable results and renames the value field label to reflect the new summary calculation.

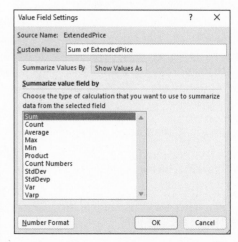

FIGURE 7-1:
Use the Value Field Settings dialog box to choose a summary calculation.

TIP

Another way to change the PivotTable summary calculation is to right-click any cell in the value field, choose the Summarize Values By command, and then select the calculation you want to use from the submenu that appears. If you don't see the calculation, choose the More Options command to open the Value Field Settings dialog box.

When you build your PivotTable, you may find that the results don't pass the smell test. For example, the numbers may appear to be far too small. In that case, check the summary calculation that Excel has applied to the field to see whether it's using Count instead of Sum. If the data field includes one or more text cells or one or more blank cells, Excel defaults to the Count summary function instead of Sum. If your field is supposed to be numeric, check the data to see whether any text values or blank cells are showing up.

When you add a second field to the row or column area, Excel displays a subtotal for each item in the outer field. (The *outer field* is the field farthest from the value area: the leftmost field if you have two fields in the row area, or the topmost field if you have two fields in the column area. The other field is called the *inner field* because it's closest to the value area.) By default, the subtotals show the sum of the data results for each outer field item. However, the same 11 summary calculations — from Average to Varp — are also available for subtotals.

Trying out the difference summary calculation

The built-in summary calculations — Sum, Count, and so on — apply over an entire field. However, a major part of data analysis involves comparing one item with another. If you're analyzing sales to customers, for example, knowing how much you sold this year is useful, but even more useful is to compare this year's sales with last year's. Are the sales up or down? By how much? Are the sales up or down with all customers or only some? These fundamental questions help managers run departments, divisions, and companies.

Excel offers two difference calculations that can help with this kind of analysis:

» **Difference From:** Compares one numeric item with another and returns the difference between them

» **% Difference From:** Compares one numeric item with another and returns the percentage difference between them

Before you set up a difference calculation, you need to decide which field in your PivotTable to use as the comparison field, or *base field,* and which item in that field to use as the basis for all the comparisons, which is called the *base item.* For example, take a peek at Figure 7-2, which uses the Order Date field to show the sales in 2022 and the sales in 2021. In this example, Order Date is the base field and 2021 is the base item.

	A	B	C	D
1				
2				
3	Sum of Extended Price	Order Date		
4	Customer	2021	2022	Grand Total
5	Alfreds Futterkiste	$2,250.50	$2,022.50	$4,273.00
6	Ana Trujillo Emparedados y helados	$603.20	$799.75	$1,402.95
7	Antonio Moreno Taquería	$1,063.20	$5,960.77	$7,023.97
8	Around the Horn	$6,983.75	$6,406.90	$13,390.65
9	Berglunds snabbköp	$11,078.57	$13,849.01	$24,927.58
10	Blauer See Delikatessen	$2,160.00	$1,079.80	$3,239.80
11	Blondel père et fils	$10,716.20	$7,817.88	$18,534.08
12	Bólido Comidas preparadas	$1,206.00	$3,026.85	$4,232.85
13	Bon app'	$10,754.89	$11,208.35	$21,963.24
14	Bottom-Dollar Markets	$13,171.35	$7,630.25	$20,801.60
15	B's Beverages	$2,910.40	$3,179.50	$6,089.90
16	Cactus Comidas para llevar	$1,576.80	$238.00	$1,814.80
17	Centro comercial Moctezuma	$100.80		$100.80
18	Chop-suey Chinese	$5,832.48	$6,516.40	$12,348.88

‹ › ⋯ PT-Invoices 2021 vs 2022   Sales   PT-S ⋯   +   ◂▬▬

FIGURE 7-2:
A PivotTable that shows sales in two years: 2021 and 2022.

Here are the steps to follow to apply a difference summary calculation to a PivotTable:

1. **Select any cell in the value field.**

2. **Choose PivotTable Analyze ➪ Field Settings.**

The Value Field Settings dialog box appears with the Summarize Values By tab displayed.

3. **Click the Show Values As tab.**

4. **In the Show Values As list, select Difference From.**

If you want to see the difference in percentage terms, select % Difference From instead.

TIP

Another way to select the Difference Summary calculation is to right-click any cell in the value field, select Show Values As, and then select Difference From.

5. **In the Base Field list, select the field from which you want Excel to calculate the difference.**

6. **In the Base Item list, select a base item.**

Figure 7-3 shows a completed Show Values As tab for the example PivotTable.

7. **Click OK.**

Excel recalculates the PivotTable results to show the difference summary calculation. Figure 7-4 shows the PivotTable from Figure 7-2 with the Difference From calculation applied.

FIGURE 7-3:
Use the Value Field Settings dialog box to choose a summary calculation.

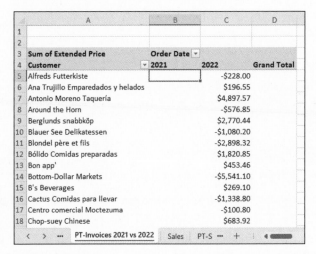

FIGURE 7-4:
The PivotTable from Figure 7-2 is now using the Difference From calculation.

Applying a percentage summary calculation

When analyzing data, comparing two or more items as a percentage is often helpful because percentage calculations enable you to make apples-to-apples comparisons between values. For example, if your PivotTable shows quarterly sales by region (see Figure 7-5), you might want to know how the results in the second, third, and fourth quarters compare, as a percentage, to the results from the first quarter.

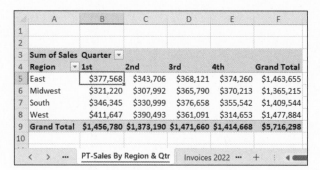

FIGURE 7-5:
A PivotTable that shows quarterly sales by region.

That kind of comparison sounds hard, but you can use Excel's percentage calculations to quickly view data items as a percentage of some other item or as a percentage of the total in the current row, column, or PivotTable. Excel offers seven percentage calculations that can help you perform this kind of analysis:

» **% Of:** Returns the percentage of each value with respect to a selected base item.

» **% of Row Total:** Returns the percentage that each value in a row represents of the total value of the row.

» **% of Column Total:** Returns the percentage that each value in a column represents of the total value of the column.

» **% of Grand Total:** Returns the percentage that each value represents of the PivotTable grand total.

» **% of Parent Row Total:** If you have multiple fields in the row area, this calculation returns the percentage that each value in an inner row represents with respect to the total of the parent item in the outer row.

» **% of Parent Column Total:** If you have multiple fields in the column area, this calculation returns the percentage that each value in an inner column represents with respect to the total of the parent item in the outer column.

» **% of Parent Total:** If you have multiple fields in the row or column area, this calculation returns the percentage of each value with respect to a selected base field in the outer row or column.

If you use the % Of calculation, you must also choose a base field and a base item upon which Excel will calculate the percentages. If you use the % of Parent Total calculation, you must also choose a base field.

Here are the steps to follow to apply a percentage summary calculation:

1. **Select any cell in the value field.**

2. **Choose PivotTable Analyze ⇨ Field Settings.**

   The Value Field Settings dialog box appears with the Summarize Values By tab displayed.

3. **Click the Show Values As tab.**

4. **In the Show Values As list, select the percentage calculation you want to use and then do the following:**

   - **If you selected % Of:** In the Base Field list, select the field from which you want Excel to calculate the percentages. In the Base Item list, select a base item. Click OK.

   - **If you selected % of Parent Total:** In the Base Field list, select the field from which you want Excel to calculate the percentages. Click OK.

   - **If you selected any other option in the list:** Click OK.

   Excel recalculates the PivotTable results to show the percentage summary calculation. Figure 7-6 shows the PivotTable from Figure 7-2 with the % Of calculation applied with Quarter as the base field and 1st as the base item.

FIGURE 7-6: The PivotTable from Figure 7-5, now using the % Of calculation.

Adding a running total summary calculation

A *running total* is the cumulative sum of the values that appear in a set of data. Most running totals accumulate over a period of time. For example, suppose you have 12 months of sales figures. In a running total calculation, the first value is the first month of sales, the second value is the sum of the first and second months, the third value is the sum of the first three months, and so on.

You use a running total in data analysis when you need to see a snapshot of the overall data at various points. For example, suppose you have a sales budget for each month. As the fiscal year progresses, comparing the running total of the budget figures with the running total of the actual sales tells you how your department or company is doing with respect to the budget. If sales are consistently below budget, you might consider lowering prices, offering customers extra discounts, or increasing your product advertising.

Creating a running total seems like a job best left to a complex Excel formula. Sure, you could create such a formula, but I'm happy to report that you don't have to bother with any of that. That's because Excel offers a built-in Running Total In summary calculation that you can apply to your PivotTable results. No muss and not even any fuss.

REMEMBER

The Running Total In summary applies to not just the Sum calculation but also related calculations, such as Count and Average.

Before you configure your PivotTable to use a Running Total In summary calculation, you must choose the field on which to base the accumulation, called the *base field*. This field will most often be a date field, but you can also create running totals based on other fields, such as customer, division, or product.

Here are the steps to follow to apply a Running Total In summary calculation to a PivotTable:

1. **Select any cell in the value field.**

   Figure 7-7 shows a value field cell selected in a PivotTable of monthly order totals.

2. **Choose PivotTable Analyze ⇨ Field Settings.**

   The Value Field Settings dialog box appears, displaying the Summarize Values By tab.

3. **Click the Show Values As tab.**

4. **In the Show Values As list, select Running Total In.**

   If you want to see the running total in percentage terms, select % Running Total In instead.

TIP

   Another way to select the Running Total In summary calculation is to right-click any cell in the value field, and then choose Show Values As ⇨ Running Total In.

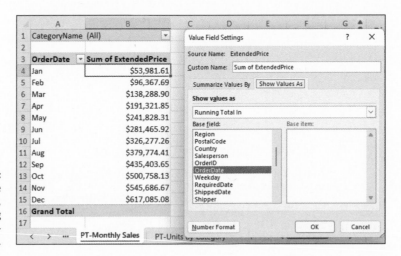

	A	B
1	CategoryName	(All)
2		
3	**OrderDate**	**Sum of ExtendedPrice**
4	Jan	$53,981.61
5	Feb	$42,386.08
6	Mar	$41,921.21
7	Apr	$53,032.95
8	May	$50,506.46
9	Jun	$39,637.61
10	Jul	$44,811.34
11	Aug	$53,497.15
12	Sep	$55,629.24
13	Oct	$65,354.48
14	Nov	$44,928.54
15	Dec	$71,398.41
16	**Grand Total**	**$617,085.08**
17		

FIGURE 7-7:
A PivotTable showing monthly order totals.

5. In the Base Field list, select the field from which you want Excel to accumulate the running totals.

6. Click OK.

Excel recalculates the PivotTable results to show the running totals. Figure 7-8 shows the PivotTable from Figure 7-7 with the Running Total In calculation applied using OrderDate as the base field.

FIGURE 7-8:
The PivotTable from Figure 7-7, with the Running Total In calculation applied.

Creating an index summary calculation

One of the most crucial aspects of data analysis is determining the relative importance of the results of your calculations. This determination is particularly vital in a PivotTable, whose results summarize a large amount of data but on the surface provide no clue as to the relative importance of the various value area results.

For example, suppose your PivotTable shows the units sold for various product categories broken down by region (see Figure 7-9). Suppose further that in Oregon, you sold 30 units of produce and 35 units of seafood. Does this mean that seafood sales are relatively more important in the Oregon market than produce sales? Not necessarily. To determine relative importance, you must take into account the larger picture, such as the total units sold of both produce and seafood across all states. Suppose the produce total is 145 units and the seafood total is 757 units. In that case, you can see that the 30 units of produce sold in Oregon represents a much higher portion of total produce sales than does Oregon's 35 units of seafood. A proper analysis would also take into account the total units sold in Oregon and the total units sold overall (the PivotTable's Grand Total).

	A	B	C	D	E
1	Country	USA ▼			
2					
3	**Sum of Quantity**	**Region** ▼			
4	**CategoryName** ▼	Idaho	Oregon	Washington	Grand Total
5	Beverages	301	71	182	554
6	Condiments	240	32	99	371
7	Confections	359	79	72	510
8	Dairy Products	343	86	54	483
9	Grains/Cereals	247	42	25	314
10	Meat/Poultry	337	6	96	439
11	Produce	110	30	5	145
12	Seafood	637	35	85	757
13	**Grand Total**	**2574**	**381**	**618**	**3573**
14					

< > ⋯ | PT-Units By Category & Region | PT-Fou ⋯ + ⋮ ◀●

FIGURE 7-9:
A PivotTable showing units sold by category and region.

Determining the relative importance of a PivotTable's results sounds headache-inducingly complex, but Excel offers the built-in Index calculation, which handles everything without the need for aspirin. The Index calculation determines the *weighted average* — the average taking into account the relative importance of each value — of each cell in the PivotTable results.

TECHNICAL STUFF

Put your math geek hat on because here's the formula Excel uses:

```
(Cell Value) * (Grand Total) / (Row Total) * (Column Total)
```

In the Index calculation results, the higher the value, the more important the cell in the overall PivotTable report.

Follow these steps to apply the Index summary calculation to a PivotTable:

1. **Select any cell in the value field.**

2. **Choose PivotTable Analyze ⇨ Field Settings.**

   The Value Field Settings dialog box appears with the Summarize Values By tab displayed.

3. **Click the Show Values As tab.**

4. **In the Show Values As list, select Index.**

   Alternatively, right-click any cell in the value field, and then choose Show Values As ⇨ Index.

TIP

5. **Click OK.**

   Excel recalculates the PivotTable results to show the Index results.

TIP

Working with the Index calculation results is much easier if you format the data field to show just two decimal places. Select any cell in the value field, choose PivotTable Analyze ⇨ Field Settings, click Number Format, select Number in the Category list, make sure that 2 appears in the Decimal places field, click OK, and then click OK again.

Figure 7-10 shows the PivotTable from Figure 7-9 with the Index calculation applied (and all the Index calculations reduced to two decimal places for easier reading). Note that under Oregon, the index value for the Produce category is 1.94, whereas the index value for Seafood is 0.43, which tells you that produce sales in Oregon are relatively more important than seafood sales.

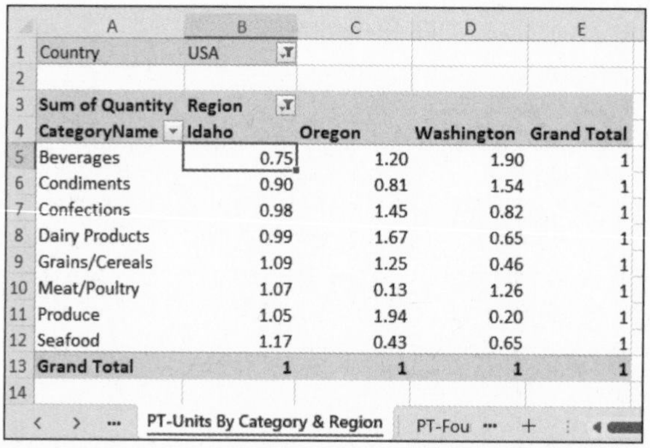

	A	B	C	D	E
1	Country	USA ⌄			
2					
3	**Sum of Quantity**	Region ⌄			
4	CategoryName ⌄	Idaho	Oregon	Washington	Grand Total
5	Beverages	0.75	1.20	1.90	1
6	Condiments	0.90	0.81	1.54	1
7	Confections	0.98	1.45	0.82	1
8	Dairy Products	0.99	1.67	0.65	1
9	Grains/Cereals	1.09	1.25	0.46	1
10	Meat/Poultry	1.07	0.13	1.26	1
11	Produce	1.05	1.94	0.20	1
12	Seafood	1.17	0.43	0.65	1
13	**Grand Total**	**1**	**1**	**1**	**1**
14					

< > ... PT-Units By Category & Region   PT-Fou ... + ⋮

FIGURE 7-10:
The PivotTable from Figure 7-9, with the Index calculation applied.

Working with PivotTable Subtotals

When you add a second field to the row or column area, as I describe in Chapter 6, Excel displays subtotals for the items in the outer field. Having these outer field subtotals available is a useful component of data analysis because it shows you not only how the data breaks down according to the items in the second (inner) field but also the total of those items for each item in the first (outer) field. However, Excel lets you turn off subtotals that you don't want to see, and it lets you add multiple subtotals. The next two sections provide the details.

Turning off subtotals for a field

If you kick things up a notch and add a third field to the row or column area, Excel displays two sets of subtotals: one for the second (middle) field and one for the first (outer) field. And for every extra field you add to the row or column area, Excel mindlessly adds yet another set of subtotals.

Believe me, a PivotTable displaying two or more sets of subtotals in one area is no picnic to read. Do yourself a favor and reduce the complexity of the PivotTable layout by turning off the subtotals for one or more of the fields. Here's how:

1. **Select any cell in the field you want to work with.**

2. **Choose PivotTable Analyze ⇨ Field Settings.**

   The Field Settings dialog box appears with the Subtotals & Filters tab displayed.

3. **In the Subtotals group, select the None radio button.**

   Alternatively, right-click any cell in the field and then deselect the Subtotal "*Field*" command, where *Field* is the name of the field.

TIP

4. **Click OK.**

   Excel hides the field's subtotals.

Displaying multiple subtotals for a field

When you add a second field to the row or column area, as I discuss in Chapter 6, Excel displays a subtotal for each item in the outer field, and that subtotal uses the Sum calculation. If you prefer to see the Average for each item or the Count, you can change the field's summary calculation; see the section "Changing the PivotTable summary calculation," previously in this chapter.

However, a common data-analysis task is to view items from several different points of view. That is, you study the results by eyeballing not just a single summary calculation, but several: Sum, Average, Count, Max, Min, and so on.

That's awesome of you, but it's not all that easy to switch from one summary calculation to another. To avoid this problem, Excel enables you to view multiple subtotals for each field, with each subtotal using a different summary calculation. It's true. You can use as many of Excel's 11 built-in summary calculations as you need. That said, using StdDev and StDevp at the same time doesn't make sense, because the former is for sample data and the latter is for population data. The same is true for the Var and Varp calculations.

Okay, here are the steps to follow to add multiple subtotals to a field:

1. **Select any cell in the field you want to mess with.**

2. **Choose PivotTable Analyze ⇨ Field Settings.**

   The Field Settings dialog box appears with the Subtotals & Filters tab displayed.

3. **In the Subtotals group, select the Custom radio button.**

4. **In the list that appears below the Custom options, select each calculation that you want to appear as a subtotal.**

   Alternatively, right-click any cell in the field and then deselect the Subtotal "*Field*" command, where *Field* is the name of the field.

TIP

5. **Click OK.**

   Excel recalculates the PivotTable to show the subtotals you selected.
   Figure 7-11 shows an example PivotTable showing the Sum, Average, Max, and Min subtotals.

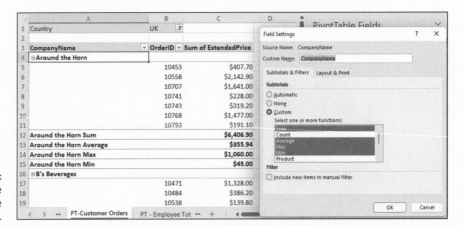

FIGURE 7-11:
A PivotTable with multiple subtotals.

Introducing Custom Calculations

A *custom calculation* is a formula that you define to produce PivotTable values that wouldn't otherwise appear in the report if you used only the source data and Excel's prefab summary calculations. Custom calculations let you to extend your data analysis to include results that are tailored to your company, your department, or the daily whims of your boss.

For example, suppose your PivotTable shows employee sales by quarter and you want to award a 10 percent bonus to each employee with sales of more than $50,000 in any quarter. That's awfully generous of you! To help, you can create a custom calculation that checks for sales greater than $50,000 and then multiplies those by 0.1 to get the bonus number.

A custom calculation is an Excel formula applied to your source data to produce a summary result. In other words, in most cases the custom calculation is just like Excel's built-in PivotTable summary calculations, except that you define the specifics of the calculation. Because you're creating a formula, you can use most of Excel's formula power, which gives you tremendous flexibility to create custom calculations that suit your data-analysis needs. And by placing these calculations in the PivotTable itself — as opposed to, for example, adding them to your source data — you can easily update the calculations as needed and refresh the report results.

Formulas for custom calculations

Custom calculations are formulas with certain restrictions imposed; see the section "Understanding custom calculation limitations," later in this chapter, for more details. A custom calculation formula always begins with an equals sign (=), followed by one or more operands and operators:

>> **Operands:** The values that the formula uses as the raw material for the calculation. In a custom PivotTable calculation, the operands can be numbers, worksheet functions, or fields from your data source.

>> **Operators:** The symbols that the formula uses to perform the calculation. In a custom PivotTable calculation, the available operators include addition (+), subtraction (–), multiplication (*), division (/), and comparison operators such as greater than (>) and less than or equal to (<=).

Checking out the custom calculation types

When building a custom calculation for a PivotTable, Excel offers two types:

» **Calculated field:** A new data field in which the values are the result of a custom calculation formula. You can display the calculated field along with another data field or on its own. A calculated field is really a custom summary calculation, so in almost all cases, the calculated field references one or more fields in the source data. See the section "Inserting a Custom Calculated Field," later in this chapter.

» **Calculated item:** A new item in a row or column field in which the values are the result of a custom calculation. In this case, the calculated item's formula references one or more items in the same field. See the section "Inserting a Custom Calculated Item," later in this chapter, for more on working with a custom calculated item.

Understanding custom calculation limitations

Custom calculations — whether they're calculated fields or calculated items — are powerful additions to your PivotTable analysis toolbox. However, although custom calculation formulas look like regular worksheet formulas, you can't assume that you can do everything with a custom PivotTable formula that you can do with a worksheet formula. In fact, Excel imposes a number of limitations on custom formulas.

The major limitation inherent in custom calculations is that, with the exception of constant values such as numbers, you can't reference anything outside the PivotTable's source data:

» You can't use a cell reference, range address, or range name as an operand in a custom calculation formula.

» You can't use any worksheet function that requires a cell reference, range, or defined name. However, you can still use many of Excel's worksheet functions by substituting either a PivotTable field or a PivotTable item in place of a cell reference or range name. For example, if you want a calculated item that returns the average of items named Jan, Feb, and Mar, you could use the following formula:

    =AVERAGE(Jan, Feb, Mar)

» You can't use the PivotTable's subtotals, row totals, column totals, or grand total as an operand in a custom calculation formula.

You also need to understand how references to other PivotTable fields work in your calculations and what limitations you face when using field references:

» **Field references:** When you reference a PivotTable field in your formula, Excel interprets this reference as the *sum* of that field's values. For example, the formula =Sales + 1 does not add 1 to each Sales value and return the sum of these results; that is, Excel does not interpret the formula as =Sum of (Sales + 1). Instead, the formula adds 1 to the sum of the Sales values, and Excel interprets the formula as =(Sum of Sales) + 1.

» **Field reference problems:** The fact that Excel defaults to a Sum calculation when you reference another field in your custom calculation can lead to problems. The trouble is that summing certain types of data doesn't make sense. For example, suppose you have inventory source data with UnitsInStock and UnitPrice fields. You want to calculate the total value of the inventory, so you create a custom field based on the following formula:

```
=UnitsInStock * UnitPrice
```

Unfortunately, this formula doesn't work because Excel treats the UnitPrice operand as Sum of UnitPrice. Adding the prices together doesn't make sense, so your formula produces an incorrect result.

Finally, Excel imposes the following limitations on the use of calculated items:

» A formula for a calculated item can't reference items from any field except the one in which the calculated item resides.

» You can't insert a calculated item into a PivotTable that has at least one grouped field. You must ungroup all the PivotTable fields before you can insert a calculated item.

» You can't group a field in a PivotTable that has at least one calculated item.

» You can't insert a calculated item into a filter field. Also, you can't move a row or column field that has a calculated item into the filter area.

» You can't insert a calculated item into a PivotTable in which a field has been used more than once.

» You can't insert a calculated item into a PivotTable that uses the Average, StdDev, StdDevp, Var, or Varp summary calculations.

Inserting a Custom Calculated Field

A custom calculated field might look much like an Excel worksheet formula, but you don't enter the formula for a calculated field into a worksheet cell. Instead, Excel offers the Calculated Field feature, which provides a dialog box for you to name the field and construct the formula. Excel then stores the formula along with the rest of the PivotTable data.

Here are the steps to follow to insert a custom calculated field into a PivotTable:

1. **Select any cell in the PivotTable's value area.**

2. **Choose PivotTable Analyze ⇨ Fields, Items, & Sets ⇨ Calculated Field.**

   The Insert Calculated Field dialog box appears.

3. **In the Name text box, enter a name for the calculated field.**

4. **In the Formula text box, start the formula.**

   Begin with an equals sign (=) and then add any constants or worksheet functions you need to get started.

5. **When you get to the point in your formula at which you need to add a field, select a field in the Fields list and then click Insert Field.**

   You can also double-click the field to add it to the formula.

6. **Keep building your formula, repeating Step 5 to add fields as needed.**

7. **When the formula is complete, click Add.**

   Figure 7-12 shows an example formula for a custom calculated field. In this case, the formula uses an IF() function to check whether the ExtendedPrice field is greater than 50,000. If it is, the formula returns the ExtendedPrice value multiplied by 0.1; otherwise, it returns 0.

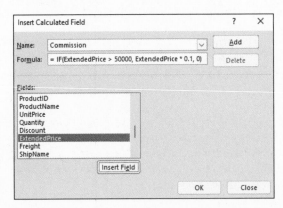

FIGURE 7-12: A custom calculated field, ready for insertion into the PivotTable.

8. **Click OK.**

Excel adds the calculated field to the PivotTable's data area, as shown in Figure 7-13. Excel adds the calculated field to the PivotTable Fields task pane.

	A	B	C
1	Country	(All)	
2			
3	Row Labels	Sum of ExtendedPrice	Sum of Commission
4	Andrew Fuller	$70,444.14	$ 7,044.41
5	Anne Dodsworth	$26,310.39	$ -
6	Janet Leverling	$108,026.13	$ 10,802.61
7	Laura Callahan	$56,032.60	$ 5,603.26
8	Margaret Peacock	$128,809.78	$ 12,880.98
9	Michael Suyama	$43,126.37	$ -
10	Nancy Davolio	$93,148.04	$ 9,314.80
11	Robert King	$60,471.19	$ 6,047.12
12	Steven Buchanan	$30,716.44	$ -
13	**Grand Total**	**$617,085.08**	**$ 61,708.51**
14			

PT - Employee Total Sales +

FIGURE 7-13: The custom calculated field in action.

WARNING

When you add a calculated field to the PivotTable, Excel also applies the custom calculation to the Grand Total value (refer to Figure 7-13). Unfortunately, this total is often inaccurate, and you should be careful not to assume that it's correct. The problem is that it's not a sum of the values in the calculated field, as you might think. Instead, Excel applies the calculated field's formula to the sum of whatever field or fields you referenced in the formula. In the example shown in Figure 7-13, Excel applies the formula to the Sum of Extended Price field's Grand Total value, which is not the correct way to calculate the total commission. If you want to see the correct total for the calculated field, set up a formula outside the PivotTable that sums the values.

Inserting a Custom Calculated Item

If your data analysis requires PivotTable results that are not available using just the data source fields and Excel's built-in summary calculations, no problem: You can insert a calculated item that uses a custom formula to derive the results you need. Sweet!

A calculated item uses a formula similar to an Excel worksheet formula, but you don't enter the formula for a calculated item into a worksheet cell. Instead, Excel offers the Calculated Item command, which displays a dialog box in which you name the item and construct the formula. Excel then stores the formula along with the rest of the PivotTable data.

The Calculated Item feature creates just a single item in a field. However, feel free to add as many calculated items as you need. For example, suppose you want to compare the sales of nonvegan items (such as meat, poultry, dairy, and seafood) with vegan items (grains, cereals, produce, and beverages). One approach would be to create one calculated item that returns the average sales of the nonvegan items and a second calculated item that returns the average sales of the vegan items.

Here are the steps to follow to insert a custom calculated item into a PivotTable:

1. **Select any cell in the field to which you want to insert the item.**

2. **Choose PivotTable Analyze ⇨ Fields, Items, & Sets ⇨ Calculated Item.**

   The Insert Calculated Item dialog box appears.

3. **In the Name text box, enter a name for the calculated field.**

4. **In the Formula text box, start the formula.**

   Begin with an equals sign (=) and then add any constants or worksheet functions you need to get started.

5. **When you get to the point in your formula at which you need to add a field, select the field in the Fields list and then click Insert Field.**

   You can also double-click the field to add it to the formula.

6. **When you get to the point in your formula at which you need to add an item, select the item in the Items list and then click Insert Item.**

   You can also double-click the item to add it to the formula.

7. **Keep building your formula, repeating Steps 5 and 6 to add fields and items as needed.**

8. **When the formula is complete, click Add.**

   Figure 7-14 shows an example formula for a custom calculated item. In this case, I use the AVERAGE() function to calculate the average of several nonvegan food categories.

9. **Click OK.**

10. **Click OK.**

    Excel adds the calculated item to the PivotTable field. Figure 7-15 shows two calculated items added to the PivotTable's row field. Note, as well, that when you select a custom calculated item, Excel shows the item's custom formula in the formula bar.

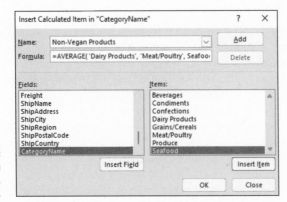

FIGURE 7-14:
A custom
calculated item,
ready for action.

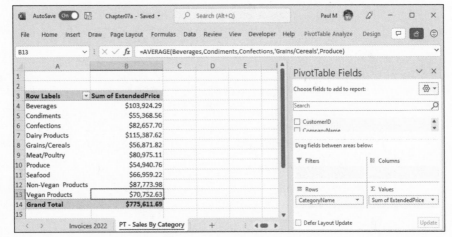

FIGURE 7-15:
Two custom
calculated items
added to the
row area.

Editing a Custom Calculation

When you add a custom calculation to a PivotTable, Excel first checks the formula to make sure that it contains no syntax errors — such as a missing comma or parenthesis — or illegal operands — such as cell addresses, unknown field or item names, or functions not supported by custom calculations. If Excel finds an error, it displays a dialog box to scold you and refuses to add the custom calculation to the PivotTable.

However, just because a formula contains no syntax errors or illegal operands doesn't necessarily mean that its results are correct. In a calculated field, you might have used the wrong function for the result you're seeking. In a calculated item involving several field items, you might have accidentally missed an item.

Alternatively, your formula may be working perfectly, but it may no longer be the result you need if your data analysis needs have changed. For example, you might have a calculated field that determines whether employees get paid a bonus by looking for sales greater than $50,000. If that threshold changes to $75,000, your calculated field will no longer produce the results you want.

Whether your custom calculation contains an error or your data analysis needs have changed, Excel enables you to edit the formula to produce the result you want. Here's how to edit a custom calculation:

1. **To edit a calculated field, select any cell in the PivotTable's data area.**

To edit a calculated item, select any cell in the field that contains the calculated item.

2. **Choose PivotTable Analyze ⇨ Fields, Items, & Sets ⇨ Calculated Field.**

The Insert Calculated Field dialog box appears.

To edit a calculated item instead, choose PivotTable Analyze ⇨ Fields, Items, & Sets ⇨ Calculated Item to open the Insert Calculated Item dialog box.

3. **In the Name list, select the calculation that you want to edit.**

4. **Edit the formula.**

5. **Click Modify.**

6. **Click OK.**

Excel updates the custom calculation's results.

You can also edit a calculated item by selecting the item's result. The formula appears in Excel's formula bar, and you can edit it from there.

TIP

Deleting a Custom Calculation

Custom calculations don't always remain a permanent part of a PivotTable report. For example, it's common to add a calculated field or item temporarily to the PivotTable to test the data or get a number to use elsewhere. Similarly, you may find that you create several versions of a custom calculation and want to keep only the final version. Finally, although custom calculations are a powerful tool, they can't do everything, so you may find that a calculation does not provide the answer you seek or help you with your data analysis.

For all these situations, Excel enables you to delete those calculated fields or items that you no longer need by following these steps:

1. **Select any cell in the PivotTable.**

2. **To delete a calculated field, choose PivotTable Analyze ⇨ Fields, Items, & Sets ⇨ Calculated Field.**

   The Insert Calculated Field dialog box appears.

   To delete a calculated item instead, choose PivotTable Analyze ⇨ Fields, Items, & Sets ⇨ Calculated Item to open the Insert Calculated Item dialog box.

3. **In the Name list, select the calculation that you want to delete.**

4. **Click Delete.**

5. **Click OK.**

   Excel removes the custom calculation.

Chapter **8**

Building PivotCharts

I f a PivotTable appeals to the left side of your brain — the analytical side that likes numbers — the PivotChart will likely appeal to the right side of your brain — the visual side that likes patterns. That's because a PivotChart is to a PivotTable what a regular chart is to a range. That is, the PivotChart is a graphical representation of the PivotTable. The PivotChart enables you to visualize the PivotTable report by displaying the value area results in chart form.

However, you can also say that a PivotChart is to a regular chart what a PivotTable is to a regular range. In other words, the PivotChart goes far beyond the capabilities of a simple chart because the PivotChart comes with most of the same features that make PivotTables so powerful: You can filter the results to see just the data you need, and you can pivot fields from one area of the PivotChart to another to get the layout you want. In this chapter, you discover what PivotCharts are all about, learn how to build PivotCharts, and explore ways to get the most out of your PivotCharts.

Introducing the PivotChart

As you might expect, PivotCharts have a number of elements in common with PivotTables, but some key differences also exist. The following list explains these differences and introduces you to some important PivotChart concepts:

>> **Chart Categories (X-Axis):** As does a PivotTable, a PivotChart automatically groups large amounts of data into smaller, more manageable groups. For example, if you have data with a Category field containing values such as Beverages, Condiments, Confections, and so on and you build your PivotChart using the Category field, the resulting chart will display one chart category (X-axis value) for each unique Category field value. The chart x-axis is the equivalent of a row field in a PivotTable.

>> **Chart Data Series:** Also, as with a PivotTable, you can break down your data in terms of a second field. For example, your data might have an Order Date field. If you add that field to the PivotChart, Excel creates one data series for each unique value in that field. The chart data series is the equivalent of a column field in a PivotTable.

>> **Chart Values (Y-Axis):** You can't have a PivotTable without a value field, and the same is true of a PivotChart. When you add a numeric field for the summary calculation, Excel displays the results as chart values (Y-axis). The chart y-axis is the equivalent of a value field in a PivotTable.

>> **Dynamic PivotCharts:** Perhaps the biggest difference between a PivotChart and a regular chart is that each PivotChart is a dynamic object that you can reconfigure as needed, just as you can with a PivotTable. You can add fields to different chart areas and you can place multiple fields in any chart area.

>> **Filtering:** As with a PivotTable, you can use the unique values in another field to filter the results that appear in the PivotChart. For example, if your source data has a Country field, you can add it to the PivotChart and use it to filter the chart results to show just those from a specific country. The chart filter is the equivalent of a filter field in a PivotTable.

Understanding PivotChart pros and cons

PivotCharts have advantages and disadvantages, and understanding their strengths and weaknesses can help you decide when and if you should use them.

On the positive side, a PivotChart is a powerful data–analysis tool because it combines the strengths of Excel's charting capabilities — including most of the options available with regular charts — with the features of a PivotTable. Also, creating a basic PivotChart is just as straightforward as creating a PivotTable. In fact, if you already have a PivotTable, you can create the equivalent PivotChart by pressing a single key.

On the negative side, PivotCharts share the same caveats that come with regular charts, particularly the fact that if you don't choose the proper chart type or layout, your data will not be readily understood. Moreover, a PivotChart can quickly become extremely confusing when you have multiple Category fields or Data Series fields. Finally, PivotCharts have inherent limitations that restrict the options and formatting that you can apply. I talk about these limitations a bit later in this chapter.

Taking a PivotChart tour

PivotCharts carry over some of the same terminology that I discuss in Chapter 6 for PivotTables, including the concepts of the *report filter, value area,* and *field button.* However, PivotCharts also use several unique terms that you need to understand to get the most out of PivotCharts (see Figure 8-1):

>> **Category items:** The unique field values that define the chart's categories.

>> **Category axis:** The chart's X-axis (that is, the horizontal axis) that displays the category items.

>> **Data series items:** The unique field values that define the chart's data series. The item names appear in the chart legend.

>> **Data series axis:** The chart's Y-axis (that is, the vertical axis) that displays the values of the data series items.

>> **Value area:** Displays the charted results of the calculation that Excel applied to a numeric field in your data.

REMEMBER

One of the main sources of PivotChart confusion is the fact that Excel uses different terminology with PivotCharts and PivotTables. In both, you have a value area that contains the numeric results, and you have a report filter that you can use to filter the data. However, understanding how Excel maps the PivotTable's row and column areas to the PivotChart is important:

>> **Row area versus category axis:** In a PivotTable, the row area contains the unique values that Excel has extracted from a field in the source data. The PivotChart equivalent is the category axis, which corresponds to the chart's X-axis. That is, each unique value from the source field has a corresponding category axis value.

>> **Column area versus series axis:** In a PivotTable, the column area contains the unique values that Excel has extracted from a field in the source data. The PivotChart equivalent is the series axis, which corresponds to the chart's Y-axis. That is, each unique value from the source field has a corresponding data series.

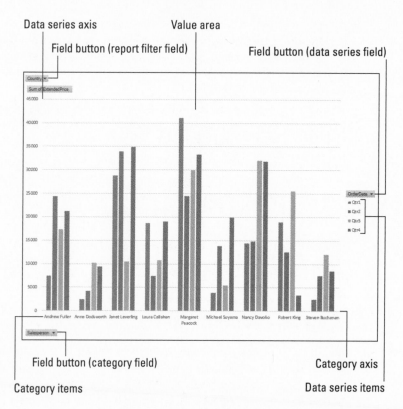

Data series axis — Value area

Field button (report filter field) — Field button (data series field)

Field button (category field) — Category axis

Category items — Data series items

FIGURE 8-1:
The major sights to see in the PivotChart landscape.

Understanding PivotChart limitations

PivotCharts are a powerful addition to your data-analysis toolkit, but they aren't always the ideal solution. Excel has rigid rules for which parts of a PivotTable report correspond to which parts of the PivotChart layout. Moving a field from one part of the PivotChart to another can easily result in a PivotChart layout that is either difficult to understand or doesn't make sense.

You also face a number of limitations that control the types of charts you can build and the formatting options you can apply:

>> **Chart types:** Excel offers a large number of chart types, and you can change the default PivotChart type to another that more closely suits your needs; see the section "Changing the PivotChart type," later in this chapter. However, the three chart types that you can't apply to a PivotChart are Bubble, XY (Scatter), and Stock.

>> **Adding and removing fields:** After you create the PivotChart, as long as you're working with the chart itself, you can't add or remove fields. If you want to reconfigure the PivotChart's fields, you have to add or remove the fields using the underlying PivotTable.

>> **Pivoting fields:** You can't pivot the fields from one part of the PivotChart to another. If you want to pivot a field, you have to use the underlying PivotTable.

Fortunately, these PivotChart limitations aren't onerous in most situations, so they should in no way dissuade you from taking advantage of the analytical and visualization power of the PivotChart.

Creating a PivotChart

Excel gives you three ways to create a PivotChart. That seems like a lot, but is that significant? Probably not, but you should at least be familiar with all three methods, which I outline in the sections that follow.

Creating a PivotChart from a PivotTable

I don't like using the word *easy* to describe anything computer related, because one person's easy is another person's I-have-no-idea-what's-going-on-here. However, if you already have a PivotTable, creating a PivotChart to visualize that PivotTable's data is as close to easy as things get in the data-analysis world. Why? Because convincing Excel to make that PivotChart requires just two measly steps:

1. **Select any cell in the PivotTable.**
2. **Press F11.**

Yep, that's all there is to it. Excel creates a new chart sheet and displays the PivotChart and the PivotChart Fields task pane.

Embedding a PivotChart on a PivotTable's worksheet

When you create a PivotChart directly from an existing PivotTable by pressing F11, as described in the preceding section, Excel places the chart in a new chart sheet. This is usually the best solution because it gives you the most room to view and manipulate the PivotChart. However, viewing the PivotChart together with its associated PivotTable is often useful. For example, when you change the Pivot-Table view, Excel automatically changes the PivotChart view in the same way. Rather than switching from one sheet to another to compare the results, having the PivotChart on the same worksheet lets you to compare the PivotChart and PivotTable immediately. Nice.

Creating a new PivotChart on the same worksheet as an existing PivotTable is called *embedding* the PivotChart. Here are the steps to follow to embed a PivotChart:

1. **Select any cell in the PivotTable.**

2. **Choose PivotTable Analyze ⇨ PivotChart.**

The Insert Chart dialog box appears.

3. **In the list of chart types on the left side of the Insert Chart dialog box, select the chart type you want.**

REMEMBER

You can't use the XY (Scatter), Bubble, or Stock chart type with a PivotChart.

Excel displays one or more chart subtypes for the chart type you selected.

4. **On the right side of the Insert Chart dialog box, select the chart subtype you want.**

5. **Click OK.**

Excel embeds the PivotChart on the PivotTable's worksheet.

Excel embeds the PivotChart in the center of the visible worksheet area. In most cases, this location means that the new PivotChart overlaps your existing PivotTable, which makes comparing them difficult. To fix this problem, you can move or resize the PivotChart:

» To move the PivotChart, move the mouse pointer over an empty part of the chart area and then drag the chart object to the new position.

» To resize the PivotChart, select the chart and then move the mouse pointer over any one of the selection handles that appear on the chart area's corners and sides. Drag a handle to the size you require.

REMEMBER

If you already have a PivotChart in a separate chart sheet, you can embed it in the PivotTable's worksheet. I describe how this works later in this chapter, in the section "Moving a PivotChart to another sheet."

Creating a PivotChart from an Excel range or table

If the data you want to summarize and visualize exists as an Excel range or table, you can build a PivotChart (and its underlying PivotTable) directly from that data. Here are the steps to follow:

1. **Select a cell in the table that you want to use as the source data.**

   If you're using a range, select any cell in the range instead.

2. **Choose Insert ⇨ PivotChart.**

   The Create PivotChart dialog box appears, with the Select a Table or Range radio button selected. The Table/Range box should show the name of your table (or the address of your range). If not, adjust the name or address as needed before moving on.

3. **Select the New Worksheet radio button.**

   Alternatively, if you want to add the PivotTable to an existing location, select the Existing Worksheet radio button and then, in the Location range box, select the worksheet and cell where you want the PivotTable to appear.

4. **Click OK.**

   Excel creates a blank PivotTable and a blank, embedded PivotChart, and it displays the PivotChart Fields task pane, as shown in Figure 8-2. This pane contains two main areas:

   - A list of the column headers from your table, each of which has a check box to its left. These are your PivotChart (and PivotTable) fields.

   - Four boxes representing the four areas of the PivotChart: Filters, Legend (Series), Axis (Categories), and Values. To complete the PivotChart, add one or more fields to some or all of these areas.

5. **Drag a text field and drop it in the Axis (Categories) area.**

   Excel adds a button for the field to the PivotChart's category (X) axis.

6. **Drag a numeric field and drop it in the Values area.**

   Excel sums the numeric values based on the row values.

7. **If desired, drag fields and drop them in the Legend (Series) area and the Filters area.**

   Each time you drop a field into an area, Excel updates the PivotChart (and its associated PivotTable) to include the new data. Figure 8-3 shows a completed PivotChart (and PivotTable), with fields in just the Axis (Categories), Values, and Filters boxes. Note, too, that when you select the PivotChart, Excel displays three contextual tabs — PivotChart Analyze, Design, and Format — that are bursting with options for manipulating and formatting your PivotChart.

If your PivotChart includes just a Category field, Excel displays the results using a standard bar chart. If the PivotChart includes both a Category field and a series field, Excel displays the results using a clustered column chart. I talk about how to view the PivotChart using a different type of chart in the section "Changing the PivotChart type," later in this chapter.

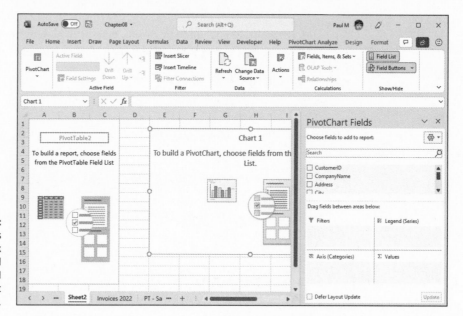

FIGURE 8-2:
Excel kicks things off with a blank PivotTable and PivotChart, and the PivotChart Fields task pane.

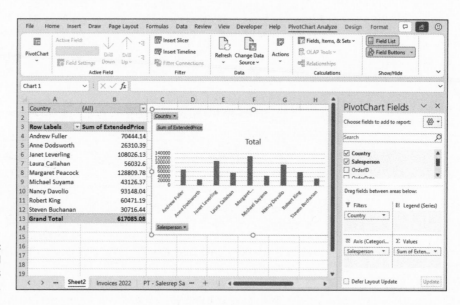

FIGURE 8-3:
An embedded PivotChart and its PivotTable.

TECHNICAL STUFF

The clustered column chart is a great way to visualize two-dimensional PivotTable results, but deciphering the chart isn't always easy — especially if you have a large number of data series, which usually means that most of the columns in each category are quite small. To get a better understanding of the chart, you might want to know what data is represented by specific columns.

You can find the specifics related to each column by moving the mouse pointer over the column in the plot area. Excel then displays a banner with data in the following format:

Series *"Series Item"* Point *"Category Item"* Value: *Value*

Here, *Series Item* is an item from the series field, *Category Item* is an item from the Category field, and *Value* is the value of the data point. For example, if the Shipper field has an item named United Package, the Salesperson field has an item named Steven Buchanan, and the value is 488, the banner shows the following:

Series "United Package" Point "Steven Buchanan" Value: 488

Working with PivotCharts

After you have a PivotChart up and charting, you might want to leave it as is. That's perfectly fine, but you're more likely to want to take advantage of the many ways Excel offers to manipulate and format a PivotChart. In the rest of this chapter, I run through a fistful of techniques for messing around with PivotCharts.

Moving a PivotChart to another sheet

In the section "Creating a PivotChart from a PivotTable," previously in this chapter, I talk about creating a new PivotChart on a separate chart sheet. However, in some situations, this separate chart sheet might not be convenient. For example, if you want to compare the PivotChart and its associated PivotTable, that comparison is more difficult if the PivotChart and PivotTable reside in separate sheets. Similarly, you might prefer to place all your PivotCharts on a single sheet so that you can compare them or they're easy to find. Finally, if you plan on creating several PivotCharts, you might not want to clutter your workbook with separate chart sheets.

The solution in all these cases is to move your PivotChart or PivotCharts to the worksheet you prefer. To that worthy end, follow these steps to move a PivotChart to a new location:

1. **Select the PivotChart you want to move.**

2. **Choose Design ⇨ Move Chart.**

   The Move Chart dialog box appears.

3. Select the Object In radio button and open its drop-down list to select the sheet where you want the PivotChart moved (see Figure 8-4).

4. Click OK.

Excel moves the PivotChart to the location you specified.

FIGURE 8-4:
Use the Move Chart dialog box to move a PivotChart to another worksheet.

TIP

The steps in this section apply both to PivotCharts embedded in separate chart sheets and to PivotChart objects embedded in worksheets. For the latter, however, you can use a second technique. Select the PivotChart and then choose Home ➪ Cut (or press Ctrl+X) to remove the PivotChart and store it in the Windows Clipboard. Switch to the sheet where you want the PivotChart moved. If you're moving the PivotChart to a worksheet, select the cell where you want the upper-left corner of the chart to appear. Choose Home ➪ Paste (or press Ctrl+V). Excel pastes the PivotChart object to the sheet. Move and resize the PivotChart object to taste.

Filtering a PivotChart

By default, each PivotChart report displays a summary for all the records in your source data, which is usually what you want to see. However, you might have situations that require you to focus more closely on some aspect of the data. You can focus on a specific item from one of the source data fields by taking advantage of the PivotChart's report filter.

For example, suppose that you're dealing with a PivotChart that summarizes data from thousands of customer invoices over some period of time. A basic PivotChart might tell you the total units sold for each product category. However, what if you want to see the units sold for each product in a specific country? If the Product field is in the PivotChart's Axis (Categories) area, you can add the Country field to the Legend (Series) area. However, dozens of countries might be involved, so that isn't an efficient way to go. Instead, you can add the Country field to the Report Filter area. You can then tell Excel to display the total sold for each product for the specific country in which you're interested.

As another example, suppose you ran a marketing campaign in the previous quarter and set up an incentive plan for your salespeople whereby they could earn bonuses for selling at least a specified number of units. Suppose, as well, that you have a PivotChart showing the sum of the units sold for each product. To see the numbers for a particular employee, you can add the Salesperson field to the Report Filter area and then select the employee you want to work with.

Here are the steps to follow to filter a PivotChart:

1. **Click the PivotChart's Report Filter button.**

Excel displays a list of the Report Filter field items.

2. **Select the item you want to view, as shown in Figure 8-5.**

If you want to display data for two or more items, select the Select Multiple Items check box and then repeat Step 2 to select the other items.

3. **Click OK.**

Excel filters the PivotChart to show only the data for the item (or items) you selected.

Report Filter field button

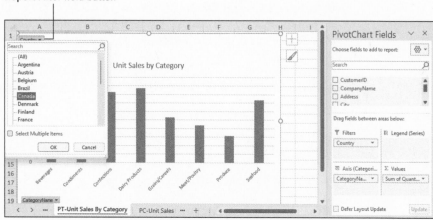

FIGURE 8-5:
Pull down the
Report Filter field
list and then
select an item.

If you want to return to seeing all the items, click the Report Filter field button, select (All), and then click OK.

You can also filter the items in the Axis (Categories) area. For example, in a PivotChart that includes items from the ProductName field in the row area, you might want to see only those products with names that begin with the letter *G* or contain the word *tofu*. You can do that by applying a filter to a Category field. Excel offers several text filters, including Equals, Doesn't Equal, Begins With, Ends With, Contains, Greater Than, and Less Than. If the field uses dates, you can apply a date filter such as Before, Yesterday, Last Month, and This Year.

In the PivotChart, click the button for the field you want to work with and then choose either the Label Filters or the Date Filters command. In the list that appears, select the filter type you want to apply, such as Begins With. Then type your filter criteria and click OK.

Changing the PivotChart type

If you don't include a series field in the PivotChart, Excel displays the report using regular columns, which is useful for comparing the values across the Category field's items. If you include a series field in the PivotChart, Excel displays the report using clustered columns, where each category shows several different-colored columns grouped beside one another, one for each item in the series field. These clustered columns are useful for comparing the series values for each item in the category.

Although these default chart types are fine for many applications, they're not always the best choice. For example, if you don't have a series field and you want to see the relative contribution of each category item to the total, a pie chart would be a better choice. If you're more interested in showing how the results trend over time, a line chart is usually the ideal type.

Whatever your needs, Excel enables you to change the default PivotChart type to any of the following types: Column, Bar, Line, Pie, Area, Doughnut, Radar, Surface, Cylinder, Cone, or Pyramid.

REMEMBER

Excel doesn't allow you to use a PivotChart with the following chart types: XY (Scatter), Bubble, or Stock.

Follow these steps to change your PivotChart's type:

1. **Select the PivotChart.**

2. **Choose Design ⇨ Change Chart Type.**

   The Change Chart Type dialog box appears.

3. **In the list of chart types on the left, select the chart type you want to use.**

   Excel displays the available chart subtypes.

4. **On the right side of the dialog box, select the Chart subtype you want to use.**

5. **Click OK.**

   Excel redisplays the PivotChart with the new chart type. For example, Figure 8-6 shows the PivotChart from Figure 8-5 displayed using the pie chart type.

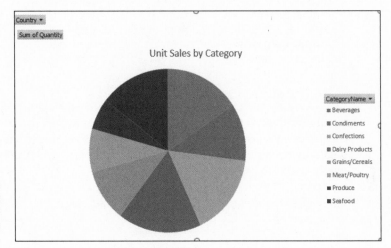

FIGURE 8-6:
The PivotChart
from Figure 8-5
now displayed as
a pie chart.

Adding data labels to your PivotChart

Depending on the chart type you choose, augmenting the chart with the values from the report is often useful. For example, with a pie chart, you can add to each slice the value as well as the percentage the value represents of the grand total. In most cases, you can also add the series name and the category name.

To add these data labels to your PivotChart, follow these steps:

1. **Select the chart.**

2. **Choose Design ⇨ Add Chart Element ⇨ Data Labels.**

   Excel displays a menu of data label types.

3. **Select the data label position you want to use.**

   The choices you see depend on the chart type.

   You can also select More Data Label Options to open the Format Data Labels task pane and then select the Value check box. Depending on the data, you might also be able to select the Series Name, Category Name, and Percentage check boxes.

Sorting the PivotChart

When you create a PivotChart and include a series field, Excel displays the data series based on the order of the field's items as they appear in the PivotTable. That is, as you move left to right through the items in the PivotTable's column field, the data series moves left to right in the PivotChart's series field (or top to bottom if you're looking at the PivotChart legend). This default series order is fine in most applications, but you might prefer to change the order. In the default clustered column chart, for example, you might prefer to reverse the data series so that they appear from right to left.

Similarly, the PivotChart categories appear in the same order as they appear in the underlying PivotTable's row field. In this case, you might prefer to display the categories in some custom order. For example, you might want to rearrange employee names so that those who have the same supervisor or who work in the same division appear together.

First, here are the steps to follow to sort the data series items:

1. **Select the PivotChart.**

2. **Select the field button for the PivotChart's Data Series field.**

   Excel displays a list of sort options for the field. The sort options you see vary depending on the field's data type:

   - **For a text field:** Sort A to Z (ascending) and Sort Z to A (descending).

   - **For a date field:** Sort Oldest to Newest (ascending) and Sort Newest to Oldest (descending).

   - **For a numeric field:** Sort Smallest to Largest (ascending) and Sort Largest to Smallest (descending).

3. **Select the sort order you want to use.**

   Excel redisplays the PivotChart using the new series order.

Follow these steps to sort the category items:

1. **Select the PivotChart.**

2. **Select the field button for the PivotChart's Category field.**

   Excel displays a list of sort options for the field.

   The sort options you see vary depending on the field's data type, and the possible options are the same as those in Step 2 of the preceding steps.

3. **Select the sort order you want to use.**

   Excel redisplays the PivotChart using the new field order.

MANUALLY SORTING DATA SERIES OR CATEGORIES

Excel enables you to sort the data series items or categories manually. Unfortunately, Excel doesn't offer a method for manually sorting series items or categories directly on the PivotChart. Instead, you must manually sort the data on the PivotTable itself. When you do this, Excel automatically applies the new sort order to the PivotChart.

To manually sort the data series items, select the PivotChart's underlying PivotTable and then select the label of the column field item you want to move. Move the mouse pointer to the right edge of the label cell so that the pointer changes into a four-headed arrow, and then drag the label left or right to the new position.

To manually sort the categories, display the PivotChart's underlying PivotTable and select the label of the row field item you want to move. Move the mouse pointer to the bottom edge of the label cell so that the pointer changes into a four-headed arrow, and then drag the label up or down to the new position.

When you return to the PivotChart, you see that the data series items or categories now appear in the new sort order.

Adding PivotChart titles

By default, Excel doesn't add titles to your PivotChart. This absence of titles isn't a big deal for most PivotCharts because the field names and item labels often provide enough context to understand the report. However, the data you use might have cryptic field names or coded item names, so the default PivotChart might be difficult to decipher. In that case, you might want to add titles to the PivotChart that make the report more comprehensible.

Excel offers three PivotChart titles:

» An overall chart title that sits above the chart's plot area or is overlaid on the plot area
» A category (X) axis title that sits below the category items
» A data series (Y) axis title that sits to the left of the data series axis labels

You can add one or more of these titles to your PivotChart. And although Excel doesn't allow you to move these titles to a different location, you can play around with the font, border, background, and text alignment.

WARNING

The downside to adding PivotChart titles is that most of them take up space in the chart area, which means you have less space to display the PivotChart itself. (The exception is an overall chart title overlaid on the plot area.) This reduced space isn't usually a problem with a simple PivotChart, but if you have a complex chart — particularly if you have a large number of category items — you might prefer not to display titles at all, or you might prefer to display only one or two.

To get the PivotChart title ball rolling, here's how you add an overall chart title:

1. Select the PivotChart.

2. Choose Design ⇨ Add Chart Element ⇨ Chart Title.

3. Select the type of chart title you want to add.

Besides None, you have two choices:

- **Above Chart:** Places the title above the PivotChart's plot area, centered on the PivotChart

- **Centered Overlay:** Places the title centered in the PivotChart's plot area

Excel adds a default title to the PivotChart. The title that Excel adds depends on your data, but it's usually something generic such as "Chart Title" or "Total."

4. Select the chart title.

5. Enter the title you want to use.

6. Click outside the chart title to set it.

Here are the steps to follow to add an axis title:

1. Select the PivotChart.

2. Choose Design ⇨ Add Chart Element ⇨ Axis Titles.

3. Select the type of chart title you want to add.

You have two choices:

- **Primary Horizontal:** Adds a category (X) axis title

- **Primary Vertical:** Adds a data series (Y) axis title

Excel adds a default axis title to the PivotChart. The title that Excel adds is usually something generic, such as "Axis Title."

4. Select the title.

5. Enter the title you want to use.

6. Click outside the chart title to set it.

To format a chart title, select the title and then choose Format ⇨ Format Selection. The task pane that appears offers two tabs:

>> **Title Options:** This tab comes with three subtabs: Fill & Line (use the Fill and Border sections to format the title's background and borders), Effects (use the Shadow, Glow, Soft Edges, and 3-D Format sections to apply these effects to the title), and Size & Properties (use the Alignment options to align the title).

>> **Text Options:** This tab comes with three subtabs: Text Fill & Outline (use the Text Fill and Text Outline sections to format the title text background and outline), Text Effects (use the Shadow, Reflection, Glow, Soft Edges, 3-D Format, and 3-D Rotation sections to apply these effects to the title text), and Textbox (use the Text Box options to align the title text).

To edit a title, either double-click the title or right-click the title and then select Edit Text.

Excel gives you three methods for removing a title from a PivotChart:

>> Follow the steps in this section, and in the menu of title options, select None.

>> Right-click the title you want to remove and choose the Delete command.

>> Select the title you want to remove and then press the Delete key.

Moving the PivotChart legend

The PivotChart legend displays the series field items along with a colored box that tells you which series belongs to which item. By default, Excel displays the legend to the right of the plot area. This position is usually the best because it doesn't interfere with other chart elements such as titles (which I describe in the preceding section, "Adding PivotChart titles") or the axis labels.

However, displaying the legend on the right does mean that it takes up space that would otherwise be used by your PivotChart. If you have a number of category items in your PivotChart report, you might prefer to display the legend above or below the plot area to give the PivotChart more horizontal room.

Excel enables you to move the legend to one of five positions with respect to the plot area: right, left, bottom, top, and upper-right corner. Excel also gives you the option of having the legend overlapping the chart, which means that Excel doesn't resize the plot area to accommodate the legend. This position is useful if you have some white space on the chart (for example, at the top) where you can place the legend so that it doesn't hide any chart data.

Follow these steps to set the position of the PivotChart legend:

1. **Select the PivotChart.**

2. **Choose Design ⇨ Add Chart Element ⇨ Legend.**

   If you want, you can select a predefined legend position: Right, Top, Left, or Bottom.

3. **Select More Legend Options.**

   The Format Legend task pane appears and displays the Legend Options tab.

4. **Click the Legend Options subtab, expand the Legend Options section, if necessary, and then select the radio button for the legend position you want.**

   To display the legend overlapping the chart, deselect the Show the Legend without Overlapping the Chart check box.

   Excel moves the legend to the new position.

In some cases, you might prefer to not display the legend. For example, if your PivotChart doesn't have a series field, Excel still displays a legend for the default "series" named Total. This legend isn't particularly useful, so you can gain some extra chart space by hiding the legend. To do this, follow the preceding Steps 1 and 2 to display the Legend menu and then select None. Alternatively, right-click the legend and choose the Delete command.

Displaying a data table with the PivotChart

The point of a PivotChart is to combine the visualization effects of an Excel chart with the pivoting and filtering capabilities of a PivotTable. The visualization part helps your data analysis because it enables you to make at-a-glance comparisons among series and categories, and it enables you to view data points relative to other parts of the report.

However, although visualizing the data is often useful, it lacks a certain precision because you don't see the underlying data. Excel offers several ways to overcome this problem, including creating the PivotChart on the same worksheet as the PivotTable (see the section "Embedding a PivotChart on a PivotTable's worksheet"), moving a chart to the PivotTable worksheet (see the section "Moving a PivotChart to another sheet"), and displaying data labels (see the section "Adding data labels to your PivotChart"), all previously in this chapter.

Yet another method is to display a data table along with the PivotChart. A *PivotChart data table* displays the chart's categories as columns and its data series as rows, with the cells filled with the actual data values. Because these values appear directly below the chart, the data table gives you an easy way to combine a visual report with the specifics of the underlying data. To display a data table with the PivotChart, follow these steps:

1. **Select the PivotChart.**

2. **Choose Design ⇨ Add Chart Element ⇨ Data Table.**

   Select a predefined data table:

   - **With Legend Keys:** Displays the data table with the same colored squares that appear in the legend to identify each series

   - **No Legend Keys:** Displays the data table without the colored squares

   Excel displays the data table below the PivotChart. Figure 8-7 shows an example.

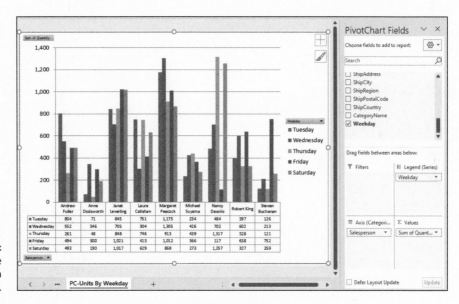

FIGURE 8-7: A data table shown below a PivotChart.

3

Discovering Advanced Data-Analysis Tools

Use a workbook Data Model to analyze related tables.

Use Excel's powerful worksheet functions and charting features to track trends over time and forecast future values.

Tap into the power of Excel's more than 70 statistical functions to calculate averages, determine ranking and percentiles, measure dispersions, and analyze distributions.

Gain extra insights into your data by using formulas, functions, and the Analysis ToolPak add-on tool for creating histograms, calculating moving averages, using exponential smoothing, and performing smart sampling.

Use the Regression and Correlation tools; the Anova data-analysis tool; and the z-Test, t-Test, and Fourier data-analysis tools to perform inferential statistics analysis.

Chapter **9**

Dealing with Data Models

I f you hang out in online places where folks talk about Excel (hey, it could happen), someone at some point will describe Excel as a "very good flat-file database management system" (or something along those lines). The operative adjectival phrase here is *flat-file,* which describes a database in which all data is stored in standalone tables that have no relationship with each other. The opposite is a *relational* database management system in which the tables are (or, at least, can be) related in some way. (You learn what these types of relationships are all about in this chapter.) Standalone tables are merely two-dimensional (hence flat), while adding a relational angle gives the data a third dimension.

At first glance, it seems as though that online opiner was right: Excel workbooks generally consist of multiple, standalone tables, so Excel really is a flat-file database. That's true, but it's also *way* out-of-date. Sure, older versions of Excel only did the flat-file thing, but more recent versions come with some powerful relational capabilities that can kick your data analysis into a higher gear. These relational features come courtesy of Excel's Data Model, which is the subject of this chapter.

Understanding Excel Data Models

When you want to analyze data in Excel, the basic approach is to convert the range to a table and then use Excel's various table-related analysis tools — such as subtotals, filtering, the Database functions, and PivotTables — to interrogate the data. For many applications, this approach works awesomely well, as I describe in previous chapters. However, what if the data you want to analyze exists in multiple tables? For example, suppose you have a workbook that contains (at least) the following two tables:

» **Orders:** This table holds data on orders placed by your customers, including the ID of the customer who placed the order and the date of the order. This table includes an Order ID column, which uniquely identifies each order.

» **Order Details:** This table holds data on the specific products that make up each order: product ID, unit price, quantity ordered, and so on. This table also includes an Order ID column, which identifies the order for each product.

Why not lump both tables into a single table? Well, that would mean that, for each product ordered, you would have to include the customer ID, the order date, and so on. If the customer purchased 10 different products, this information would be repeated 10 times.

To avoid such data redundancy, the data is kept in separate tables. That sounds great, but what if you want to analyze orders based on data that exists in both tables? For example, maybe you want to examine quantities ordered over a specific time frame. How do you do that when the quantities ordered are in the Order Details table and the order dates are in the Orders table?

The answer is that you need to set up a relationship between the two tables. You set up this relationship by connecting the tables using a column they have in common, as follows:

» One of the tables must include a column that contains values that uniquely identify each item in the table. This column is known as the *primary key*. In our example, the Orders table's Order ID column is the primary key.

» The other table includes the first table's primary key column — where it's known as the *foreign key* — but the values in this second table's column aren't usually unique. In our example, most customer orders would include multiple products, so for every order in the Orders table, there will likely be multiple records in the Order Details table.

The following two figures show how this works. In Figure 9-1, the first record in the Orders table refers to Order ID 10248. If you look at the Order Details table in Figure 9-2, you see that the first three records also have an Order ID of 10248. Those three records make up the entire order that uses ID 10248.

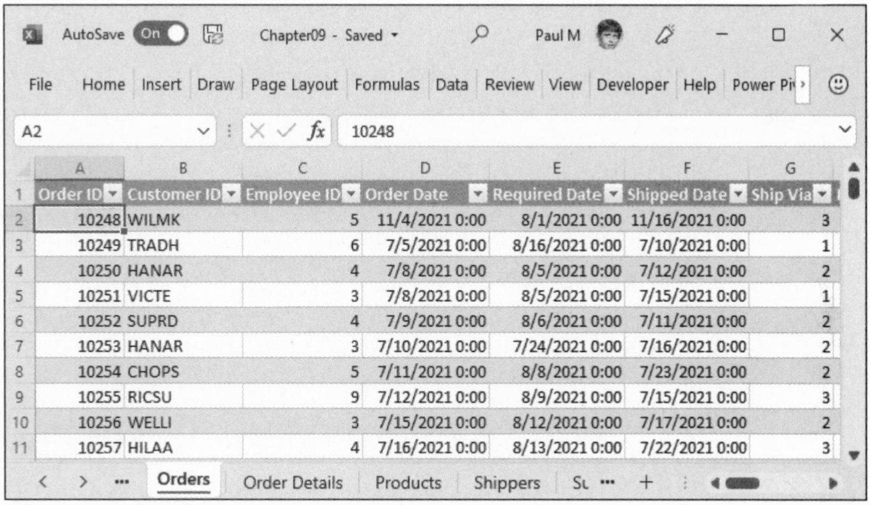

Order ID	Customer ID	Employee ID	Order Date	Required Date	Shipped Date	Ship Via
10248	WILMK	5	11/4/2021 0:00	8/1/2021 0:00	11/16/2021 0:00	3
10249	TRADH	6	7/5/2021 0:00	8/16/2021 0:00	7/10/2021 0:00	1
10250	HANAR	4	7/8/2021 0:00	8/5/2021 0:00	7/12/2021 0:00	2
10251	VICTE	3	7/8/2021 0:00	8/5/2021 0:00	7/15/2021 0:00	1
10252	SUPRD	4	7/9/2021 0:00	8/6/2021 0:00	7/11/2021 0:00	2
10253	HANAR	3	7/10/2021 0:00	7/24/2021 0:00	7/16/2021 0:00	2
10254	CHOPS	5	7/11/2021 0:00	8/8/2021 0:00	7/23/2021 0:00	2
10255	RICSU	9	7/12/2021 0:00	8/9/2021 0:00	7/15/2021 0:00	3
10256	WELLI	3	7/15/2021 0:00	8/12/2021 0:00	7/17/2021 0:00	2
10257	HILAA	4	7/16/2021 0:00	8/13/2021 0:00	7/22/2021 0:00	3

FIGURE 9-1: In the Orders table, the first record has an Order ID value of 10248.

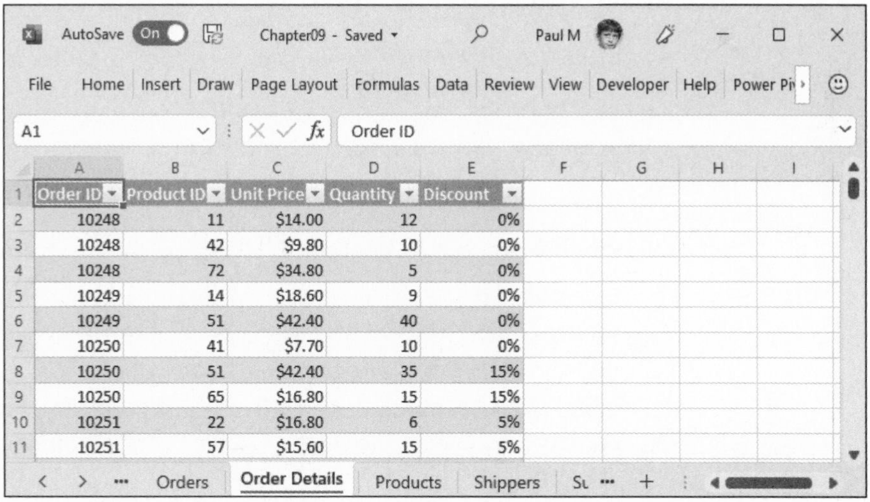

Order ID	Product ID	Unit Price	Quantity	Discount
10248	11	$14.00	12	0%
10248	42	$9.80	10	0%
10248	72	$34.80	5	0%
10249	14	$18.60	9	0%
10249	51	$42.40	40	0%
10250	41	$7.70	10	0%
10250	51	$42.40	35	15%
10250	65	$16.80	15	15%
10251	22	$16.80	6	5%
10251	57	$15.60	15	5%

FIGURE 9-2: In the Order Details table, the first three records have an Order ID value of 10248.

You can work with the data in both tables if you set up a relationship between them based on the common Order ID column. When you have two or more tables that are related in this way, you're now working with an Excel *Data Model*.

Excel supports two types of relationships — or, in the vernacular, two types of *cardinality* — in a Data Model:

>> **One-to-many:** Each unique value in the primary key can be related to multiple values in the foreign key. In our example, each record in the Orders table can be related to multiple records in the Order Details table (since every order can contain multiple items), so these tables would have a one-to-many cardinality.

>> **One-to-one:** Each unique value in the primary key can be related to only one value in the foreign key. For example, suppose you have a table of employees and a table of office locations. Each table contains only unique entries and you can assign only one office to one employee, so these tables would have a one-to-one cardinality.

REMEMBER

You can have only one Data Model in each of your workbooks, but each Data Model can contain as many tables as your multi-table analysis needs dictate.

Creating a relationship between tables

Assuming you have a couple of tables with primary key and foreign key columns that can have a one-to-many or one-to-one relationship, follow these steps to set up that relationship between the tables:

1. **Make sure that the workbook containing the two tables is open in Excel.**

2. **Choose Data ⇨ Data Tools ⇨ Relationships.**

   Excel opens the Manage Relationships dialog box.

3. **Click New.**

   Excel opens the Create Relationship dialog box.

4. **In the Table drop-down list, select the table that contains the foreign key column. Then in the Column (Foreign) drop-down list, select the table's foreign key column.**

5. **In the Related Table drop-down list, select the table that contains the primary key column. Then in the Related Column (Primary) drop-down list, select the table's primary key column.**

REMEMBER

The primary key and foreign key columns don't need to have the same name. As long as the values in the foreign key column are taken from the unique values found in the primary key column, you can set up the relationship even if the two columns use different names.

Figure 9-3 shows a completed version of the Create Relationship dialog box using the Order Details and Orders tables from the previous example. Note that I'm relating the tables using the common Order ID column.

6. **Click OK.**

   Excel returns you to the Manage Relationships dialog box, where your new relationship appears in the list.

   Note that if you need to make adjustments to the relationship, you can select the relationship in the list and then click Edit. If you no longer need the relationship, select it and then click Delete.

7. **Click Close.**

   Excel closes the dialog box and add the two related tables to the workbook's Data Model.

Importing related external data tables

If you want to work with multiple, related tables that reside in an external data source, rather than importing each table and creating the relationships manually, you can save a ton of time by importing the data directly into your workbook's Data Model. To show you how this works, here are the steps to follow to import multiple, related tables from an Access database:

1. **Open or create the workbook in which you want to create your Data Model.**

2. **Choose Data ⇨ Get Data ⇨ From Database ⇨ From Microsoft Access Database.**

   The Import Data dialog box appears.

3. **Select the Access database file that contains the tables you want to import, and then click Import.**

   The Navigator window appears and displays a list of tables in the Access database.

4. **Select the Select Multiple Items check box.**

5. **In the list of tables, select the check box beside a table you want to import.**

6. **Click Select Related Tables.**

   Excel examines the tables and selects the check box beside each related table (see Figure 9-4).

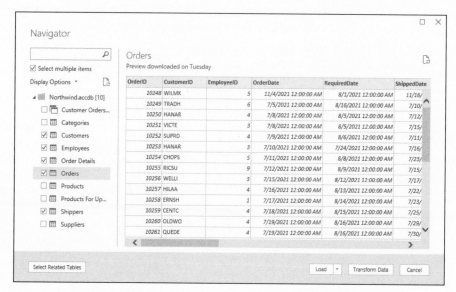

FIGURE 9-4: You can click Select Related Tables to have Excel figure out which tables are related to the selected table.

7. **Repeat Steps 5 and 6 until you've selected all the data you want to import.**

8. **Click the Load drop-down arrow and then click Load To.**

   Excel opens the Import Data dialog box, as shown in Figure 9-5.

   Note that, by default, Excel selects the Only Create Connection option. This option tells Excel to create a connection to the external data instead of adding the data to a worksheet. This is the way to go if you'll be managing your Data Model using the Power Pivot add-in, as described later in this chapter. If you instead want the data imported into Excel as tables, select the Table option; if you prefer to import the data as a PivotTable, select the PivotTable Report option; finally, if you want to import the data as a PivotChart, select the PivotChart option.

   Also, be sure to leave the Add This Data to the Data Model check box selected.

9. **Click OK.**

   Excel imports the external data to your workbook's Data Model and displays the connection details in the Queries tab of the Queries and Connections task pane.

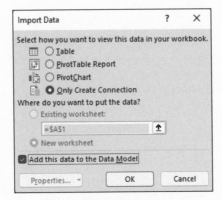

FIGURE 9-5:
When you import multiple, related tables, you can opt to create only a connection to the data.

Basing a PivotTable on multiple, related tables

Once you've set up a relationship between two tables, you can use that relationship to combine the columns from those two tables in a single PivotTable. This powerful data-analysis magic works as follows:

1. **Select a cell in one of the related tables that you want to include in your PivotTable.**

2. **Choose Insert ➪ PivotTable.**

   The PivotTable from Table or Range dialog box shows up. The name of the table from Step 1 appears in the dialog box.

REMEMBER

   If you imported your related tables using the Only Create Connection option, as I describe in the preceding section, you can create a PivotTable from your Data Model by selecting Insert ➪ PivotTable ➪ From Data Model.

3. **(Optional) If you want your PivotTable to reside in an existing worksheet, select the Existing Worksheet option and use the Location range box to select the cell that will be the upper-left corner of the PivotTable.**

4. **Select the Add This Data to the Data Model check box, as shown in Figure 9-6.**

Selecting this option is the crucial difference between creating a regular one-table PivotTable and a multi-table PivotTable.

REMEMBER

5. **Click OK.**

Excel creates a blank PivotTable and displays the PivotTable Fields task pane.

At first glance, everything in the new worksheet looks the same as it does when you're creating a garden-variety, one-table PivotTable. Not so fast. Take a closer look at the PivotTable Fields task pane: The pane now displays a couple of tabs at the top: Active and All. The Active tab displays the fields from the table you selected in Step 1; the All tab displays a list all the tables in your workbook and the fields they contain.

6. **On the Active tab, add to the PivotTable areas whatever fields you need from the current table.**

7. **On the All tab, add to the PivotTable areas whatever fields you need from the related table.**

Once you add at least one field from the related table, Excel displays that table's fields in the Active tab, as shown in Figure 9-7. In this example, I've added the Orders table's Order ID field to the Rows area and the Order Details table's Quantity field to the Values area, so this PivotTable shows the sum of the products in each order.

8. **Repeat Steps 6 and 7 until your PivotTable is complete.**

When you're building your PivotTable, what happens if you try to add a field from a table that's not in your Data Model (that is, from a table that has no relationship with a table in your model)? In that case, Excel displays the message "Relationships between tables may be needed," as shown in Figure 9-8.

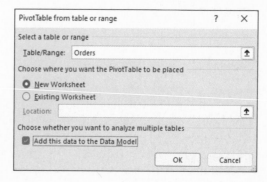

FIGURE 9-6:
Be sure to select the Add This Data to the Data Model check box.

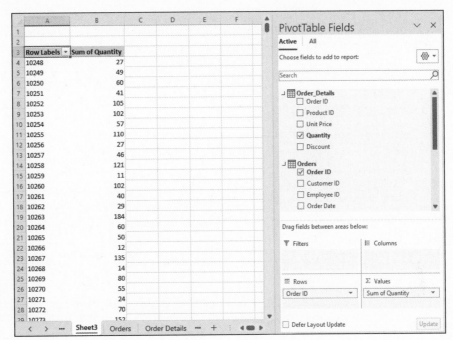

FIGURE 9-7:
A PivotTable that summarizes data from two related tables: Orders and Order Details.

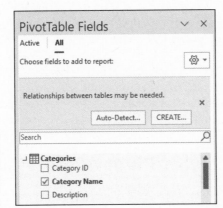

FIGURE 9-8:
Excel displays this message if you try to add a field from an unrelated table.

You have three ways to handle things from here:

» If you change your mind and decide you don't want the field in your PivotTable, deselect the field's check box in the PivotTable Fields task pane.

» To create the required relationship manually, click Create. Excel opens the Create Relationship dialog box (refer to Figure 9-3), where you select your related tables and the appropriate foreign key and primary key columns.

>> To have Excel attempt to create the relationship automatically, click Auto-Detect. If Excel is successful, you see the version of the Auto-Detect Relationships dialog box, as shown in Figure 9-9. Click Close to proceed.

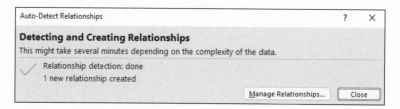

Managing a Data Model with Power Pivot

The Data Model lurks behind the scenes of your workbook. If all you want to do is use your related tables to build PivotTable reports and PivotCharts, you can safely ignore the Data Model and get on with your life. That simple approach is usually fine if you're just working with two or three related tables. However, the more tables in your Data Model, the more complex everything becomes and the greater the need to manage that complexity and the greater the need for tools to take full advantage of all those relationships.

Managing and analyzing the relational data in an Excel Data Model is the bailiwick of the Power Pivot add-in. With Power Pivot on the job, you can add tables to your Data Mode, create, edit, and view relationships, transform data, build PivotTables, and more.

Enabling the Power Pivot add-in

Power Pivot is a COM add-in that needs to be enabled before you can use it to raise your data-analysis game. Here are the steps to run through:

1. **Choose File ➪ Options.**

2. **Click Add-ins.**

3. **In the Manage list, choose COM Add-ins and then click Go.**

   The COM Add-ins dialog box appears.

4. **Select the Microsoft Power Pivot for Excel check box.**

5. **Click OK.**

   Excel enables Power Pivot and adds the Power Pivot tab to the Ribbon.

Adding a table to the Data Model

You normally add a table to the Data Model by creating a relationship between that table and another. However, if that's not possible, you can add a table directly to the Data Model by using Power Pivot. Here's how:

1. Select a cell in the table that you want to add to the workbook Data Model.

2. Choose Power Pivot ⇨ Add to Data Model.

Power Pivot opens and adds the table to the Data Model.

Importing related tables from an external data source

If the data you need for your Data Model resides in an external data source, you can use Power Pivot to import a table and its related tables. Here are the steps to follow to use Power Pivot to import multiple, related tables from an Access database:

1. If you don't have Power Pivot open, choose Power Pivot ⇨ Manage (or Data ⇨ Data Tools ⇨ Manage Data Model).

2. Choose Home ⇨ Get External Data ⇨ From Database ⇨ From Access.

Although this example uses a Microsoft Access file as the data source, Power Pivot also enables you to import external data from SQL Server, Azure Analysis Services, an OData data feed, Azure SQL, an Excel workbook, a text file, and more.

The Table Import Wizard dialog box appears.

3. Click Browse.

Power Pivot displays the Open dialog box.

4. Select the Access database file that contains the tables you want to import, and then click Open.

Power Pivot returns you to the Table Import Wizard.

5. (Optional) If your data source requires a login, fill in the required credentials using the User Name and Password text boxes.

Once you've completed the login credentials, it's a good idea to click Test Connection to make sure everything works.

6. **Click Next.**

The Table Import Wizard asks you to choose how you want to import the data.

7. **Select the Select from a List of Tables and Views to Choose the Data to Import option and then click Next.**

Alternatively, you can select the Write a Query That Will Specify the Data to Import option and then, when you click Next, enter a SQL query to define the data you want to bring aboard.

8. **In the list of tables, select the check box beside a table you want to import.**

9. **Click Select Related Tables.**

Power Pivot examines the tables and selects the check box beside each related table (see Figure 9-10).

10. **Repeat Steps 8 and 9 until you've selected all the data you want to import.**

11. **Click Finish.**

Power Pivot imports the external data to the Data Model and Table Import Wizard shows you the result of the import.

12. **Click Close.**

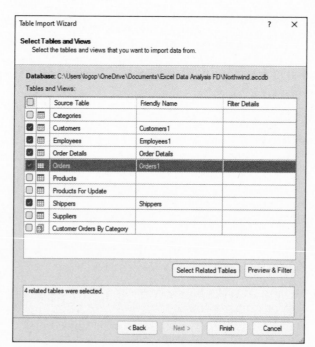

FIGURE 9-10:
Click Select Related Tables and Power Pivot will automatically select the tables related to the selected table.

Viewing table relationships

Having related tables can get fairly complex even with only a few tables in your Data Model. One way that Power Pivot helps is by offering a diagram view feature, which gives you a visual view of the tables in your Data Model and their relationships.

To switch to diagram view, follow these steps:

1. **If you don't have Power Pivot open, choose Power Pivot ⇨ Manage (or Data ⇨ Data Tools ⇨ Manage Data Model).**

2. **Choose Home ⇨ Diagram View.**

Power Pivot switches from its default data view to diagram view, as shown in Figure 9-11.

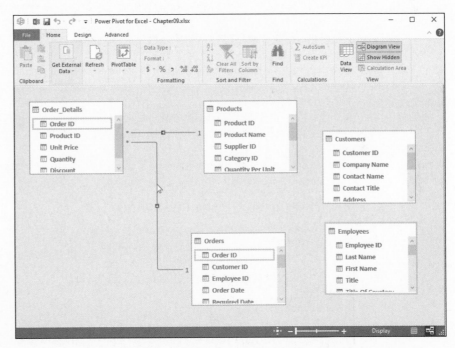

FIGURE 9-11: Visualize your Data Model tables and relationships with diagram view.

Here are a few notes to bear in mind when you work in diagram view:

>> Each box represents a table in your Data Model. You can move a box by dragging its header and size a box by dragging its borders.

>> Two related tables are joined by a connector. The arrow in the middle of the connector indicates the direction of the relationship (that is, from the primary key to the foreign key).

>> At the end of each connector you see either a 1 or an * (asterisk). The * symbol means *many*, so a connector with 1 at one end and * at the other tells you the tables are related by a one-to-many cardinality. A 1 at both ends of the connector tells you the tables are related using a one-to-one cardinality.

>> To see which columns are related in each table, hover the mouse pointer over the connector (refer to Figure 9-10). Power Pivot highlights the related columns in both tables.

>> Tables that have no connectors are currently unrelated to any tables in the Data Model. This happens, for example, if you import a table by using Power Pivot, as I describe previously in the "Adding a table to the Data Model" section.

Viewing relationship details

Another way to examine the details of your Data Model relationships is to use Power Pivot's Manage Relationships dialog box. This tool shows you the names of the tables involved in a relationship, the cardinality type, and the direction of the relationship. You can also use the Manage Relationships dialog box to create, edit, and delete relationships. Follow these steps:

1. **If you don't have Power Pivot open, choose Power Pivot ⇨ Manage (or Data ⇨ Data Tools ⇨ Manage Data Model).**

2. **Choose Design ⇨ Manage Relationships.**

Power Pivot opens the Manage Relationships dialog box, as shown in Figure 9-12.

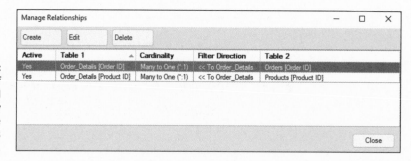

FIGURE 9-12:
See the details of your Data Model relationships by using the Manage Relationships dialog box.

From here, you can not only view the specifics of each relationship but also use the following buttons to manage those relationships:

- **Create:** Click this button to display the Create Relationship dialog box, which enables you to forge a new relationship between tables, as I discuss in the next section.

- **Edit:** Select a relationship and then click this button to open the Edit Relationship dialog box, which enables you to change the tables or columns or both used in the selected relationship.

- **Delete:** Select a relationship and then click this button to remove the selected relationship. When Power Pivot asks you to confirm, click OK.

Creating a relationship between tables with Power Pivot

Although your Data Model tables usually already have a relationship defined with another table, that doesn't mean your work is done. A single table can easily have relationships with two or more tables. In the Orders table example presented previously (refer to Figure 9-1), note that the table has a Customer ID column and an Employee ID column. These correspond to the columns of the same name in a Customers table and an Employees table, respectively. Therefore, you can use Power Pivot to create relationships between the Orders table and the Customers and Employees tables (where the Customer ID and Employee ID columns in the Orders table are foreign keys and the corresponding columns in the Customers and Employees tables are primary keys).

You can create a relationship by choosing columns or by using diagram view.

Creating a relationship by choosing columns

To create a relationship by choosing columns, follow these steps:

1. **In Power Pivot, choose Design ⇨ Create Relationship.**

   Or, if you happen to have the Manage Relationships dialog box onscreen (Design ⇨ Manage Relationships), you can click the Create button.

   Power Pivot displays the Create Relationship dialog box.

2. **In the Table 1 drop-down list, select the table that contains the primary key column.**

3. **In the Columns list below Table 1, select the primary key column.**

4. **In the Table 2 drop-down list, select the table that contains the foreign key column.**

5. **In the Columns list below Table 2, select the foreign key column.**

6. **Click OK.**

   Power Pivot creates the relationship.

Creating a relationship in diagram view

If you're working in diagram view, follow these steps to create a relationship:

1. **In Power Pivot, hover the mouse pointer over the primary key column of the table you want to relate.**

2. **Click and drag the primary key column over to the table that contains the foreign key column.**

   As you drag the column, Power Pivot extends a line from table that contains the primary key.

3. **Drop the primary key column on the foreign key column.**

   Power Pivot creates the relationship.

Refreshing the Data Model

If you imported external data into your Data Model and you know (or suspect) that the original tables have new or modified data, you need to refresh the Data Model to get the most up-to-date info. Power Pivot gives you two ways to proceed here:

>> **Refresh a single table:** Click the table's tab and then choose Home ⇨ Refresh.

>> **Refresh all the tables:** Choose Home ⇨ Refresh ⇨ Refresh All.

Either way, Power Pivot displays the Data Refresh dialog box to show you the progress of the refresh operation, as shown in Figure 9-13. If you find the refresh is taking too long, you can click Stop Refresh.

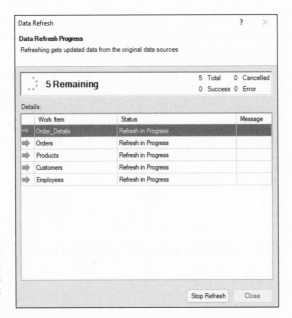

FIGURE 9-13:
The Data Refresh
dialog box shows
you the progress
of the refresh.

Transforming Data

Once you have a table in your Data Model, you can use Power Pivot to transform that data in multiple ways. For example, you can change a column's data type or numeric format; you can delete, freeze, or set the width of a column; and you can rename a column. Here are the techniques you can use:

>> **Changing the data type of a column:** Click anywhere in the column, choose Home ⇨ Data Type, and then click the data type you want to use from the drop-down menu that appears. When Power Pivot asks you to confirm, click OK.

>> **Changing the data format of a column:** Click anywhere in the column, choose Home ⇨ Format, and then click the format you want to use from the drop-down menu that appears. You can also use the buttons in the Home tab's Formatting group to adjust the formatting (for example, by increasing or decreasing the number of decimal places).

>> **Deleting a column:** Click anywhere in the column, choose Design ⇨ Delete, and then click Yes when Power Pivot asks you to confirm the deletion.

>> **Freezing a column:** Click anywhere in the column and then choose Design ⇨ Freeze. Power Pivot moves the column to the left side of the grid and keeps the column in view as you scroll the grid to the right.

>> **Unfreezing a column:** Click anywhere in the frozen column and then choose Design ⇨ Freeze ⇨ Unfreeze.

>> **Setting a column's width:** Click anywhere in the column and choose Design ⇨ Width to open the Column Width dialog box. Type the new width and then click OK. You can change a column's width also by dragging the right edge of the column's header. To automatically adjust the column's width to fit its widest entry, double-click the right edge of the column header.

>> **Renaming a column:** Right-click the column's header, click Rename Column, type the new name, and then press Enter.

Creating a PivotTable or PivotChart from Your Data Model

Once you've added your tables to the Data Model, set up all the relationships, and transformed your data as needed, you can analyze your data by creating a Pivot-Table or a PivotChart (or both). And since you're working with tables in your Data Model, you're free to use multiple related tables in your report or chart.

Power Pivot provides no less than eight possible PivotTable and PivotChart combinations:

>> **PivotTable:** Creates just a PivotTable.

>> **PivotChart:** Creates just a PivotChart.

>> **Chart and Table (Horizontal):** Creates both a PivotTable and PivotChart, which appear side-by-side on the worksheet (with the PivotChart to the left of the PivotTable).

>> **Chart and Table (Vertical):** Creates both a PivotTable and PivotChart, which appear one-over-the-other on the worksheet (with the PivotChart above the PivotTable).

>> **Two Charts (Horizontal):** Creates two PivotCharts, which appear side-by-side on the worksheet.

>> **Two Charts (Vertical):** Creates two PivotCharts, which appear one-over-the-other on the worksheet.

>> **Four Charts:** Creates four PivotCharts, which appear in a rectangular arrangement on the worksheet.

>> **Flattened PivotTable:** Creates a flattened PivotTable, which collapses a multi-field Row (or Column) area to show each field in its own PivotTable column (or row).

Here are the steps to follow:

1. **To create just a PivotTable, choose Home ⇨ PivotTable.**

Otherwise, click the PivotTable button's drop-down arrow and then select the type of report you want: PivotChart, Chart and Table (Horizontal), and so on.

Power Pivot displays a dialog box asking where you want the report displayed.

2. **(Optional) If you want your report to appear on an existing worksheet, select the Existing Worksheet option and use the Location range box to select the cell that will be the upper-left corner of the PivotTable.**

3. **Click OK.**

Excel creates a blank PivotTable and displays the PivotTable Fields or PivotChart Fields task pane with the All tab selected.

4. **On the All tab, add to the PivotTable areas whatever fields you need from any of the related tables.**

5. **Repeat Step 4 until your PivotTable or PivotChart is complete.**

6. **If your report includes multiple PivotCharts, click in each PivotChart and repeat Steps 4 and 5.**

As you make your changes, Excel updates the PivotCharts on-the-fly.

Chapter **10**

Tracking Trends and Making Forecasts

When you're analyzing data, it certainly helps to run basic calculations such as sum and average and to summarize the data either by using Excel's database functions or, even better, by constructing a PivotTable or PivotChart. It's all good. However, as useful as these tools are, they can't answer one seemingly fundamental question: Given some historical data — it could be profits or sales or expenses or defects or customer complaints — what's the overall direction of that data? Are profits going up? Are defects going down? Are sales cyclical (say, down in the winter but up in the summer)? Answering these types of questions falls under the heading of *trend analysis,* and in this chapter you discover the powerful Excel tools that not only help you see the trends hiding in your data but also let you make forecasts of future values. It's all quite slick, as you soon see.

Plotting a Best-Fit Trend Line

If you want to get a sense of the overall trend displayed by a set of data, the easiest way is to use a chart to plot a *best-fit trend line.* This is a straight line through the chart's data points where the differences between the chart points that reside above the line and those that reside below the line cancel each other out.

A best-fit trend line is an example of *regression analysis,* which is a statistical tool for analyzing the relationship between two phenomena, with one depending on the other. For example, housing sales depend on interest rates:

>> When interest rates go down, housing sales go up.

>> When interest rates go up, housing sales go down.

In regression analysis lingo, housing sales are known as the *dependent variable* and interest rates are called the *independent variable.*

When you're working with historical data — for example, sales over time — time is the independent variable and the item you're measuring (such as sales) is the dependent variable.

REMEMBER

To add a best-fit trend line, you must plot your data series as an XY (Scatter) chart.

If you've already built an Excel chart for your data, here are the steps to follow to plot a best-fit trend line on that chart:

1. **Click the chart to select it.**

2. **If your chart has multiple data series, click the series you want to analyze.**

3. **Choose Chart Design ⇨ Add Chart Element ⇨ Trendline ⇨ More Trendline Options.**

   The Format Trendline task pane appears.

4. **Click the Trendline Options tab.**

5. **Select the Linear radio button.**

   Excel plots the best-fit trend line.

   If you want to see just the trend line, feel free to pass over Steps 6 and 7, which introduce a bit of math to the trend analysis. It's useful math, however, so if you're interested, do Steps 6 and 7 and then read my explanation of what these numbers mean, which follows these steps.

6. (Optional) Select the Display Equation on Chart check box.

7. (Optional) Select the Display R-Squared Value on Chart check box.

8. Click X (close) in the upper-right corner.

Excel displays the regression equation and the R^2 value (described next). Figure 10-1 shows a chart with the plotted trend line, the regression equation, and the R^2 value.

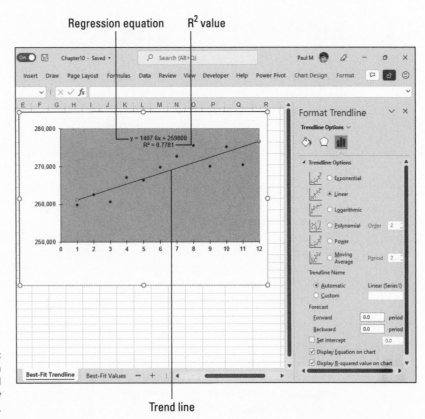

FIGURE 10-1: A chart with a trend line and some geeky numbers.

TECHNICAL STUFF

Okay, so what's up with those scary-looking numbers added to the chart above the trend line in Figure 10-1? The top line is called the regression equation and the bottom line is called the R2 value.

The *regression equation* tells you the exact relationship between the dependent variable and the independent variable. With *linear regression*, in which the best-fit trend line is a straight line, the regression equation looks like this:

```
y = mx + b
```

y is the dependent variable; x is the independent variable; m is the slope of the trend line; and b is the starting value for the trend.

R^2 is the *coefficient of determination,* which is the square of the correlation, and it tells you how well the trend line fits the data. In general, the closer R^2 is to 1, the better the fit. Values of R^2 below 0.7 mean that the trend line isn't a very good fit for the data. I go on and on about correlation in Chapter 11.

Calculating Best-Fit Values

If your analysis requires exact trend values, you could plot the best-fit trend line and then use the regression equation to calculate the values. However, if the data values change, you need to recalculate the values. A better solution is to use the TREND function. TREND takes up to four arguments:

```
TREND(known_ys, known_xs, new_xs, const)
```

The only required argument is *known_ys,* which is a range reference or array of the dependent values. The *known_xs* argument is a range reference or array of the independent values (the default is the array {1,2,3,...},n}, where n is the number of *known_ys*). The *new_xs* argument is for forecasting, so it's not required here. (I talk about it a bit later in the "Calculating Forecasted Linear Values" section.) The *const* argument determines the y-intercept: FALSE places it at 0, and TRUE (the default) calculates the y-intercept based on the *known_ys*. (The *y-intercept* is the value of y at the point where the trend line crosses the y-axis.)

Here's the procedure to follow to calculate best-fit values using the TREND function:

1. **Select the first cell of the range where you want the best-fit values to appear.**

   Step 1 assumes you want to build a dynamic array, which makes your worksheet compatible with only Excel 2019 or later. If you need your model to work with earlier versions of Excel, you must create a traditional array formula, so start by selecting all the cells in which you want the best-fit values to appear.

2. **Type =trend(.**

3. **Type a reference or array that represents the dependent values.**

4. **Type a comma and then type a reference or array that represents the independent values.**

5. **If you prefer to use a trend starting point of 0, type two commas and then type** FALSE.

6. **Type**).

7. **Click the Enter button on the formula bar or press Enter.**

   If you're creating a traditional array for compatibility, press and hold down Ctrl+Shift and then click the Enter button or press Enter.

   Excel calculates the best-fit trend values and enters them as an array.

Figure 10-2 shows a worksheet that lists sales (column D) over three years by fiscal quarter. The TREND array is in column F, and you can see that the dependent variable (that is, the sales) is referenced by the range D2:D13, and the independent variable (that is, the period numbers) is referenced by the range C2:C13.

	F2		fx	=TREND(D2:D13, C2:C13)		
	A	B	C	D	E	F	G
1	**Sales**		**Period**	**Actual**	**Trend (Equation)**	**TREND**	
2		1st Quarter	1	259,846	261,208	261,208	
3	**Fiscal**	2nd Quarter	2	262,587	262,615	262,615	
4	**2020**	3rd Quarter	3	260,643	264,023	264,023	
5		4th Quarter	4	267,129	265,430	265,431	
6		1st Quarter	5	266,471	266,838	266,838	
7	**Fiscal**	2nd Quarter	6	269,843	268,246	268,246	
8	**2021**	3rd Quarter	7	272,803	269,653	269,654	
9		4th Quarter	8	275,649	271,061	271,061	
10		1st Quarter	9	270,117	272,468	272,469	
11	**Fiscal**	2nd Quarter	10	275,315	273,876	273,876	
12	**2022**	3rd Quarter	11	270,451	275,284	275,284	
13		4th Quarter	12	276,543	276,691	276,692	
14							
		Best-Fit Values	LINEST	+			

FIGURE 10-2: An array of best-fit trend values (column F).

REMEMBER

In the example shown in Figure 10-2, the independent values are the period numbers 1, 2, 3, and so on. However, these are the default values for the *known_xs* argument, so technically you could omit this argument in this example.

For the "fun" of it, column E shows the best-fit trend values calculated using the regression equation shown previously in Figure 10-1:

```
y = 1407.6x + 259800
```

For example, to calculate x for period 1 (cell C2), cell E2 contains the following formula:

```
y = 1407.6 * C2 + 259800
```

USING LINEST TO GET EXACT VALUES FOR THE REGRESSION EQUATION

How do I know the exact value of the trend line slope? I used Excel's LINEST function, which can calculate not only the slope (m) but also the y-intercept (b), which you can then plug into the general regression equation (y = mx + b) to calculate individual trend values. LINEST uses the following syntax:

```
LINEST(known_ys, known_xs, const, stats)
```

The first three arguments — *known_ys*, *known_xs*, and *const* — are identical to those used in the TREND function. A fourth argument, named stats, is an optional Boolean value that determines whether LINEST returns additional regression statistics besides the slope and intercept. The default is FALSE. When you use LINEST without the stats argument (or with *stats* set to FALSE), enter the function as a 1x2 array, where the value in the first column is the slope of the trend line and the value in the second column is the intercept. With stats set to TRUE, enter the function as a 5x2 array. Note that in this larger array, the R^2 value (the coefficient of determination) is given in the first column of the third row.

The results in Columns E and F are identical for the most part, but not in every case. Why not? Because the TREND function uses higher precision than the regression equation. For example, while the regression equation uses 1407.6 for the slope of the trend line, the actual value (and the one used by TREND) is 1407.625874.

Plotting Forecasted Values

So far, I've mentioned two ways to determine the R^2 value (the coefficient of determination) that tells you whether the dependent and independent variables are well correlated:

>> Plot the best-fit trend line and select the Display R-Squared Value on Chart check box.

>> Use the LINEST function with the stats argument set to TRUE and read the R^2 value in the first column of the third row.

If you find that either method indicates that the dependent and independent variables are well correlated (that is, the R^2 value is 0.7 or higher), give yourself a high-five and then take advantage of that correlation to forecast future values.

This sounds like magic, but it's only statistics. The key here is the assumption that the major factors underlying the existing data will remain more or less constant over the number of periods in your forecast. If you're about to acquire another company or shed product lines, any forecast you produce based on your old data is likely to be useless.

With that caveat in mind, the most straightforward way to calculate forecasted values is to use a chart to extend the best-fit trend line into one or more future periods. Note, however, that to work with a best-fit trend line and use it to plot forecasted values, you must plot your data series as an XY (Scatter) chart.

Here are the steps to follow:

1. **Click the chart to select it.**

2. **If your chart has multiple data series, click the series you want to analyze.**

3. **Choose Chart Design ⇨ Add Chart Element ⇨ Trendline ⇨ More Trendline Options.**

   The Format Trendline task pane appears.

4. **Click the Trendline Options tab.**

5. **Select the Linear radio button.**

   Excel plots the best-fit trend line.

6. **In the Forecast section, use the Forward text box to type the number of units you want to project the trend line into in the future.**

   Excel extends the best-fit trend line, as shown in Figure 10-3.

7. **(Optional) Select the Display Equation on Chart check box.**

8. **(Optional) Select the Display R-Squared Value on Chart check box.**

9. **Click X (close) in the upper right.**

   Excel displays the regression equation and the R^2 value beside the extended trend line.

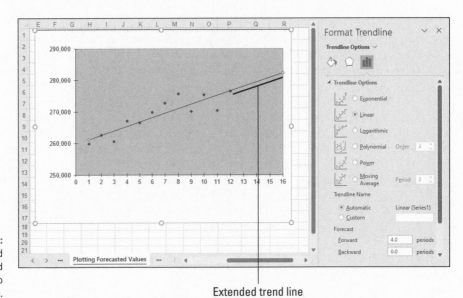

FIGURE 10-3:
A best-fit trend
line, extended
four periods into
the future.

Extended trend line

**TECHNICAL
STUFF**

Another way to come up with forecasted dependent variable values is to calculate them directly using the regression equation that Excel generates when you select the Display Equation on Chart check box in the Format Trendline task pane. The general regression equation for a linear model is as follows:

$$y = mx + b$$

y is the dependent variable; x is the independent variable; m is the slope of the trend line; and b is the starting value for the trend. Both m and b are constants, so to calculate the dependent variable value for the next period in your forecast, substitute that period's independent variable value for x.

Extending a Linear Trend

With a *linear trend*, the dependent variable is related to the independent variable by some constant amount. For example, you might find that housing sales (the dependent variable) increase by 100,000 units whenever interest rates (the independent variable) decrease by 1 percent. Similarly, you might find that company revenue (the dependent variable) increases by $250,000 for every $50,000 you spend on advertising (the independent variable).

If forecasting is part of your data analysis, you can take advantage of a linear relationship to forecast future periods. Excel kindly offers a couple of tools you can use to extend a linear trend into one or more future periods: the fill handle and the Series command.

Extending a linear trend using the fill handle

Excel's fill handle — the little green square that appears in the lower-right corner of the selected cell or range — wears many hats, but perhaps the most surprising use for this handy tool is to extend a linear trend one or more periods into the future. Here's how it works:

1. **Select the existing data.**

The fill handle appears in the lower-right corner of the selected range.

2. **Click and drag the fill handle to extend the selection over the number of future periods you want to forecast.**

Excel extends the existing data with the forecasted values.

Extending a linear trend using the Series command

The second method that Excel offers for extending a linear trend is the Series command. Here's how it works:

1. **Select the existing data and the cells where you want the forecasted data to appear.**

2. **Choose Home ⇨ Fill ⇨ Series.**

Excel displays the Series dialog box, shown in Figure 10-4. Note that Excel automatically fills in the Step Value text box with the slope of the trend line for the existing data.

3. **Select the AutoFill radio button.**

4. **Click OK.**

Excel extends the existing linear trend with the forecasted values.

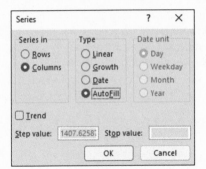

FIGURE 10-4:
The Series dialog box: your best-fit trend best friend.

TIP

If your data analysis requires that you see the values that make up a linear trend, the Series command can help:

1. **Copy the historical data into an adjacent row or column.**

2. **Select the range that includes both the copied historical data and the blank cells that will contain the projections.**

3. **Choose Home ➪ Fill ➪ Series.**

   Excel displays the Series dialog box.

4. **Select the Linear radio button.**

5. **Select the Trend check box.**

6. **Click OK.**

   Excel replaces the copied historical data with the best-fit trend numbers and projects the trend onto the blank cells.

Calculating Forecasted Linear Values

If your analysis requires exact forecast values, you could extend the best-fit trend line and then use the regression equation to calculate the values, or you could use the fill handle or Series command to extend the linear trend. These are straight-forward methods, but if the historical values change, you need to repeat these procedures to recalculate the forecasted values. A more efficient solution is to use the TREND function. Here's a recap of the TREND syntax:

```
TREND(known_ys, known_xs, new_xs, const)
```

In this situation, you need to use TREND not only with the *known_ys* argument (a reference to the dependent values) and optionally the *known_xs* argument (a reference to the independent values), but also the *new_xs* argument. The *new_xs* argument is a range reference or array that represents the new independent values for which you want forecasted dependent values.

Here's the procedure to follow to calculate forecasted linear trend values using the TREND function:

1. **Select the first cell of the range where you want the best-fit values to appear.**

   Step 1 assumes you want to build a dynamic array, which makes your worksheet compatible with Excel 2019 or later. If you need your model to work with earlier versions of Excel, you must create a traditional array formula, so start by selecting all the cells in which you want the forecasted values to appear.

2. **Type** =trend(.

3. **Type a reference or array that represents the dependent values.**

4. **Type a comma and then type a reference or array that represents the independent values.**

5. **Type a comma and then a reference or array that represents the new independent values.**

6. **If you prefer to use a trend starting point of 0, type a comma and then type** FALSE.

7. **Type**).

8. **Click the Enter button on the formula bar or press Enter.**

   If you're creating a traditional array for compatibility, press and hold down Ctrl+Shift and then click the Enter button or press Enter.

   Excel calculates the forecasted trend values and enters them as an array.

Figure 10-5 shows a worksheet that lists historical sales (D2:D13) over three years by fiscal quarter. The TREND forecast array is in D14:D17.

TECHNICAL
STUFF

When you use the LINEST function to calculate the linear trend's slope (m) and y-intercept (b), you can use these results to forecast new values. That is, given a new independent value x, the forecasted dependent value is given by the regression equation:

```
y = mx + b
```

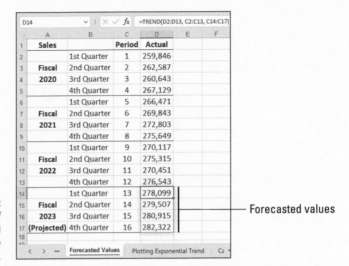

FIGURE 10-5:
An array of forecasted trend values (see the range D14:D17).

You can also calculate a forecasted linear trend value by using the FORECAST. LINEAR function, which takes three arguments:

```
TREND(x, known_ys, known_xs)
```

x is the new independent value for which you want to forecast a new dependent value; *known_ys* and *known_xs* are the same as with the TREND function, except that with FORECAST.LINEAR, the *known_xs* argument is required.

Plotting an Exponential Trend Line

Up to now, you've learned how to perform regression analysis on only linear data, which changes at a constant rate. However, you can also apply regression analysis to nonlinear data, where the trend line isn't straight.

A common example of nonlinear data is an *exponential trend*, which rises or falls at an increasing rate. It's called exponential because the trend line resembles the graph of a number being raised to successively higher values of an exponent. For example, the series 2^1, 2^2, 2^3 starts off slowly (2, 4, 8, and so on), but by the time you get to 2^{20}, the series value is up to 1,048,576, and 2^{100} is a number that's 31 digits long!

To visualize such a trend, you can plot an *exponential trend line.* This is a curved line through the data points where the differences between the points on one side of the line and those on the other side of the line cancel each other out.

Here are the steps to follow to plot an exponential trend line:

1. **Click the chart to select it.**

2. **If your chart has multiple data series, click the series you want to analyze.**

3. **Choose Chart Design ⇨ Add Chart Element ⇨ Trendline ⇨ More Trendline Options.**

   The Format Trendline task pane appears.

4. **Click the Trendline Options tab.**

5. **Select the Exponential radio button.**

   Excel plots the exponential trend line.

6. **(Optional) Select the Display Equation on Chart check box.**

   If you just want to see the trend line, feel free to pass over Steps 6 and 7.

7. **(Optional) Select the Display R-Squared Value on Chart check box.**

8. **Click X (close) in the upper right.**

   Excel displays the regression equation and the R^2 value (described next). Figure 10-6 shows a chart with the plotted exponential trend line, the regression equation, and the R^2 value.

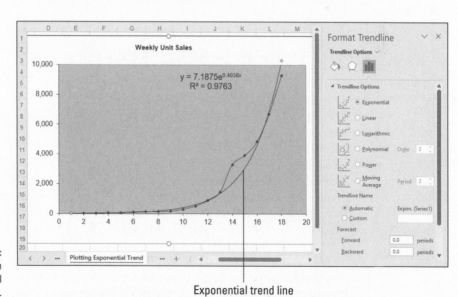

FIGURE 10-6: A chart with an exponential trend line.

Exponential trend line

With nonlinear regression, when the best-fit trend line is an exponential curve, the regression equation takes the following general form:

$$y = be^{mx}$$

y is the dependent variable; x is the independent variable; b and m are constants; and e is a constant (approximately 2.71828) that represents the base of the natural logarithm.

Calculating Exponential Trend Values

Eyeballing an exponential trend line, as I discuss in the preceding section, is a fun way to pass the time. The trend line is a great visual tool, but it doesn't help if you require exact exponential trend values. Yep, you could plot the trend line and then use the exponential version of the regression equation to calculate the exact values:

$$y = be^{mx}$$

However, if the data values change, you need to replot the trend line and recalculate the trend values. Too much work!

A better solution is to use the GROWTH function, which takes up to four arguments:

```
GROWTH(known_ys, known_xs, new_xs, const)
```

The *known_ys* argument is required and is a reference to the dependent values. The *known_xs* argument is a reference to the independent values (the default is the array $\{1,2,3,\ldots\},n\}$, where n is the number of *known_ys*). The *new_xs* argument is a reference to the new independent values for which you want forecasted dependent values. The *const* argument determines the value of b in the exponential regression equation: FALSE places it at 1, whereas TRUE (the default) calculates b based on the *known_ys*.

Here are the steps to follow to calculate exponential trend values using the GROWTH function:

1. **Select the first cell of the range where you want the best-fit values to appear.**

    Step 1 assumes you want to build a dynamic array, which makes your worksheet compatible with Excel 2019 or later. If your model must work with earlier versions of Excel, you need to create a traditional array formula, so start by selecting all the cells in which you want the best-fit values to appear.

2. **Type** =growth(.

3. **Type a reference or array that represents the dependent values.**

4. **Type a comma and then type a reference or array that represents the independent values.**

5. **Type a comma and then type a reference or array that represents the new independent values.**

6. **If you prefer to use a trend starting point of 1, type a comma and then type** FALSE.

7. **Type).**

8. **Click the Enter button on the formula bar or press Enter.**

If you're creating a traditional array for compatibility, press and hold down Ctrl+Shift and then click the Enter button or press Enter.

Excel calculates the exponential trend values and enters them as an array.

Figure 10-7 shows a worksheet that lists units sold (column B) over 18 weeks. The GROWTH array for the historical trend is in column C, and you can see that the dependent variable (that is, the units sold) is referenced by the range B3:B20, and the independent variable (that is, the week numbers) is referenced by the range A3:A20.

<table>
<tr><td colspan="2">C3</td><td>∨ ⋮ × ✓ fx</td><td colspan="3">=GROWTH(B3:B20, A3:A20)</td></tr>
<tr><td>A</td><td>B</td><td>C</td><td>D</td><td>E</td><td>F</td></tr>
<tr><td colspan="3">1 Historical Data</td><td></td><td colspan="2">Future Data</td></tr>
<tr><td>2 Week</td><td>Units</td><td>Trend</td><td></td><td>Week</td><td>Forecast</td></tr>
<tr><td>3   1</td><td>11</td><td>11</td><td></td><td>19</td><td></td></tr>
<tr><td>4   2</td><td>15</td><td>16</td><td></td><td>20</td><td></td></tr>
<tr><td>5   3</td><td>27</td><td>24</td><td></td><td>21</td><td></td></tr>
<tr><td>6   4</td><td>44</td><td>36</td><td></td><td>22</td><td></td></tr>
<tr><td>7   5</td><td>59</td><td>54</td><td></td><td></td><td></td></tr>
<tr><td>8   6</td><td>112</td><td>81</td><td></td><td></td><td></td></tr>
<tr><td>9   7</td><td>125</td><td>121</td><td></td><td></td><td></td></tr>
<tr><td>10   8</td><td>136</td><td>182</td><td></td><td></td><td></td></tr>
<tr><td>11   9</td><td>157</td><td>272</td><td></td><td></td><td></td></tr>
<tr><td>12   10</td><td>298</td><td>408</td><td></td><td></td><td></td></tr>
<tr><td>13   11</td><td>503</td><td>610</td><td></td><td></td><td></td></tr>
<tr><td>14   12</td><td>875</td><td>914</td><td></td><td></td><td></td></tr>
<tr><td>15   13</td><td>1,452</td><td>1,369</td><td></td><td></td><td></td></tr>
<tr><td>16   14</td><td>3,293</td><td>2,049</td><td></td><td></td><td></td></tr>
<tr><td>17   15</td><td>3,902</td><td>3,069</td><td></td><td></td><td></td></tr>
<tr><td>18   16</td><td>4,837</td><td>4,596</td><td></td><td></td><td></td></tr>
<tr><td>19   17</td><td>6,693</td><td>6,882</td><td></td><td></td><td></td></tr>
<tr><td>20   18</td><td>9,283</td><td>10,306</td><td></td><td></td><td></td></tr>
<tr><td colspan="3">‹ › ⋯ Calculating Exponential Trend</td><td></td><td>LOGEST</td><td>Plotting a</td></tr>
</table>

FIGURE 10-7:
An array of exponential trend values (column C) and forecast values (column F).

TECHNICAL STUFF

USING LOGEST TO GET EXACT VALUES FOR THE EXPONENTIAL REGRESSION EQUATION

You can use the LOGEST function to calculate the exponential trend equation's m and b constants, which you can then plug into the equation, $y = be^{mx}$, to calculate individual trend values. LOGEST uses the syntax shown here:

```
LOGEST(known_ys, known_xs, const, stats)
```

The first three arguments — *known_ys*, *known_xs*, and *const* — are the same as those used in the GROWTH function. A fourth argument, named `stats`, is an optional Boolean value that determines whether LOGEST returns additional regression statistics. The default is FALSE. When you use LOGEST without the `stats` argument (or with `stats` set to FALSE), enter the function as a 1x2 array, where the value in the second column is b; to derive m, you must use the LN function to take the natural logarithm of the value in the first column of the array. With `stats` set to TRUE, enter the function as a 5x2 array. Note that in this larger array, the R^2 value (the coefficient of determination) is given in the first column of the third row.

REMEMBER

In the example shown in Figure 10-7, the independent values are the week numbers 1, 2, 3, and so on. However, these are the default values for the *known_xs* argument, so technically you could omit this argument in this example.

Plotting a Logarithmic Trend Line

A *logarithmic trend* is one in which the data rises or falls very quickly at the beginning but then slows down and levels off over time. An example of a logarithmic trend is the sales pattern of a highly anticipated new product, which typically sells in large quantities for a short time and then levels off.

To visualize such a trend, you can plot a *logarithmic trend line.* This is a curved line through the data points where the differences between the points on one side of the line and those on the other side of the line cancel each other out.

Here are the steps to follow to plot a logarithmic trend line:

1. **Click the chart to select it.**

2. **If your chart has multiple data series, click the series you want to analyze.**

3. **Choose Chart Design ⇨ Add Chart Element ⇨ Trendline ⇨ More Trendline Options.**

The Format Trendline task pane appears.

4. **Click the Trendline Options tab.**

5. **Select the Logarithmic radio button.**

Excel plots the logarithmic trend line.

6. **(Optional) Select the Display Equation on Chart check box.**

If you just want to see the trend line, feel free to pass over Steps 6 and 7.

7. **(Optional) Select the Display R-Squared Value on Chart check box.**

8. **Click X (close) in the upper right.**

Excel displays the regression equation and the R^2 value (described next). Figure 10-8 shows a chart with the plotted exponential trend line, the regression equation, and the R^2 value.

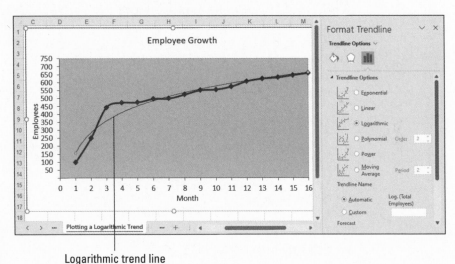

FIGURE 10-8:
A chart with a logarithmic trend line.

Logarithmic trend line

When the best-fit trend line is a logarithmic curve, the regression equation takes the following general form:

```
y = m * ln(x) + b
```

y is the dependent variable; x is the independent variable; b and m are constants; and ln is the natural logarithm, for which you can use the Excel function LN.

**TECHNICAL
STUFF**

Excel doesn't have a function that calculates the values of b and m directly. However, you can use the LINEST function if you "straighten out" the logarithmic curve by using a logarithmic scale for the independent values:

```
{=LINEST(known_ys, LN(known_xs), const, stats)}
```

Plotting a Power Trend Line

In many cases of regression analysis, the best fit is provided by a *power trend*, in which the data increases or decreases steadily. Such a trend is clearly not exponential or logarithmic, both of which imply extreme behavior, either at the end of the trend (in the case of exponential) or at the beginning of the trend (in the case of logarithmic). Examples of power trends include revenues, profits, and margins in successful companies, all of which show steady increases in the rate of growth year after year.

A power trend sounds linear, but plotting the *power trend line* shows a curved best-fit line through the data points. In your analysis of such data, it's usually best to try a linear trend line first. If that doesn't give a good fit, switch to a power trend line.

Follow these steps to plot a power trend line:

1. **Click the chart to select it.**

2. **If your chart has multiple data series, click the series you want to analyze.**

3. **Choose Chart Design ⇨ Add Chart Element ⇨ Trendline ⇨ More Trendline Options.**

The Format Trendline task pane appears.

4. **Click the Trendline Options tab.**

5. **Select the Power radio button.**

Excel plots the power trend line.

6. **(Optional) Select the Display Equation on Chart check box.**

If you just want to see the trend line, skip Steps 6 and 7.

7. (Optional) Select the Display R-Squared Value on Chart check box.

8. Click X (close).

Excel displays the regression equation and the R^2 value (described next). Figure 10-9 shows a chart with the plotted power trend line, the regression equation, and the R^2 value.

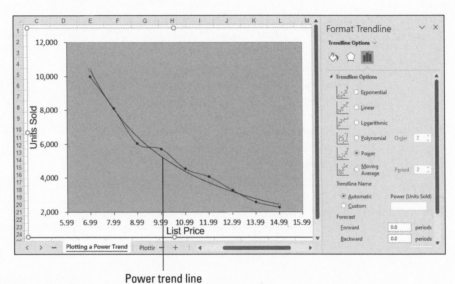

FIGURE 10-9:
A chart with a power trend line.

Power trend line

When the best-fit trend line is a power curve, the regression equation takes the following general form:

$$y = m * x^b$$

y is the dependent variable; x is the independent variable; and b and m are constants.

TECHNICAL STUFF

There's no worksheet function available to directly calculate the values of b and m. However, you can use the LINEST function if you "straighten out" the power curve by applying a logarithmic scale to the dependent and independent values:

```
{=LINEST(LN(known_ys), LN(known_xs), const, stats)}
```

Plotting a Polynomial Trend Line

In many real-world scenarios, the relationship between the dependent and independent variables doesn't move in a single direction. That would be too easy. For example, rather than constantly rising — uniformly (as in a linear trend), sharply (as in an exponential or logarithmic trend), or steadily (as in a power trend) — data such as unit sales, profits, and costs might move up and down.

To visualize such a trend, you can plot a *polynomial trend line,* which is a best-fit line of multiple curves derived using an equation that uses multiple powers of x. The number of powers of x is the *order* of the polynomial equation. Generally, the higher the order, the tighter the curve fits your existing data, but the more unpredictable your forecasted values are.

If you have a chart already, follow these steps to add a polynomial trend line:

1. Click the chart to select it.

2. If your chart has multiple data series, click the series you want to analyze.

3. Choose Chart Design ➪ Add Chart Element ➪ Trendline ➪ More Trendline Options.

The Format Trendline task pane appears.

4. Click the Trendline Options tab.

5. Select the Polynomial radio button.

6. Click the Order spin button arrows to set the order of the polynomial equation you want.

Excel plots the polynomial trend line.

7. (Optional) Select the Display Equation on Chart check box.

If you just want to see the trend line, bypass Steps 7 and 8.

8. (Optional) Select the Display R-Squared Value on Chart check box.

9. Click X (close) in the upper right.

Excel displays the regression equation and the R^2 value. Figure 10-10 shows a chart with the plotted polynomial trend line, the regression equation, and the R^2 value.

Polynomial trend line

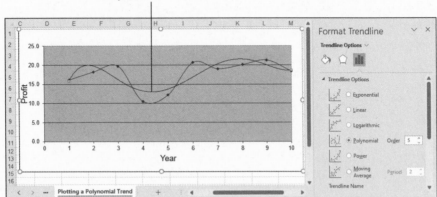

FIGURE 10-10:
A chart with a
polynomial
trend line.

When the best-fit trend line is a polynomial curve, the regression equation takes the following form:

$$y = m_n x^n + \ldots + m_2 x^2 + m_1 x + b$$

y is the dependent variable; x is the independent variable; and b and mn through m1 are constants.

TECHNICAL
STUFF

To calculate the values b and mn through m1, you can use LINEST if you raise the *known_xs* values to the powers from 1 to n for an nth-order polynomial:

$$\{=LINEST(known\_ys,\ known\_xs\ \wedge\ \{1,2,\ldots,n\},\ const,\ stats)\}$$

Alternatively, you can use the TREND function:

$$\{=TREND(known\_ys,\ known\_xs\ \wedge\ \{1,2,\ldots,n\},\ new\_xs,\ const)\}$$

Creating a Forecast Sheet

Excel features such as AutoFill, the Trendline chart element, and worksheet functions such as TREND and GROWTH are powerful forecasting tools. However, there might be times when you prefer Excel to do most of the forecasting work. Hey, no judgment from here.

To get Excel to assume the forecasting duties, take advantage of the Forecast Sheet feature, which enables you to take a worksheet full of historical data and create a new worksheet with a visual forecast. That forecast has three items:

>> **Forecast:** These values are the trendline values based on your historic data.

>> **Lower Confidence Bound:** For each forecast period, these values represent the low prediction for that period.

>> **Upper Confidence Bound:** For each forecast period, these values represent the high prediction for that period.

By default, Excel's Forecast Sheet feature implements a statistical method that uses a 95 percent confidence interval, which means you can be 95 percent sure that, for each forecast period, the actual value will fall somewhere within the range created by the low and high prediction values. You can adjust this default confidence interval up or down, as needed.

Here are the steps you need to run through:

1. **In the worksheet that contains your historical data, select a cell any-where in the data range or table.**

2. **Choose Data ⇨ Forecast Sheet.**

    Excel selects all the historical data and displays the Create Forecast Worksheet dialog box, shown in Figure 10-11.

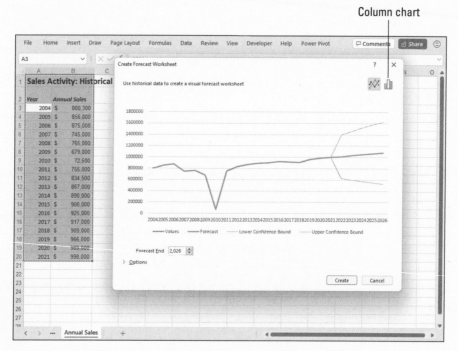

Column chart

FIGURE 10-11:
You use the
Create Forecast
Worksheet
dialog box to
set up your
forecast sheet.

3. **(Optional) If you'd prefer to visualize the trend by using a column chart instead of Excel's default line chart, click the Column Chart icon (labeled in Figure 10-11).**

4. **In the Forecast End spin box, specify the date when you want your forecast to end.**

5. **(Optional) For a bit more control over your forecast, click Options to expand the dialog box and displays the following options:**

   - **Forecast Start:** Select a starting date for your historical data.

   - **Confidence Interval:** Select a new degree of confidence that Excel uses to set the forecast's Lower Confidence Bound and Upper Confidence Bound lines that appear in the default line chart. In general, the lower the confidence interval, the closer the Lower Confidence Bound and Upper Confidence Bound lines appear in the forecast. In other words, if you want a smaller range of possible future values, the trade-off is having lower confidence that the actual values will fall within those narrower bounds. Note, too, that the highest possible confidence interval is 99.99%. There are no 100% guarantees here!

   - **Seasonality:** If you change this option from Detect Automatically to Set Manually, you can enter a value that indicates the number of points in the values range of your data table that are part of a recurring seasonal pattern. When Excel can't automatically detect seasonality in your worksheet data, a warning appears, suggesting that you select the Set Manually option button (and leave the default setting at 0) to get better results in the forecast.

   - **Include Forecast Statistics:** Select this check box to have Excel include a table of forecast accuracy metrics and smoothing factors in the forecast worksheet.

   - **Timeline Range:** Specifies the range containing the dates in your historical data.

   - **Values Range:** Specifies the range containing the values in your historical data.

   - **Fill Missing Points Using:** Specifies how Excel automatically fills in any missing data points it finds in the worksheet table. You can have Excel fill the missing points with zeroes or interpolate the missing points based on the existing values that surround the missing values.

   - **Aggregate Duplicates Using:** Specifies how Excel handles duplicate values.

6. Click Create.

Excel creates a new forecast worksheet that contains a table with your historical data and the forecast values, as well as an embedded line or column chart depicting the historical values and the trend range for the forecast values. Figure 10-12 shows an example.

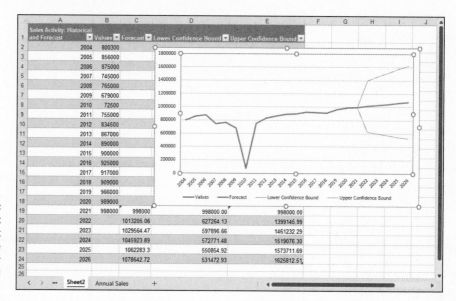

FIGURE 10-12:
The new forecast worksheet showing a table and line chart for the historic and forecast values.

Sales Activity: Historical and Forecast	Values	Forecast	Lower Confidence Bound	Upper Confidence Bound
2004	800300			
2005	856000			
2006	875000			
2007	745000			
2008	765000			
2009	679000			
2010	72500			
2011	755000			
2012	834500			
2013	867000			
2014	890000			
2015	900000			
2016	925000			
2017	917000			
2018	909000			
2019	966000			
2020	989000			
2021	998000	998000	998000.00	998000.00
2022		1013205.06	627264.13	1399145.99
2023		1029564.47	597896.66	1461232.29
2024		1045923.89	572771.48	1519076.30
2025		1062283.3	550854.92	1573711.69
2026		1078642.72	531472.93	1625812.51

Chapter **11**

Analyzing Data Using Statistics

xcel is a statistics powerhouse that boasts more than 100 statistical work-sheet functions. That's great if you're a statistician, but do you really need all that stats muscle if you're just doing basic data analysis? You'll no doubt be relieved to hear that the answer is a resounding "No!" Most of Excel's statistical features redefine the word *esoteric*. Believe me when I tell you that you can safely do without Excel features such as cumulative beta probability density and Fourier analysis. I merrily skip over those features and many more in this chapter as I focus on Excel's most important and most useful statistical methods, including calculating the average, rank, largest and smallest values, variance, standard deviation, and correlation. Will it be fun? No, don't be silly. Will it be useful? You can count on it.

Counting Things

The simplest statistical method you can apply to your data is to count the items in that data set. Of course, Excel being Excel, just because counting things is simple, counting things in Excel is complex because the program offers — count 'em — *five* functions related to counting items a worksheet: COUNT, COUNTA, COUNTBLANK, COUNTIF, and COUNTIFS. As if that's not enough, Excel also provides two extra functions that handle permutations and combinations, respectively — PERMUT and COMBIN.

Counting numbers

The COUNT function tallies the number of cells within a specified range that hold numeric values. That is, COUNT ignores cells that contain text (including numbers that are formatted as text), cells that contain the logical values TRUE or FALSE, and cells that are empty. (It's worth noting that COUNT does include cells that contain dates or times because Excel treats those data types as numbers.) Here's the syntax:

```
=COUNT(value1[, value2, ...])
```

Here, *value1*, *value2*, and so on are cell or range references. For example, to use the COUNT function to return how many numeric values are in the range B3:B12 in the worksheet shown in Figure 11-1, use the following formula:

```
=COUNT(B3:B12)
```

As shown in cell E3, COUNT returns 6 (five numbers plus one date).

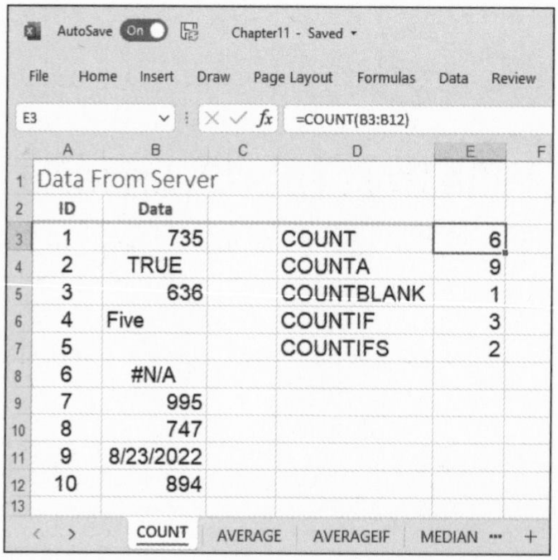

FIGURE 11-1: COUNT returns the tally of the numeric values in a range.

Counting nonempty cells

The COUNTA function counts the number of cells within a specified range that are nonempty. It doesn't matter what data types the cells use — they could be numbers, dates, times, logical values, or text. As long as a cell contains something, it gets included in the COUNTA total. Here's the COUNTA syntax:

```
=COUNTA(value1[, value2, ...])
```

Here, *value1*, *value2*, and so on are cell or range references. For example, to use COUNTA to calculate how many nonempty values are in the range B3:B12 in the worksheet shown previously in Figure 11-1, use the following formula:

```
=COUNTA(B3:B12)
```

As you can see in cell E4 in Figure 11-1, COUNTA returns the value 9.

Counting empty cells

The COUNTBLANK function is the functional opposite of COUNTA in that it counts the number of cells within a specified range that are empty. Here's the COUNTBLANK syntax:

```
=COUNTBLANK(value1[, value2, ...])
```

Here, *value1*, *value2*, and so on are cell or range references. For example, to use COUNTBLANK to return how many empty values are in the range B3:B12 in the worksheet shown previously in Figure 11-1, use the following formula:

```
=COUNTBLANK(B3:B12)
```

As you can see in cell E5 in Figure 11-1, COUNTBLANK returns the value 1.

Counting cells that match criteria

The COUNT, COUNTA, and COUNTBLANK functions count numbers, nonempty cells, and empty cells, respectively, so they have, in a sense, built-in criteria for what they count and what they ignore. If you have your own criteria for what should get counted and what shouldn't, you can turn to the COUNTIF function to apply that condition. Here's the syntax:

```
=COUNTIF(range, criteria)
```

Here, *range* is the worksheet range over which you want to count cells, and *criteria* is a logical expression, enclosed in quotation marks, that specifies which cells in the range should be counted.

For example, looking back at the range B3:B12 in Figure 11-1, suppose you want to know how many cells contain a value greater than 800. Here's a formula that'll get the job done:

```
=COUNTIF(B3:B12,">800")
```

As you can see in cell E6 in Figure 11-1, this formula returns the value 3. (There are two numbers greater than 800, plus the date value is equal to 43700, so it also meets the criteria.)

TIP

You can use any of the standard logical operators when building your criteria expression: Use the < operator for a less-than comparison; the <= operator for a less-than-or-equal-to comparison; the > operator for a greater-than comparison; the >= operator for a greater-than-or-equal-to comparison; the = operator for an equal-to comparison; and the <> operator for a not-equal-to comparison.

Counting cells that match multiple criteria

The COUNTIF function applies a single condition to a single range, but sometimes you might need to apply multiple criteria

>> To a single range

>> To multiple ranges

To handle both scenarios, may I introduce you to the COUNTIFS function, which uses the following syntax:

```
=COUNTIFS(range1, criteria1[, range2, criteria2, ...])
```

Here, *criteria1* gets applied to *range1*, *criteria2* gets applied to *range2*, and so on. COUNTIFS includes in the tally only those cells that match all the criteria.

For example, looking back at the range B3:B12 in Figure 11-1, suppose you want to know how many cells contain a value greater than 800 but less than 1000. Here's a formula that will do just that:

```
=COUNTIFS(B3:B12, ">800", B3:B12, "<1000")
```

As you can see in cell E7 in Figure 11-1, this formula returns the value 2.

Counting permutations

An often useful way to count things is to calculate the *permutations,* which, given a data set, are the number of ways that a subset of that data can be grouped, in any order, without repeats. For example, suppose your data set consists of the letters A, B, C, D. Here are all the ways you can group any two of these letters, without repeats:

AB, AC, AD, BA, BC, BD, CA, CB, CD, DA, DB, DC

The two crucial characteristics of a permutation are as follows:

>> Order is important, so AB and BA are different groupings.

>> Repeats aren't allowed, so the groupings AA, BB, CC, and DD aren't included in the permutations.

Excel's PERMUT function counts the number of permutations possible when selecting a subset from a data set (or a sample from a population). Here's the PERMUT syntax:

```
=PERMUT(number, number_chosen)
```

Here, *number* is the number of items in the set, and *number_chosen* is the number of items in each subset. Given a population of four items and two items in each subset, for example, you calculate the number of permutations by using the formula

```
=PERMUT(4, 2)
```

The function returns the value 12, indicating that 12 different ways exist in which two items can be selected from a set of four.

A variation on the permutation theme is when you allow repetitions in the subset (such as AA, BB, CC, and DD from the ABCD set). In that case, you need to use Excel's PERMUTATIONA function, which uses the same syntax as PERMUT:

```
=PERMUTATIONA(number, number_chosen)
```

For example, to calculate the number of permutations in which two items are selected from a population of four items, with repeats allowed, you use the following formula:

```
=PERMUTATIONA(4, 2)
```

The result is 16.

Counting combinations

It's often useful to count things by calculating the *combinations,* which, given a data set, are the number of ways that a subset of that data can be grouped, without repeats, when the order isn't important (that is, each subset is unique). For example, suppose your data set consists of the letters A, B, C, D. Here are all the unique ways you can group any two of these letters, without repeats:

AB, AC, AD, BC, BD, CD

A combination has two key characteristics:

>> The subsets must be unique, which is another way of saying that order isn't important. For example, the subsets AB and BA are the same subset.

>> Repeats aren't allowed, so the groupings AA, BB, CC, and DD aren't included in the combinations.

Excel's COMBIN function counts the number of combinations possible when selecting unique subsets from a data set (or a sample from a population). Here's the COMBIN syntax:

```
=COMBIN(number, number_chosen)
```

Here, *number* is the number of items in the set, and *number_chosen* is the number of items in each subset. Given a population of four items and two items in each subset, for example, you calculate the number of combinations by using the formula

```
=COMBIN(4, 2)
```

The function returns the value 6, indicating that six different ways exist in which two items can be selected uniquely from a set of four.

If you want repeats included (such as AA, BB, CC, and DD from the ABCD set), use Excel's COMBINA function, which uses the same syntax as COMBIN:

```
=COMBINA(number, number_chosen)
```

For example, to calculate the number of unique combinations in which two items are selected from a population of four items, with repeats allowed, you use the following formula:

```
=COMBINA(4, 2)
```

The result is 10.

Averaging Things

An *average* is the sum of two or more numeric values divided by the count of the numeric values. You can calculate the average by creating a custom formula, but that's practical for only a small number of items. For larger collections, using the Excel worksheet functions for calculating averages is way faster and more efficient.

REMEMBER

Statisticians refer to an average as the *mean. Central tendency* is defined as a typical value in a distribution or a value that represents the majority of cases. The most commonly used measures of central tendency are mean, median, and mode.

Calculating an average

The go-to worksheet function for calculating the average (or mean) of a set of values is the AVERAGE function, which uses the following syntax:

```
AVERAGE(number1[, number2, ...])
```

You can enter up to 255 arguments, and each can be a number, a cell, a range, a range name, or an array (that is, a list of values enclosed in curly braces, such as {20, 25, 25, 30}). If a cell contains zero, Excel includes it in the calculation; but if a cell is blank, Excel doesn't include it.

For example, to determine the average of the values in the range D3:D19, you use the following formula:

```
=AVERAGE(D3:D19)
```

Calculating a conditional average

In your data analysis, you might need to average the values in a range, but only those values that satisfy some condition. You can do this by using the AVERAGEIF function, an amalgam of AVERAGE and IF, which averages only those cells in a range that meet the condition you specify. AVERAGEIF takes up to three arguments:

```
=AVERAGEIF(range, criteria[, average_range])
```

The *range* argument is the range of cells you want to use to test the condition; the *criteria* argument is a logical expression, surrounded by double quotation marks, that determines which cells in *range* to average; and the optional *average_range* argument is the range from which you want the average values to be taken. If you omit *average_range*, Excel uses *range* for the average.

Excel sums only those cells in *average_range* that correspond to the cells in *range* and meet the `criteria`.

For example, consider the parts database shown in Figure 11-2. If you want to get the average of the values in the Gross Margin column, you use the AVERAGE function:

```
=AVERAGE(H3:H10)
```

But if, instead, you want the average of the Gross Margin values, but only for those parts with a Cost value under $10, you're into AVERAGEIF territory:

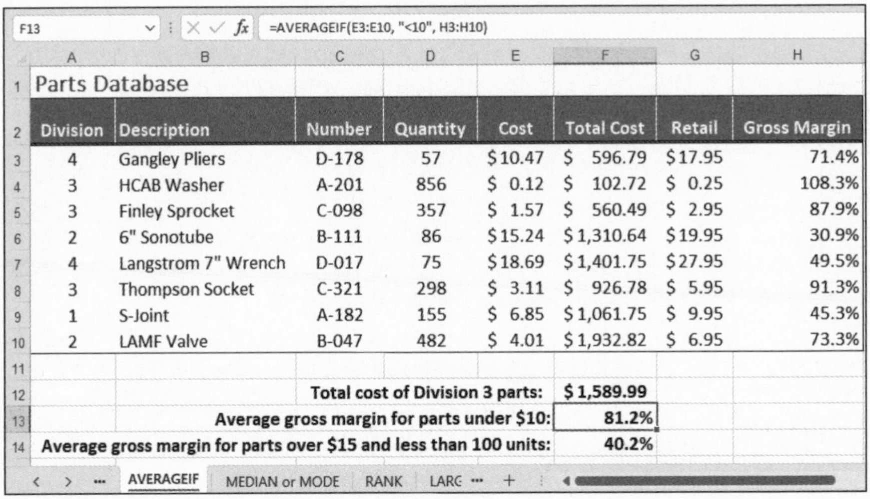

	A	B	C	D	E	F	G	H
1	Parts Database							
2	Division	Description	Number	Quantity	Cost	Total Cost	Retail	Gross Margin
3	4	Gangley Pliers	D-178	57	$10.47	$ 596.79	$17.95	71.4%
4	3	HCAB Washer	A-201	856	$ 0.12	$ 102.72	$ 0.25	108.3%
5	3	Finley Sprocket	C-098	357	$ 1.57	$ 560.49	$ 2.95	87.9%
6	2	6" Sonotube	B-111	86	$15.24	$1,310.64	$19.95	30.9%
7	4	Langstrom 7" Wrench	D-017	75	$18.69	$1,401.75	$27.95	49.5%
8	3	Thompson Socket	C-321	298	$ 3.11	$ 926.78	$ 5.95	91.3%
9	1	S-Joint	A-182	155	$ 6.85	$1,061.75	$ 9.95	45.3%
10	2	LAMF Valve	B-047	482	$ 4.01	$1,932.82	$ 6.95	73.3%
11								
12			Total cost of Division 3 parts:			$1,589.99		
13			Average gross margin for parts under $10:			81.2%		
14		Average gross margin for parts over $15 and less than 100 units:				40.2%		

FIGURE 11-2:
A parts database.

```
=AVERAGEIF(E3:E10, "<10", H3:H10)
```

This function says to Excel, in effect, "look in the range E3:E10, and each time you come across a value that's less than 10, grab the corresponding value from the range H3:H10 and include that value in the average. Best regards, AVERAGEIF."

Calculating an average based on multiple conditions

If you want to calculate an average based on multiple criteria applied to one or more ranges, check out the AVERAGEIFS function:

```
=AVERAGEIFS(average_range, range1, criteria1[, range2,
    criteria2...])
```

The *average_range* argument is the range from which you want the average values to be taken. *criteria1* gets applied to *range1*, *criteria2* gets applied to *range2*, and so on. AVERAGEIFS includes in the calculation only those cells that match all the criteria.

Referring back to the parts database shown in Figure 11-2, suppose you want the average of the Gross Margin values, but only for those parts with a Quantity value (D3:D10) less than 100 and a Cost value (E3:E10) greater than $15. AVERAGEIFS is on it:

```
=AVERAGEIFS(H3:H10, D3:D10, "<100", E3:E10, ">15")
```

This formula appears in cell F14 of Figure 11-2, and you can see that the result is 40.2%.

Calculating the median

When analyzing data, you may need to find the *median*, which is the midpoint in a series of numbers: the point at which half the values are greater and half the values are less when you arrange the values in numerical order. What about when you have an even number of values? Great question! In that case, the median is the average of the two values that lie in the middle.

To calculate the median, you use Excel's MEDIAN function:

```
MEDIAN(number1[, number2, ...])
```

You can enter up to 255 arguments, and each can be a number, cell, range, range name, or array. Excel includes zeroes in the calculation, but not blanks.

In the Product Defects worksheet shown in Figure 11-3, the median value of the Defects column (D3:D19) is given by the following formula in cell I2:

```
=MEDIAN(D3:D19)
```

Calculating the mode

The *mode* is the most common value in a list of values. To calculate the mode for a set of numbers, fire up Excel's MODE function:

```
MODE(number1[, number2, ...])
```

You can specify up to 255 arguments; each argument can be a number, cell, range, range name, or array. Excel includes zeroes in the calculation, but it doesn't include blanks. If there is no most common value (that is, if all values are unique), Excel returns the #N/A error.

| I2 | | f_x | =MEDIAN(D3:D19) | | | | | |

Product Defects

Workgroup	Group Leader	Defects	Units	% Defective
A	Hammond	8	969	0.8%
B	Hammond	4	815	0.5%
C	Hammond	14	1,625	0.9%
D	Hammond	3	1,453	0.2%
E	Hammond	9	767	1.2%
F	Hammond	11	1,023	1.1%
G	Hammond	15	1,256	1.2%
H	Hammond	8	781	1.0%
L	Bolter	7	1,109	0.6%
M	Bolter	11	1,021	1.1%
N	Bolter	6	812	0.7%
O	Bolter	11	977	1.1%
P	Bolter	5	1,182	0.4%
Q	Bolter	7	961	0.7%
R	Bolter	12	689	1.7%
T	Bolter	19	1,308	1.5%

Median Defects: 9
Mode Defects: 11

MEDIAN or MODE   RANK   LARGE or SMALL

FIGURE 11-3: MEDIAN returns the median value of a set of numeric values.

In the Product Defects worksheet, shown previously in Figure 11-3, the mode value of the Defects column (D3:D19) is given by the following formula in cell I3:

```
=MODE(D3:D19)
```

REMEMBER Excel interprets the logical value TRUE as 1 and the logical value FALSE as 0, so you can use logical values as arguments when calculating the median or mode. However, if an array or a range of cells contains a logical value, MEDIAN and MODE don't include them in the calculation.

Finding the Rank

Finding how one item ranks relative to the other items in a list is often useful. For example, you might want to find out how a student's test score ranks in relation to the other students. You can do this by sorting the list, but in some situations, sorting isn't advisable. For example, if the original data was constantly changing, it would require constant resorting. Instead, you can use Excel's RANK.EQ function to determine an item's rank relative to other items in a list:

```
RANK.EQ(number, ref[, order])
```

RANK.EQ takes three arguments: *number* is the item you want to rank; *ref* is the range that holds the list of items; and *order* is the optional sort order you want Excel to use. The default is descending, but you can use any nonzero value for ascending.

For example, Figure 11-4 shows a worksheet that contains student grades in the range B3:B48. To find out the rank of the grade in cell B3, you use the following formula:

```
=RANK.EQ(B3, $B$3:$B$48)
```

As you can see in cell C3, the returned value is 6.

	A	B	C	D	E	F
	C3		f_x =RANK.EQ(B3, $B$3:$B$48)			
1	Student Grades					
2	Student ID	Grade	Rank			
3	64947	82	6			
4	69630	66	28			
5	18324	52	44			
6	89826	94	1			
7	63600	40	46			
8	25089	62	39			
9	89923	88	2			
10	13000	75	10			
11	16895	66	28			
12	24918	62	39			
13	45107	71	19			
14	64090	53	43			
15	94395	74	14			
16	58749	65	34			
17	26916	66	28			
18	59033	67	27			
19	15450	68	25			
	< > ...	RANK	LARGE or SMALL	FREQUENCY	VAR	

FIGURE 11-4:
RANK returns the ranking of a value in a set.

TIP

Note the use of absolute references for the *ref* argument in Figure 11-4. I used absolute references because after entering the formula in cell C3, I filled the formula down from C4 to C48. By using an absolute range reference, I ensured that the *ref* argument is the same for all the filled cells.

You can also use the RANK.AVG function to calculate the rank. With RANK.AVG, if two or more numbers have the same rank, Excel averages the rank. For example, in the list 100, 95, 90, 85, 85, 80, 70, the RANK.AVG function ranks the number 85 as 4.5, which is the average of 4 and 5. By contrast, RANK.EQ would give both instances of 85 the rank 4. With both RANK.EQ and RANK.AVG, if two or more numbers have the same rank, subsequent numbers are affected. In the preceding list, the number 80 ranks sixth. The RANK.AVG function takes the same three arguments as RANK.EQ:

```
RANK.AVG(number, ref[, order])
```

While you're here, I might as well mention Excel's PERCENTRANK.INC function, which you can wield to determine the rank of a value as a percentage of all the values in your data set. PERCENTRANK.INC takes three arguments:

```
PERCENTRANK.INC(array, x[, significance])
```

Here, *array* is the array or range you want to use; *x* is the value you want to rank; *and* *significance* is the optional number of significant digits you want your results to return (the default is three). PERCENTRANK.INC gives equal values the same rank.

Excel also includes PERCENTRANK.EXC to comply with industry standards for calculating the rank of a value as a percentage of all the values in a data set:

```
PERCENTRANK.EXC(array, x[, significance])
```

As you can see, PERCENTRANK.EXC takes the same arguments as PERCENTRANK.INC, but it excludes the ranks of 0 and 100.

Determining the Nth Largest or Smallest Value

When given a list of values and an item from that list, you can use RANK.EQ (or RANK.AVG) to determine that item's rank (ascending or descending) in that list. A slightly different approach to this problem is to determine, given a list of values, what item in that list has a specified rank, such as first, third, or tenth.

You can solve this problem by sorting the list, but if the values change constantly, a better approach is to use Excel's LARGE or SMALL function, as I describe in the next two sections.

Calculating the nth highest value

Excel's LARGE worksheet function returns the *n*th highest value in a list. Here's the syntax:

```
LARGE(array, n)
```

LARGE takes two arguments: *array* is the array or range you want to work with, and *n* is the rank order of the value you seek.

For example, given a list of student grades shown in the range B3:B48 in Figure 11-5, what's the minimum mark required to crack the top 10 grades? That's a piece of cake for the LARGE function, where the following formula (see cell D4 in Figure 11-5) returns the value 75:

```
=LARGE(B3:B48, 10)
```

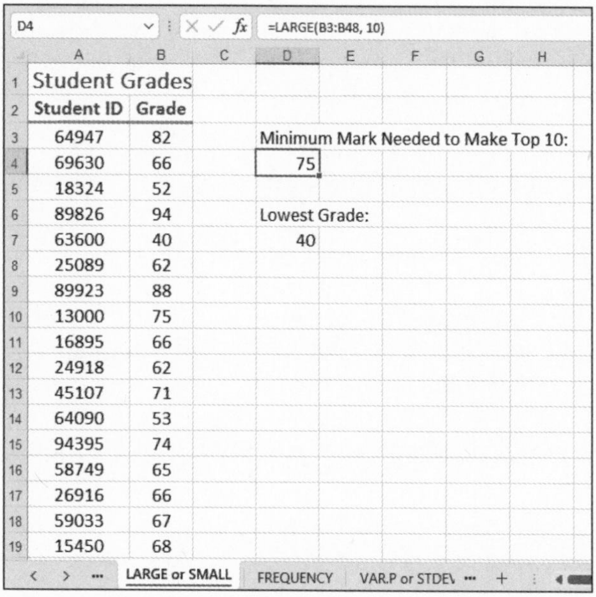

FIGURE 11-5: LARGE returns the *n*th largest value in a range or array.

Calculating the nth smallest value

Excel's SMALL worksheet function returns the *n*th smallest value in an array or range. Here's the syntax:

```
SMALL(array, n)
```

SMALL takes two arguments: *array* is the array or range you want to work with, and *n* is the rank order of the value you want.

For example, given the student grades shown in the range B3:B48 in Figure 11-5, what's the lowest grade? The following formula (see cell D7 in Figure 11-5) returns the value 40:

```
=SMALL(B3:B48, 1)
```

Creating a Grouped Frequency Distribution

Organizing a large amount of data into a grouped frequency distribution can help you see patterns in the data. With student test scores, for example, the first group might be scores less than or equal to 50, the second group might be 51 to 60, and so on, up to scores between 91 and 100. You can use the Excel FREQUENCY function to return the number of occurrences in each group:

```
FREQUENCY(data_array, bins_array)
```

FREQUENCY takes two arguments: $data\_array$ is the list of values you want to group; $bins\_array$ is the list of groupings (known as *bins*) you want to use. You enter FREQUENCY either as a dynamic array formula or as an old-fashioned array formula into the same number of cells as you have groups (for example, if you have six groups, you enter the formula into six cells). Here are the steps to follow:

1. **Select the first cell where you want the grouped frequency distribution to appear.**

   If you want to enter the function as an old-fashioned array, select all the cells where you want the grouped frequency distribution to appear.

2. **Type =frequency(.**

3. **Enter or select the items you want to group.**

4. **Type a comma and then enter or select the list of groupings.**

   When you create your frequency distribution, keep the number of groups reasonable: between five and ten is good. If you have too few or too many groups, you can lose your ability to convey information easily. Too few intervals can hide trends, and too many intervals can mask details. You should also keep your intervals simple. Intervals of 5, 10, or 20 are good because they are easy to understand. Start your interval with a value that's divisible by the interval size, which will make your frequency distribution easy to read. Finally, all intervals should have the same number of values. Again, this makes your frequency distribution easy to understand.

5. Type).

6. Press Enter.

If you want to enter the function as an old-fashioned array, either hold down Ctrl+Shift and then click the Enter button or press Ctrl+Shift+Enter.

Excel enters the array formula and returns the number of items in each grouping. Figure 11-6 shows a FREQUENCY array formula entered into the range E3:E8.

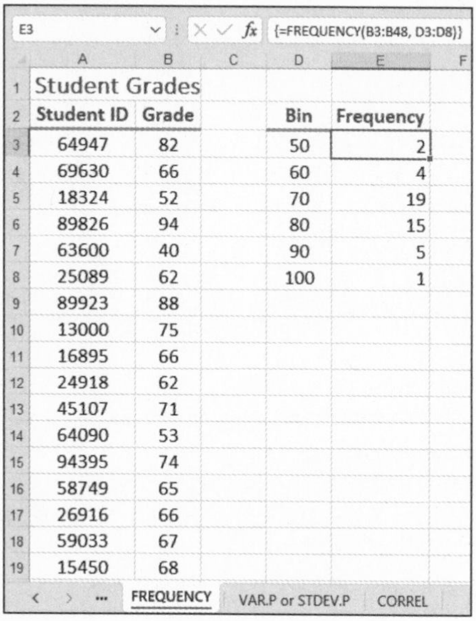

	A	B	C	D	E	F
	Student Grades					
2	Student ID	Grade		Bin	Frequency	
3	64947	82		50	2	
4	69630	66		60	4	
5	18324	52		70	19	
6	89826	94		80	15	
7	63600	40		90	5	
8	25089	62		100	1	
9	89923	88				
10	13000	75				
11	16895	66				
12	24918	62				
13	45107	71				
14	64090	53				
15	94395	74				
16	58749	65				
17	26916	66				
18	59033	67				
19	15450	68				

E3 — fx {=FREQUENCY(B3:B48, D3:D8)}

FREQUENCY | VAR.P or STDEV.P | CORREL

FIGURE 11-6: FREQUENCY tells you how many items in a range appear in each bin.

Calculating the Variance

Part of your analysis might involve determining how, on average, some values deviate from the mean. One method is to take the difference each number varies from the mean, square those differences, sum those squares, and then divide by the number of values. The result is called the *variance*, and in Excel you calculate it using VAR.S or VAR.P:

```
VAR.S(number1[, number2, ...])
VAR.P(number1[, number2, ...])
```

Use VAR.S if your data represents a sample of a larger population; use VAR.P if your data represents the entire population. In both cases, you can enter up to 255 arguments.

For example, in the Product Defects worksheet, shown in Figure 11-7, I calculate the variance of the Defects column (D3:D19) with the following formula (see cell H3):

```
=VAR.P(D3:D19)
```

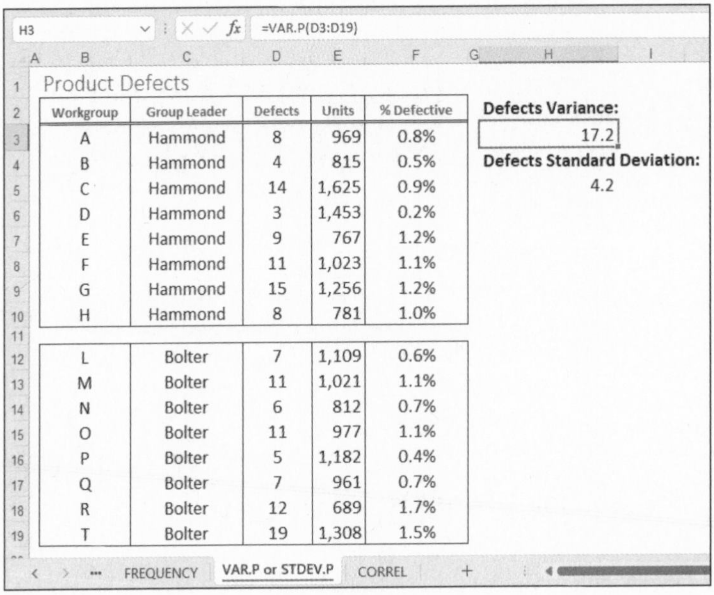

H3		✓ fx	=VAR.P(D3:D19)					

	A	B	C	D	E	F	G	H	I
1	Product Defects								
2		Workgroup	Group Leader	Defects	Units	% Defective		Defects Variance:	
3		A	Hammond	8	969	0.8%		17.2	
4		B	Hammond	4	815	0.5%		Defects Standard Deviation:	
5		C	Hammond	14	1,625	0.9%		4.2	
6		D	Hammond	3	1,453	0.2%			
7		E	Hammond	9	767	1.2%			
8		F	Hammond	11	1,023	1.1%			
9		G	Hammond	15	1,256	1.2%			
10		H	Hammond	8	781	1.0%			
11									
12		L	Bolter	7	1,109	0.6%			
13		M	Bolter	11	1,021	1.1%			
14		N	Bolter	6	812	0.7%			
15		O	Bolter	11	977	1.1%			
16		P	Bolter	5	1,182	0.4%			
17		Q	Bolter	7	961	0.7%			
18		R	Bolter	12	689	1.7%			
19		T	Bolter	19	1,308	1.5%			

< > ··· FREQUENCY VAR.P or STDEV.P CORREL +

FIGURE 11-7: VAR.P returns the variance of data that represents an entire population.

Calculating the Standard Deviation

I introduce the variance in the preceding section, but because the variance is a squared value, it's difficult to interpret relative to the mean. Therefore, statisticians often calculate the *standard deviation*, which is the square root of the variance.

If two data sets have a similar mean, the set with a higher standard deviation has more variable data. If your data is distributed normally, about 68 percent of the data is found within one standard deviation of the mean; about 95 percent is within two standard deviations; and about 99 percent is within three standard deviations.

To calculate the standard deviation, you can use the STDEV.S or STDEV.P function.

```
STDEV.S(number1[, number2, ...])
STDEV.P(number1[, number2, ...])
```

Use STDEV.S if your data is a sample of a population; use STDEV.P if your data is the entire population. In both cases, you can enter up to 255 arguments.

For example, in the Product Defects worksheet shown previously in Figure 11-7, I calculated the standard deviation of the Defects column (D3:D19) with the following formula (see cell H3):

```
=STDEV.P(D3:D19)
```

WARNING

The relation of the values to each other in the data set affects the standard deviation. For example, a single outlier can distort the standard deviation, and a data set consisting of identical values gives you a standard deviation of zero.

Finding the Correlation

Correlation is a measure of the relationship between two sets of data. For example, if you have monthly figures for advertising expenses and sales, you might wonder whether higher advertising expenses lead to more sales, that is, whether the two values are related.

WARNING

Keep in mind that a correlation does not prove that one thing causes another. The most you can say is that one number varies with the other.

To find a correlation in Excel, you use the CORREL function:

```
CORREL(array1, array2)
```

CORREL takes two arguments: *array1* and *array2*, which are two lists of numbers. CORREL returns the *correlation coefficient*, which is a number between –1 and 1. The sign suggests whether the relationship is positive (+) or negative (–). See the following table to help interpret the result.

Correlation Coefficient	Interpretation
1	The data sets are perfectly and positively correlated. For example, a 10 percent increase in advertising produces a 10 percent increase in sales.
Between 0 and 1	The data sets are positively correlated. The higher the number is, the higher the correlation is between the data.
0	No correlation exists between the data.
Between 0 and –1	The data sets are negatively correlated. The lower the number is, the more negatively correlated the data is.
–1	The data sets have a perfect negative correlation. For example, a 10-percent increase in advertising leads to a 10-percent decrease in sales.

Figure 11-8 shows a worksheet that has advertising costs in the range C3:C14 and sales in the range D3:D14. Cell F3 calculates the correlation between these two ranges as follows:

```
=CORREL(C3:C14, D3:D14)
```

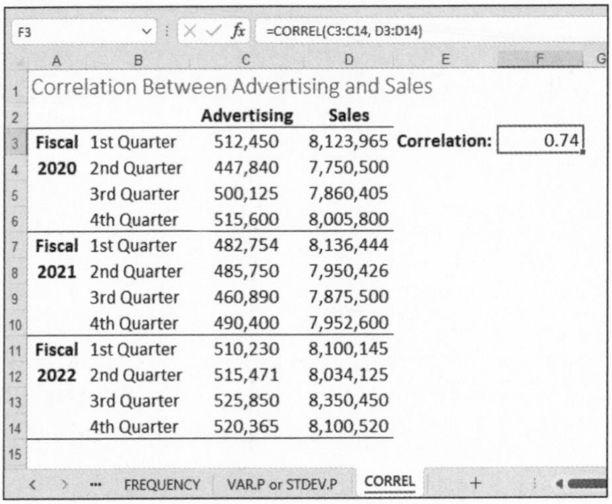

FIGURE 11-8:
CORREL
calculates the
correlation
between two sets
of values.

IN THIS CHAPTER

» **Getting Excel's Analysis ToolPak on the job**

» **Generating oodles of descriptive statistics**

» **Calculating moving averages, ranks, and percentiles**

» **Generating random numbers, for some reason**

» **Creating frequency distributions and histograms**

Chapter **12**

Analyzing Data Using Descriptive Statistics

When you're analyzing your Excel data using statistics, you can generate results that either describe something about the data or let you infer something about the data.

Describing the data, statistically speaking, means measuring various aspects of the data, including the sum, count, average, maximum, minimum, standard deviation, and so on. All these measures fall under the heading of *descriptive statistics.*

Making inferences about the data means taking a subset of the total population (for example, people, products, or panda bears) and measuring various aspects of the data that enable you to reach conclusions — *inferences* — about the population as a whole. The tools and techniques that enable you to analyze your data in this way fall under the heading of *inferential statistics.*

In this chapter, you dive into the useful world of descriptive statistics, particularly those you can generate with just a few clicks and keypresses using Excel's powerful Analysis ToolPak add-in. For the inferential statistics fun, you'll have to wait until Chapter 13.

Loading the Analysis ToolPak

You can get access to a number of powerful statistical analysis tools by loading Excel's Analysis ToolPak add-in. The Analysis ToolPak consists of 19 statistical tools that calculate not only a basic set of descriptive statistics (such as the sum, average, and standard deviation) but also more sophisticated results, such as the moving average and the rank and percentile. You can also use the analysis tools to generate random numbers and frequency distributions, and to perform inferential statistical analysis, such as correlation and regression.

Many of these tools have equivalent worksheet functions. For example, you can calculate correlation using the CORREL function, rank and percentile using the RANK.* and PERCENTILE.* functions, and so on. However, each Analysis ToolPak tool displays a dialog box that makes it easier for you to configure the tool and select the options you need for your analysis.

If all that sounds too good to be true, know that using the Analysis ToolPak has a downside: All the tool results are static values, not formulas, so if your data changes, you need to run the tool all over again.

Here are the steps to plow through to load the Analysis ToolPak:

1. **Choose File ⇨ Options.**

   The Excel Options dialog box appears.

2. **Click Add-Ins.**

3. **In the Manage drop-down list, click Excel Add-ins and then click Go.**

   The Add-Ins dialog box appears.

4. **Select the Analysis ToolPak check box, as shown in Figure 12-1, and then click OK.**

   Excel loads the Analysis ToolPak add-in.

FIGURE 12-1:
Loading the
Analysis ToolPak
add-in.

The Analysis ToolPak creates a new group named Analyze on the Ribbon's Data tab. To use one of the Analysis ToolPak's statistical tools, choose Data ➪ Data Analysis. In the Data Analysis dialog box that appears (see Figure 12-2), click the tool you want to use and then click OK. Excel displays a dialog box for the tool. In the dialog box, specify the tool settings you want to use (the controls vary from tool to tool), and then click OK.

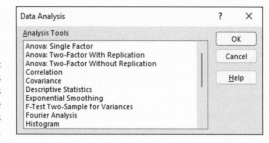

FIGURE 12-2:
The Analysis
ToolPak's tools
appear in the
Data Analysis
dialog box.

If you no longer need the Analysis ToolPak, you can disable the add-in to reduce clutter on the Ribbon's Data tab and to save space on your computer's hard drive. Follow Steps 1 through 3 to display the Add-Ins dialog box, deselect the Analysis ToolPak check box, and then click OK.

Generating Descriptive Statistics

You can speed up your data analysis by using the Descriptive Statistics tool to quickly generate up to 16 different statistical measurements. When you use this tool on a range of data, Excel assumes that you're working with a sample of a larger population and produces a table containing statistical calculations for that sample data, including the measures outlined in Table 12-1.

TABLE 12-1 **Measures Generated by the Descriptive Statistics Tool**

Measure	What It Returns
Mean	The average of the sample data.
Standard Error	The standard error of the sample data, which is a measure of how much the sample data's mean deviates from the population's mean.
Median	The middle value in the sample data (that is, the value that separates the largest half of the values from the smallest half of the values).
Mode	The most common value (if one exists) in the sample data.
Standard Deviation	The standard deviation measure of the sample data. This is a measure of the relative spread of the data: A larger standard deviation means that the data is more spread out; a smaller standard deviation means that the data is bunched together.
Sample Variance	The variance for the sample data. The variance is the square of the standard deviation.
Kurtosis	A measure that indicates whether the curve formed by the sample data (if you charted it) is peaked (positive kurtosis) or flat (negative kurtosis).
Skewness	A measure that indicates whether the curve formed by the charted sample data is bunched below the mean (positive skewness) or above the mean (negative skewness).
Range	The difference between the largest and smallest values in the sample data.
Minimum	The smallest value in the sample data.
Maximum	The largest value in the sample data.
Sum	The total of all the values in the sample data.
Count	The number of values in the sample data.
Largest(X)	The Xth largest value in the sample data.
Smallest(X)	The Xth smallest value in the sample data.
Confidence Level(X%)	The confidence interval for the mean, which is the sample mean plus or minus the returned value. There is X% probability that the mean value for the population data falls within the confidence interval.

The sharp-eyed reader will have noticed two things about the Confidence Level statistic. First, that it's slightly misnamed because it actually returns the confidence interval, not the confidence level. Second, because it enables you to infer something about the population from the sample, it's really an inferential statistic, not a descriptive statistic.

No matter; here are the steps to follow to generate all these statistics for your data:

1. **Choose Data ⇨ Data Analysis.**

   The Data Analysis dialog box appears.

2. **In the Analysis Tools list, select Descriptive Statistics and then click OK.**

   The Descriptive Statistics dialog box appears.

3. **In the Input Range box, specify the range of cells you want to analyze.**

   Most data will be in columns, but if your data is in rows, be sure to select the Rows radio button. Also, if your data range has labels, select the Labels in First Row check box (or the Labels in First Column check box, if your data is in rows).

4. **To specify a location for the output data, select the Output Range radio button and then type or click the upper-left corner of the output range.**

   Alternatively, you can select New Worksheet Ply to plop the stats in a new worksheet or select New Workbook to create an entirely new file for the results.

5. **Select the Summary Statistics check box.**

   This tells Excel to generate the mean, standard error, median, mode, standard deviation, sample variance, kurtosis, skewness, range, minimum, maximum, sum, and count.

6. **To calculate the confidence interval, select the Confidence Level for Mean check box and then type the confidence level in the text box.**

   Remember that the confidence level is the probability that the population mean falls with the calculated confidence interval of the sample mean. The default confidence level of 95% is fine for most uses.

7. **To calculate the Kth largest value in the sample data, select the Kth Largest check box and then type a value for K in the text box.**

8. **To calculate the Kth smallest value in the sample data, select the Kth Smallest check box and then type a value for K in the text box.**

   Figure 12-3 shows a completed version of the Descriptive Statistics dialog box.

9. **Click OK.**

   Excel calculates the descriptive statistics and then displays them in the location you specified in Step 4. Figure 12-4 shows an example. In this case, the sample data is the Defects column of the table (D3:D22).

   For easier analysis, you need to format the Descriptive Statistics tool's results. Select the output range, click the Home tab, and select Number in the Number Format list.

TIP

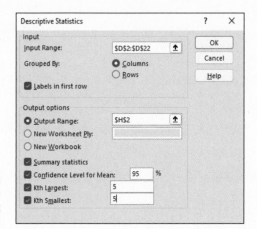

FIGURE 12-4:
The statistics
generated by the
Descriptive
Statistics tool.

Workgroup	Group Leader	Defects	Units	% Defective
A	Hammond	8	969	0.8%
B	Brimson	4	816	0.5%
C	Reilly	14	1,625	0.9%
D	Richardson	3	1,453	0.2%
E	Durbin	9	767	1.2%
F	O'Donoghue	10	1,024	1.0%
G	Voyatzis	15	1,256	1.2%
H	Granick	8	782	1.0%
I	Aster	13	999	1.3%
J	Shore	9	1,172	0.8%
K	Fox	0	936	0.0%
L	Bolter	7	1,109	0.6%
M	Renaud	8	1,022	0.8%
N	Ibbitson	6	812	0.7%
O	Harper	11	978	1.1%
P	Ferry	5	1,183	0.4%
Q	Richens	7	961	0.7%
R	Munson	12	690	1.7%
S	Little	10	1,105	0.9%
T	Jones	19	1,309	1.5%

Product Defects Database

Defects	
Mean	8.90
Standard Error	0.99
Median	8.50
Mode	8.00
Standard Deviation	4.41
Sample Variance	19.46
Kurtosis	0.51
Skewness	0.25
Range	19.00
Minimum	0.00
Maximum	19.00
Sum	178.00
Count	20.00
Largest(5)	12.00
Smallest(5)	6.00
Confidence Level(95.0%)	2.06

Calculating a Moving Average

A *moving average* smooths a data series by averaging the series values over a spec-ified number of preceding periods. For example, a seven-day moving average takes the average of the first seven days; then, for each subsequent day to the end of the series, calculates a new average based on the previous seven days (days two through eight, days three through nine, and so on). In this example, seven is called the *interval* of the moving average.

Using a moving average can reveal trends that are masked when you use a simple average because a simple average gives equal weight to each value. A moving average weighs recent values equally and ignores older values, thereby enabling you to spot trends. You can use a moving average to forecast sales, stock prices, or other trends.

Follow these steps to crank out some moving averages for your data:

1. **Choose Data ⇨ Data Analysis.**

   Excel displays the Data Analysis dialog box.

2. **In the Analysis Tools list, select Moving Average and then click OK.**

   The Moving Average dialog box shows up.

3. **In the Input Range box, specify the range of cells you want to analyze.**

   Your range reference should use absolute cell addresses, where you precede both the column letter and the row number with $, as in $C$2:$C$121.

   If your data range has labels, select the Labels in First Row check box.

4. **In the Interval text box, enter the interval you want to use for the moving average.**

5. **In the Output Range box, enter (or click the upper-left corner of) the range where you want the results to appear.**

   Alternatively, you can select New Worksheet Ply to plop the stats in a new worksheet or select New Workbook to create a new file for the results.

6. **(Optional) To display a chart that plots the moving average results, select the Chart Output check box.**

7. **(Optional) If you want to calculate standard errors for the data, select the Standard Errors check box.**

   Excel places standard error values next to the moving average values.

   Figure 12-5 shows a completed version of the Moving Average dialog box.

8. **Click OK.**

   Excel calculates the moving averages and then displays them in the location you specified in Step 5, as shown in Figure 12-6. In this case, the sample data is the Actual column of the worksheet (C2:C:121). In this example, cell D13 shows the moving average for cells C2 through C13.

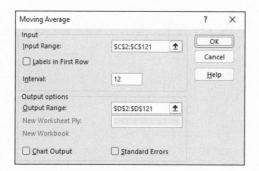

FIGURE 12-5:
The Moving
Average dialog
box, good to go.

	A	B	C	D
1	Monthly Sales - Data		Actual	12-Month Moving Avg
2		January, 2013	90.0	#N/A
3		February, 2013	95.0	#N/A
4		March, 2013	110.0	#N/A
5		April, 2013	105.0	#N/A
6		May, 2013	100.0	#N/A
7	2013	June, 2013	100.0	#N/A
8		July, 2013	105.0	#N/A
9		August, 2013	105.0	#N/A
10		September, 2013	110.0	#N/A
11		October, 2013	120.0	#N/A
12		November, 2013	130.0	#N/A
13		December, 2013	140.0	109.17
14		January, 2014	90.0	109.17
15		February, 2014	95.0	109.17
16		March, 2014	115.0	109.58
17		April, 2014	110.0	110.00
18		May, 2014	105.0	110.42
19	2014	June, 2014	105.0	110.83
20		July, 2014	110.0	111.25
21		August, 2014	115.0	112.08
22		September, 2014	115.0	112.50
23		October. 2014	125.0	112.92

< > ⋯ **Moving Average**   Rank & Percentile   Random Number Gene ⋯   +

FIGURE 12-6:
Some moving
averages
generated by
the Moving
Average tool.

When you use the Moving Average tool, the first few values in the column contain the value #N/A (see, for example, the range D2:D12 in Figure 12-6). The number of cells that contain #N/A is one less than the number specified for the Interval value because for those initial cells, Excel doesn't yet have enough values to calculate the moving average.

TIP

To use a formula to create a custom moving average of interval *n* using the AVERAGE function, enter the initial formula =AVERAGE(*range*), where *range* is a reference to the first *n* values in the series. Be sure to use relative references in the range coordinates. That way, when you fill the formula down to the subsequent cells to the end of the series, Excel updates the formula to automatically create a moving average. Thanks!

Determining Rank and Percentile

One common form of data analysis is calculating where an item ranks relative to the other items in a group. For example, in a data set that shows the number of product defects by workgroup, you might want to find out how one group's defects total ranks in relation to the other groups. You might also want to calculate the *percentile*, which is the percentage of items in the sample that are at the same level or a lower level than a given value.

As I talk about in Chapter 11, you can calculate the rank using Excel's RANK.EQ and RANK.AVG functions, and you can calculate the percentile using the PERCENTILE.EXC and PERCENTILE.INC functions. These are perfectly good worksheet functions, but if you don't mind using static results, you can calculate these values faster and with less effort by using the Analysis ToolPak's Rank and Percentile tool.

Here's how it works:

1. Choose Data ⇨ Data Analysis.

Excel opens the Data Analysis dialog box.

2. In the Analysis Tools list, select Rank and Percentile and then click OK.

Excel opens the Rank and Percentile dialog box.

3. In the Input Range box, specify the range of cells you want to analyze.

If your data is in rows, be sure to select the Rows radio button. Also, if your data range has labels, select the Labels in First Row check box (or the Labels in First Column check box, if your data is in rows).

4. In the Output Range box, enter or click the upper-left corner of the range where you want the results to appear.

Alternatively, you can select New Worksheet Ply to toss the stats into a new worksheet or select New Workbook to create a new file to hold the results.

Figure 12-7 shows a completed version of the Rank and Percentile dialog box.

5. Click OK.

Excel calculates the rank and percentile values and displays them in the location you specified in Step 4, as shown in Figure 12-8. In this case, the sample data is the Defects column of the worksheet (D3:D:22).

Excel creates a four-column table containing the rank and percentile data. Table 12-2 explains what each column tells you.

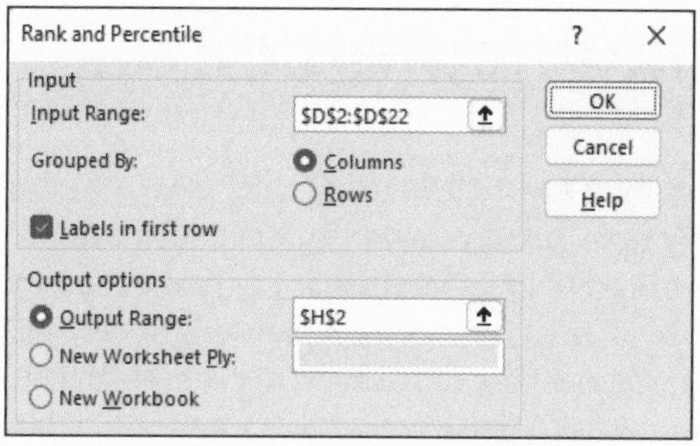

FIGURE 12-7:
A completed version of the Rank and Percentile dialog box.

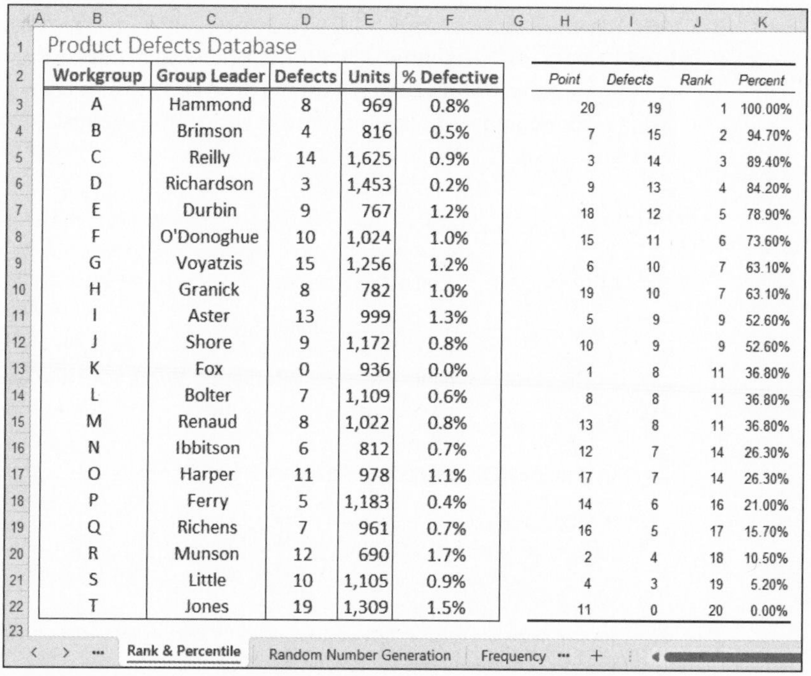

A	B	C	D	E	F	G	H	I	J	K
1	Product Defects Database									
2	Workgroup	Group Leader	Defects	Units	% Defective		Point	Defects	Rank	Percent
3	A	Hammond	8	969	0.8%		20	19	1	100.00%
4	B	Brimson	4	816	0.5%		7	15	2	94.70%
5	C	Reilly	14	1,625	0.9%		3	14	3	89.40%
6	D	Richardson	3	1,453	0.2%		9	13	4	84.20%
7	E	Durbin	9	767	1.2%		18	12	5	78.90%
8	F	O'Donoghue	10	1,024	1.0%		15	11	6	73.60%
9	G	Voyatzis	15	1,256	1.2%		6	10	7	63.10%
10	H	Granick	8	782	1.0%		19	10	7	63.10%
11	I	Aster	13	999	1.3%		5	9	9	52.60%
12	J	Shore	9	1,172	0.8%		10	9	9	52.60%
13	K	Fox	0	936	0.0%		1	8	11	36.80%
14	L	Bolter	7	1,109	0.6%		8	8	11	36.80%
15	M	Renaud	8	1,022	0.8%		13	8	11	36.80%
16	N	Ibbitson	6	812	0.7%		12	7	14	26.30%
17	O	Harper	11	978	1.1%		17	7	14	26.30%
18	P	Ferry	5	1,183	0.4%		14	6	16	21.00%
19	Q	Richens	7	961	0.7%		16	5	17	15.70%
20	R	Munson	12	690	1.7%		2	4	18	10.50%
21	S	Little	10	1,105	0.9%		4	3	19	5.20%
22	T	Jones	19	1,309	1.5%		11	0	20	0.00%
23										

⟨ ⟩ ⋯ **Rank & Percentile** Random Number Generation Frequency ⋯ +

FIGURE 12-8:
The product defects with their respective ranks and percentiles.

TABLE 12-2 ## The Rank and Percentile Tool's Output Columns

Column	Description
Point	The location of the data value within the specified input range. For example, if the value was originally the third numeric value in the input data, the point value is 3.
Column Name	The input values, sorted based upon their ranking. *Column Name* refers to the name of the original input data column.
Rank	The rank for each input value, with 1 being the highest-ranking value in the list.
Percent	The percentile result for each input value.

Generating Random Numbers

When you're building a data-analysis model in Excel, that model won't be worth a hill of beans if it doesn't contain any data so that you can take the model for a test drive. If you don't have data lying around, you can enter some placeholder test values by hand, but that's way too much work. Fortunately, you can skip that tedious and time-consuming chore in favor of a faster and more efficient approach: the Analysis ToolPak's Random Number Generation tool, which is happy to generate a set of random values for your model.

True, Excel offers worksheet functions for generating random numbers, but these functions, although useful, have limited capabilities. For example, the RAND function generates random numbers between 0 and 1, and the RANDBETWEEN function generates random numbers between two specified values. If either function provides what you need for your data, go for it.

However, in many cases, the numbers coughed up by RAND and RANDBETWEEN aren't useful because they aren't realistic. For example, if your data model uses student test scores, random numbers between, say, 40 and 100 are unrealistic because student scores are almost always distributed as a bell curve, with most of the result bunched in the middle, and just a few results on the high and low ends.

To help you get more realistic random numbers, the Random Number Generation tool enables you to generate random values using various *distributions* that specify the pattern of the values. Here's a quick look:

>> **Uniform:** Generates numbers with equal probability from the range of values you provide (which makes the Uniform distribution similar to the RANDBETWEEN worksheet function).

>> **Normal:** Produces numbers in a bell curve distribution based on a mean and standard deviation.

>> **Bernoulli:** Generates a random series of 1s and 0s based on the probability of success on a single trial.

>> **Binomial:** Generates random numbers characterized by the probability of success over a number of trials.

>> **Poisson:** Generates random numbers based on the probability of a designated number of events occurring in a time frame.

>> **Patterned:** Generates random numbers according to a pattern given by a lower and upper bound, step value, and repetition rate.

>> **Discrete:** Generates random numbers from a series of values and probabilities for these values.

Don't worry if you don't understand all these distributions or if you aren't sure how to even pronounce some of them. Feel free to experiment with each one to see the results you get.

Here are the steps to follow to use the Random Number Generation tool:

1. **Choose Data ⇨ Data Analysis.**

   Excel displays the Data Analysis dialog box.

2. **In the Analysis Tools list, select Random Number Generation and then click OK.**

   The Random Number Generation dialog box appears.

3. **Specify how many random numbers you want to generate.**

   In the Number of Variables text box, enter how many random number sets you want. This is the number of columns that will appear in the generated output.

   In the Number of Random Numbers text box, enter how many random numbers you want in each set. This is the number of rows that will appear in the generated output.

4. **In the Distribution list, select the type of distribution you want to use.**

5. **Use the controls in the Parameters group to specify the distribution parameters.**

   The options you see depend on the distribution you selected in Step 4. For example, the Random Number Generation dialog box shown in Figure 12-9 shows the Normal distribution selected, so the parameters are a mean value and a standard deviation.

6. **(Optional) In the Random Seed text box, enter a starting point for the random number generation.**

   You have the option of entering a value that Excel will use to start its generation of random numbers. The benefit of using a Random Seed value, as Excel calls it, is that you can later produce the same set of random numbers by planting the same "seed."

7. **In the Output Range box, enter (or click the upper-left corner of) the range where you want the random numbers to appear.**

   Alternatively, you can select New Worksheet Ply to add the random numbers to a new worksheet or select New Workbook to create a new file for the output.

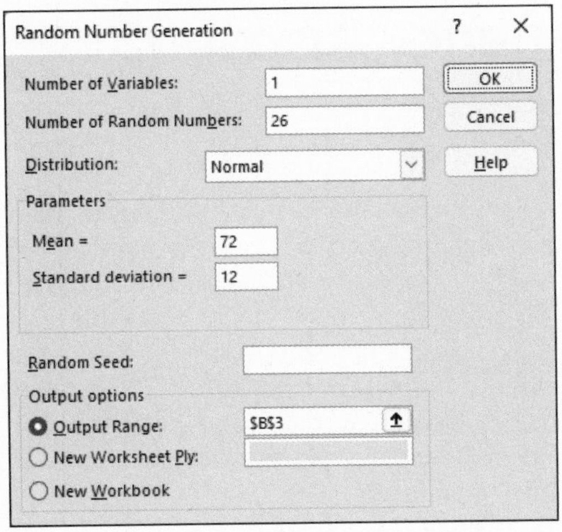

FIGURE 12-9: The parameters change depending on the Distribution value.

8. **Click OK.**

   Excel generates the random numbers and then displays them in the location you specified in Step 7, as shown in Figure 12-10.

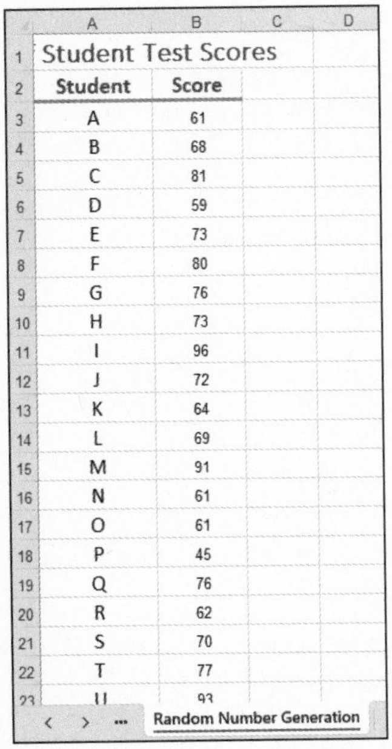

Student Test Scores

Student	Score
A	61
B	68
C	81
D	59
E	73
F	80
G	76
H	73
I	96
J	72
K	64
L	69
M	91
N	61
O	61
P	45
Q	76
R	62
S	70
T	77
U	93

FIGURE 12-10: Random test scores generated by the Random Number Generation tool.

Creating a Frequency Distribution

When analyzing a large amount of data, you might require a *frequency distribution,* which organizes the data into numeric ranges called *bins* and then tells you the number of observations that fall in each bin. For example, when analyzing student grades, you might want to know the number of students who received grades between 90 and 100, between 80 and 89, between 70 and 79, and so on.

Although you could generate a frequency distribution using Excel's FREQUENCY function (as I describe in Chapter 11), Excel offers an easier and faster method: the Analysis ToolPak's Histogram tool. This tool requires two worksheet ranges: the *input range* of observations and the *bin range,* which is a range of numbers in which each number defines a boundary of the bin. In Figure 12-11, for example, the grades in column C (C3:C48) are the input range, and the numbers in column E (E3:E8) are the bin range. In this case, there are six bins: 0–50, 51–60, 61–70, 71–80, 81–90, and 91–100.

	A	B	C	D	E	F	G
1		Student Grades					
2		Student ID	Grade		Bin		
3		64947	82		50		
4		69630	66		60		
5		18324	52		70		
6		89826	94		80		
7		63600	40		90		
8		25089	62		100		
9		89923	88				
10		13000	75				
11		16895	67				
12		24918	62				
13		45107	71				
14		64090	53				
15		94395	74				
16		58749	65				
17		26916	66				
18		59033	67				
19		15450	68				
20		56415	69				
21		88069	69				
22		75784	68				
23		51262	71				
24		96452	72				
25		87415	75				
26		56961	58				
27		19102	65				

< > ··· **Frequency Distribution** F-Test for Variances

FIGURE 12-11: A worksheet with student grades and a bin range for the distribution.

REMEMBER

Why is it called the Histogram tool and not, say, the Frequency Distribution tool? No idea. However, I can tell you that a *histogram* is a chart of a frequency distribution and, as I show in the steps that follow, the Histogram tool does offer an option for including a chart in the output.

Here are the steps to follow to create a frequency distribution using the Histogram tool:

1. Choose Data ⇨ Data Analysis.

Excel displays the Data Analysis dialog box.

2. In the Analysis Tools list, select Histogram and then click OK.

The Histogram dialog box appears.

3. In the Input Range box, specify the range of cells you want to analyze.

4. In the Bin Range box, specify the range of cells that contain your bins.

If your input and bin ranges have labels, select the Labels check box.

5. In the Output Range box, enter (or click the upper-left corner of) the range where you want the results to appear.

Alternatively, you can select New Worksheet Ply to add the frequency distribution to a new worksheet or select New Workbook to create a new file for the output.

6. (Optional) Customize the histogram.

Select the Pareto (Sorted Histogram) check box to have Excel sort the bins in descending order.

Select the Cumulative Percentage check box to have Excel add a Cumulative % column to the output. This column adds the bin percentages as it moves down the bins.

Select the Chart Output check box to have Excel include a histogram chart with the frequency distribution. If you selected the Cumulative Percentage check box, Excel also includes in the histogram a line showing the cumulative percentages.

Figure 12-12 shows a ready-to-roll version of the Histogram dialog box.

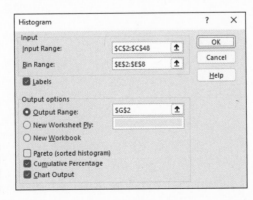

FIGURE 12-12:
The Histogram dialog box, all dressed up.

7. Click OK.

Excel calculates the frequency distribution and then displays the bin frequencies in the location you specified in Step 5, as shown in Figure 12-13. In this case, the bin values are repeated in column G, the frequencies appear in column H, and (because I selected the Cumulative Percentage check box in Figure 12-12) the cumulative percentages in column I. Figure 12-13 also shows an example histogram (because I selected the Chart Output check box in Figure 12-12).

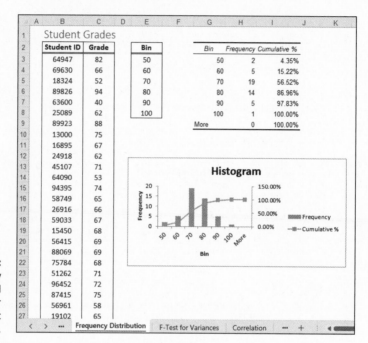

FIGURE 12-13: A frequency distribution and histogram for some student grades.

Chapter **13**

Analyzing Data Using Inferential Statistics

In this chapter, I talk about some of the more sophisticated tools provided by the Excel Analysis ToolPak add-in: Sampling, t-Test, z-Test, Scatter Plot, Regression, Correlation, ANOVA, and f-Test. With these tools, you can perform inferential statistics, which you use to first look at a set of sample observations drawn from a population and then draw conclusions — that is, make inferences — about the population's characteristics. (To read about the simpler descriptive statistical tools that Excel supplies in the Analysis ToolPak add-in, skip back to Chapter 12. You should jump back to Chapter 12 also to learn how to install the Analysis ToolPak add-in, if you haven't done so already.)

It's worth pointing out right off the top that to use these tools, you need to have a decent background in statistics. I'm talking a good basic statistics course in college or graduate school, and perhaps even a follow-up course. Armed with this reasonable knowledge of statistics and a bit of patience, you can use all these tools to good advantage.

Sampling Data

With the Sampling tool that's part of the Analysis ToolPak, you can select items from a data set either randomly or regularly, with *regular* meaning that you select every *n*th item. Why would you want to do such a thing? The most common reason is that your full data set (the population) is huge, so analyzing it would take too much time and use up too many computing resources. So instead, you extract a sample and then use this chapter's inferential statistical techniques on the sample to draw conclusions about the population.

For example, suppose that as part of an internal audit, you want to randomly select 20 orders from a table of invoices. Why, that's a perfect task for the Sampling tool! As an example, I use the table of invoices shown in Figure 13-1.

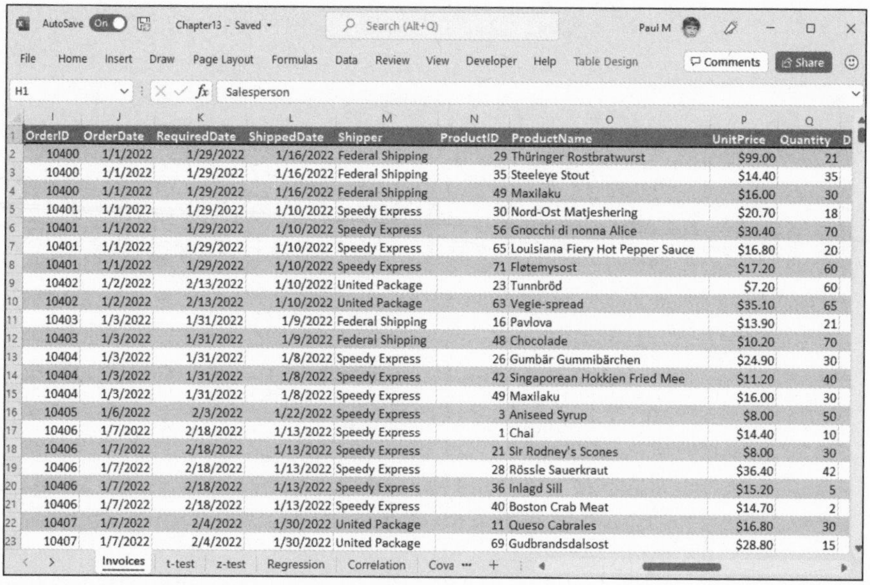

OrderID	OrderDate	RequiredDate	ShippedDate	Shipper	ProductID	ProductName	UnitPrice	Quantity
10400	1/1/2022	1/29/2022	1/16/2022	Federal Shipping	29	Thüringer Rostbratwurst	$99.00	21
10400	1/1/2022	1/29/2022	1/16/2022	Federal Shipping	35	Steeleye Stout	$14.40	35
10400	1/1/2022	1/29/2022	1/16/2022	Federal Shipping	49	Maxilaku	$16.00	30
10401	1/1/2022	1/29/2022	1/10/2022	Speedy Express	30	Nord-Ost Matjeshering	$20.70	18
10401	1/1/2022	1/29/2022	1/10/2022	Speedy Express	56	Gnocchi di nonna Alice	$30.40	70
10401	1/1/2022	1/29/2022	1/10/2022	Speedy Express	65	Louisiana Fiery Hot Pepper Sauce	$16.80	20
10401	1/1/2022	1/29/2022	1/10/2022	Speedy Express	71	Fløtemysost	$17.20	60
10402	1/2/2022	2/13/2022	1/10/2022	United Package	23	Tunnbröd	$7.20	60
10402	1/2/2022	2/13/2022	1/10/2022	United Package	63	Vegie-spread	$35.10	65
10403	1/3/2022	1/31/2022	1/9/2022	Federal Shipping	16	Pavlova	$13.90	21
10403	1/3/2022	1/31/2022	1/9/2022	Federal Shipping	48	Chocolade	$10.20	70
10404	1/3/2022	1/31/2022	1/8/2022	Speedy Express	26	Gumbär Gummibärchen	$24.90	30
10404	1/3/2022	1/31/2022	1/8/2022	Speedy Express	42	Singaporean Hokkien Fried Mee	$11.20	40
10404	1/3/2022	1/31/2022	1/8/2022	Speedy Express	49	Maxilaku	$16.00	30
10405	1/6/2022	2/3/2022	1/22/2022	Speedy Express	3	Aniseed Syrup	$8.00	50
10406	1/7/2022	2/18/2022	1/13/2022	Speedy Express	1	Chai	$14.40	10
10406	1/7/2022	2/18/2022	1/13/2022	Speedy Express	21	Sir Rodney's Scones	$8.00	30
10406	1/7/2022	2/18/2022	1/13/2022	Speedy Express	28	Rössle Sauerkraut	$36.40	42
10406	1/7/2022	2/18/2022	1/13/2022	Speedy Express	36	Inlagd Sill	$15.20	5
10406	1/7/2022	2/18/2022	1/13/2022	Speedy Express	40	Boston Crab Meat	$14.70	2
10407	1/7/2022	2/4/2022	1/30/2022	United Package	11	Queso Cabrales	$16.80	30
10407	1/7/2022	2/4/2022	1/30/2022	United Package	69	Gudbrandsdalsost	$28.80	15

FIGURE 13-1: A table of invoice data from which you might select a sample.

To sample items from a worksheet like the one shown in Figure 13-1, take the following steps:

1. **Choose Data ➪ Data Analysis.**

   The Data Analysis dialog box appears.

2. **In the Analysis Tools list, select Sampling and then click OK.**

   The Sampling dialog box appears.

3. **In the Input Range box, specify the range of cells from which you want to extract your sample.**

The range you select must contain only numeric values. If your data range has a label, select the Labels check box.

4. **Choose a sampling method.**

Excel provides two sampling methods for extracting items in your data set:

- **Periodic:** Extracts every *n*th item from the data set, such as every fifth item or every tenth item. To use this method, select the Periodic radio button and then enter the period you want to use in the Period text box.

- **Random:** Extracts items randomly from the data set. To use this method, select the Random radio button and then enter the number of items that you want to extract in the Number of Samples text box.

5. **To specify a location for the output data, select the Output Range radio button and then type (or click the upper-left corner of) the output range.**

Alternatively, you can select New Worksheet Ply to plop the sample in a new worksheet or select New Workbook to create a new file for the results.

Figure 13-2 shows a completed version of the Sampling dialog box. In this case, I ask for a random sample of 20 items from Q2:Q1060, which is the Quantity column in the Invoices table, to be output to a new worksheet.

6. **Click OK.**

Excel extracts the sample and displays it in the location you specified in Step 5. Figure 13-3 shows an example.

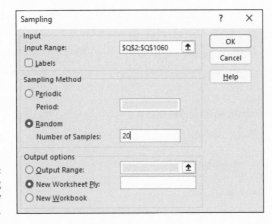

FIGURE 13-2:
The Sampling dialog box, ready to sample.

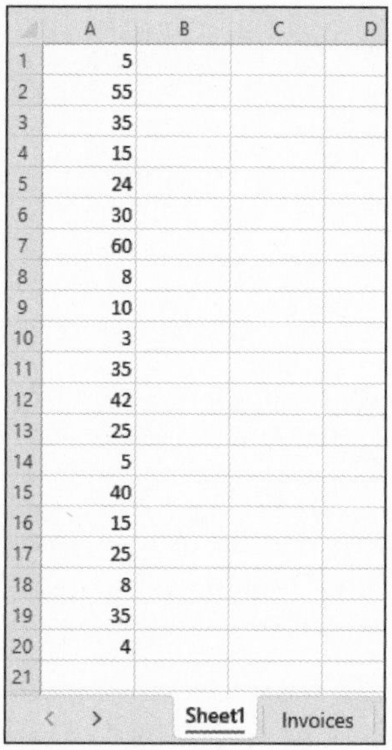

	A	B	C	D
1	5			
2	55			
3	35			
4	15			
5	24			
6	30			
7	60			
8	8			
9	10			
10	3			
11	35			
12	42			
13	25			
14	5			
15	40			
16	15			
17	25			
18	8			
19	35			
20	4			
21				

FIGURE 13-3: The sample extracted by the Sampling tool.

Using the t-Test Tools

The Excel Analysis ToolPak add-in provides three tools for working with t-values and t-tests, which can be useful when you want to make inferences about very small data sets:

- t-Test: Paired Two Sample for Means
- t-Test: Two-Sample Assuming Equal Variances
- t-Test: Two-Sample Assuming Unequal Variances

Briefly, here's how these three tools work. For the sake of illustration, assume that you're working with the values shown in Figure 13-4. The worksheet range A1:A21 contains the first set of values. The worksheet range B1:B21 contains the second set of values.

To perform a t-test calculation, follow these steps:

1. **Choose Data ➪ Data Analysis.**

   The Data Analysis dialog box appears.

	A	B	C
1	Sample 1	Sample 2	
2	0.390639	0.597253	
3	0.960314	0.247645	
4	0.002978	0.76919	
5	0.073425	0.83317	
6	0.311795	0.450877	
7	0.451693	0.08733	
8	0.989853	0.247164	
9	0.946743	0.036413	
10	0.88257	0.591507	
11	0.846565	0.475535	
12	0.817594	0.06112	
13	0.933039	0.703724	
14	0.013688	0.003346	
15	0.08753	0.887344	
16	0.017276	0.11998	
17	0.642356	0.393307	
18	0.782696	0.070239	
19	0.391383	0.837355	
20	0.142597	0.707126	
21	0.241643	0.757264	
22			

< > ... t-test z-test

FIGURE 13-4: Some sample data you can use to perform t-test calculations.

2. **In the Analysis Tools list, select the t-Test tool you want to use and then click OK.**

   - **t-Test: Paired Two Sample for Means:** Choose this tool when you want to perform a paired two-sample t-test.
   - **t-Test: Two-Sample Assuming Equal Variances:** Choose this tool when you want to perform a two-sample test and you have reason to assume that the variances of both samples equal each other.
   - **t-Test: Two-Sample Assuming Unequal Variances:** Choose this tool when you want to perform a two-sample test, but you assume that the two sample variances are unequal.

   Excel displays the corresponding t-test dialog box. Figure 13-5 shows the t-Test: Two-Sample Assuming Equal Variances dialog box. The other t-test dialog boxes are similar.

3. **In the Variable 1 Range and Variable 2 Range input text boxes, identify the sample values by telling Excel in what worksheet ranges you've stored the two samples.**

   Enter a range address in these text boxes, or click in the text box and then select a range by clicking and dragging. If the first cell in the variable range holds a label and you want to include the label in your range selection, select the Labels check box.

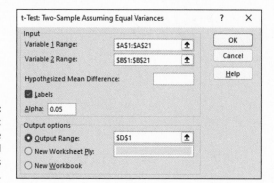

FIGURE 13-5:
The t-Test:
Two-Sample
Assuming Equal
Variances
dialog box.

4. **Use the Hypothesized Mean Difference text box to indicate whether you hypothesize that the means are equal.**

   If you think that the means of the samples are equal, either enter **0** (zero) in this text box or leave the text box empty. If you hypothesize that the means are not equal, enter the mean difference.

5. **In the Alpha text box, state the confidence level for your t-test calculation.**

   The confidence level is between 0 and 1. By default, the confidence level is equal to 0.05, which is equivalent to a 5-percent confidence level.

6. **In the Output Options section, indicate where the t-Test tool results should be stored.**

   Select one of the radio buttons and enter information in the text boxes to specify where Excel should place the results of the t-test analysis. For example, to place the t-test results into a range in an existing worksheet, select the Output Range radio button and then identify the range address in the Output Range text box. If you want to place the t-test results someplace else, select one of the other radio buttons.

7. **Click OK.**

   Excel calculates the t-test results. Figure 13-6 shows the t-test results for a Two-Sample Assuming Equal Variances test. The t-test results show the mean for each of the data sets, the variance, the number of observations, the pooled variance value, the hypothesized mean difference, the degrees of freedom (abbreviated as *df*), the t-value (or t-stat), and the probability values for one-tail and two-tail tests.

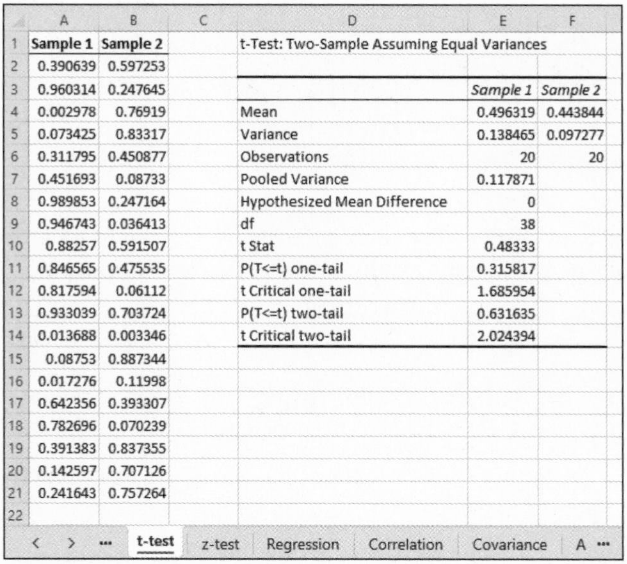

	A	B	C	D	E	F
1	Sample 1	Sample 2		t-Test: Two-Sample Assuming Equal Variances		
2	0.390639	0.597253				
3	0.960314	0.247645			Sample 1	Sample 2
4	0.002978	0.76919		Mean	0.496319	0.443844
5	0.073425	0.83317		Variance	0.138465	0.097277
6	0.311795	0.450877		Observations	20	20
7	0.451693	0.08733		Pooled Variance	0.117871	
8	0.989853	0.247164		Hypothesized Mean Difference	0	
9	0.946743	0.036413		df	38	
10	0.88257	0.591507		t Stat	0.48333	
11	0.846565	0.475535		P(T<=t) one-tail	0.315817	
12	0.817594	0.06112		t Critical one-tail	1.685954	
13	0.933039	0.703724		P(T<=t) two-tail	0.631635	
14	0.013688	0.003346		t Critical two-tail	2.024394	
15	0.08753	0.887344				
16	0.017276	0.11998				
17	0.642356	0.393307				
18	0.782696	0.070239				
19	0.391383	0.837355				
20	0.142597	0.707126				
21	0.241643	0.757264				
22						

⟨ ⟩ ⋯ **t-test** z-test Regression Correlation Covariance A ⋯

FIGURE 13-6:
The results of
a t-test.

Performing a z-Test

If you know the variance or standard deviation of the underlying population, you can calculate z-test values by using the Analysis ToolPak's z-Test: Two Sample for Means tool. You might typically work with z-test values to calculate confidence levels and confidence intervals for normally distributed data. To perform a z-test, take these steps:

1. Choose Data ⇨ Data Analysis.

The Data Analysis dialog box appears.

2. In the Analysis Tools list, select the z-Test: Two Sample for Means tool and then click OK.

Excel displays the z-Test: Two Sample for Means dialog box.

3. In the Variable 1 Range and Variable 2 Range text boxes, identify the sample values by telling Excel in what worksheet ranges you've stored the two samples.

Enter a range address in the text boxes, or click in the text box and then select a range by clicking and dragging. If the first cell in the variable range holds a label and you want to include the label in your range selection, select the Labels check box.

4. **Use the Hypothesized Mean Difference text box to indicate whether you hypothesize that the means are equal.**

   If you think that the means of the samples are equal, enter **0** (zero) into this text box or leave the text box empty. If you hypothesize that the means are not equal, enter the difference.

5. **In the Variable 1 Variance (Known) and Variable 2 Variance (Known) text boxes, provide the population variance for the first and second samples.**

6. **In the Alpha text box, state the confidence level for your z-test calculation.**

   The confidence level is between 0 and 1. By default, the confidence level equals 0.05 (equivalent to a 5-percent confidence level).

7. **In the Output Options section, indicate where the z-Test tool results should be stored.**

   To place the z-test results into a range in an existing worksheet, select the Output Range radio button and then identify the range address in the Output Range text box. If you want to place the z-test results someplace else, use one of the other radio buttons.

   Figure 13-7 shows a completed version of the dialog box (using the same sample data shown previously in Figure 13-4).

8. **Click OK.**

   Excel calculates the z-test results. Figure 13-8 shows the z-test results for a Two Sample for Means test. The z-test results show the mean for each of the data sets, the variance, the number of observations, the hypothesized mean difference, the z-value, and the probability values for one-tail and two-tail tests.

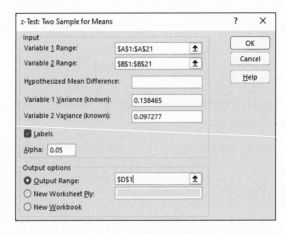

FIGURE 13-7:
The z-Test: Two Sample for Means dialog box.

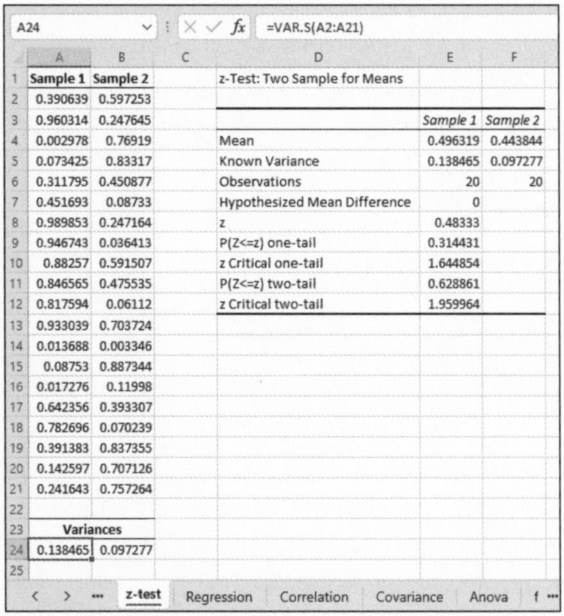

Cell reference box: `A24` | `fx` | `=VAR.S(A2:A21)`

	A	B	C	D	E	F
1	Sample 1	Sample 2		z-Test: Two Sample for Means		
2	0.390639	0.597253				
3	0.960314	0.247645			Sample 1	Sample 2
4	0.002978	0.76919		Mean	0.496319	0.443844
5	0.073425	0.83317		Known Variance	0.138465	0.097277
6	0.311795	0.450877		Observations	20	20
7	0.451693	0.08733		Hypothesized Mean Difference	0	
8	0.989853	0.247164		z	0.48333	
9	0.946743	0.036413		P(Z<=z) one-tail	0.314431	
10	0.88257	0.591507		z Critical one-tail	1.644854	
11	0.846565	0.475535		P(Z<=z) two-tail	0.628861	
12	0.817594	0.06112		z Critical two-tail	1.959964	
13	0.933039	0.703724				
14	0.013688	0.003346				
15	0.08753	0.887344				
16	0.017276	0.11998				
17	0.642356	0.393307				
18	0.782696	0.070239				
19	0.391383	0.837355				
20	0.142597	0.707126				
21	0.241643	0.757264				
22						
23	Variances					
24	0.138465	0.097277				
25						

Sheet tabs: z-test | Regression | Correlation | Covariance | Anova | f

FIGURE 13-8:
The z-test calculation results.

Determining the Regression

In Chapter 10, I talk about adding trend lines to scatter charts to help you visualize the overall trend of your data. You can move beyond the visual regression analysis that the scatter plot technique provides by using the Analysis ToolPak's Regression tool. For example, say that you used the scatter plotting technique, as I describe earlier, to begin looking at a simple data set. And, after that initial examination, suppose that you want to look more closely at the data by using full-blown, take-no-prisoners regression. To perform regression analysis by using the Regression tool, do the following:

1. Choose Data ⇨ Data Analysis.

The Data Analysis dialog box appears.

2. In the Analysis Tools list, select the Regression tool and then click OK.

Excel displays the Regression dialog box.

3. Identify your Y and X values.

In the Input Y Range text box, identify the worksheet range holding your dependent variables. Then in the Input X Range text box, identify the worksheet range reference holding your independent variables.

If your input ranges include labels, select the Labels check box.

4. (Optional) Set the constant to zero.

If the regression line should start at zero — in other words, if the dependent value should equal zero when the independent value equals zero — select the Constant Is Zero check box.

5. (Optional) Calculate a confidence level in your regression analysis.

To do this, select the Confidence Level check box and then (in the Confidence Level text box) enter the confidence level you want to use.

6. Select a location for the regression analysis results.

Use the Output Options radio buttons and text boxes to specify where Excel should place the results of the regression analysis. To place the regression results into a range in an existing worksheet, for example, select the Output Range radio button and then identify the range address in the Output Range text box. To place the regression results someplace else, select one of the other radio buttons.

7. Identify what data you want returned.

In the Residuals area, select check boxes to specify what residuals results you want returned as part of the regression analysis.

Similarly, select the Normal Probability Plots check box to add normal probability information to the regression analysis results.

Figure 13-9 shows a completed version of the dialog box.

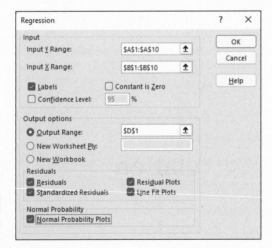

FIGURE 13-9:
The completed Regression dialog box.

8. **Click OK.**

Figure 13-10 shows a portion of the regression analysis results including three stacked visual data plots. A range supplies some basic regression statistics, including the R-square value, the standard error, and the number of observations. Below that information, the Regression tool supplies *analysis of variance* (or ANOVA) data, including information about the degrees of freedom, sum-of-squares value, mean square value, the f-value, and the significance of F. Beneath the ANOVA information, the Regression tool supplies information about the regression line calculated from the data, including the coefficient, standard error, t-stat, and probability values for the intercept — as well as the same information for the independent variable, which is the number of ads in the example I discuss here. Excel also plots some of the regression data using simple scatter charts. In Figure 13-10, for example, Excel plots residuals, predicted dependent values, and probabilities.

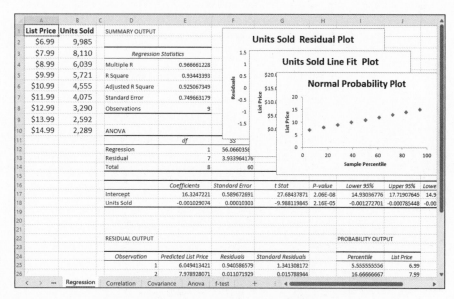

FIGURE 13-10:
The regression analysis results.

Calculating the Correlation

The Correlation analysis tool (which is available also through the Analysis Tool-Pak) quantifies the relationship between two sets of data. You might use this tool to explore such things as the effect of advertising on sales, for example. To use the Correlation analysis tool, follow these steps:

1. **Choose Data ➪ Data Analysis.**

The Data Analysis dialog box appears.

2. **In the Analysis Tools list, select the Correlation tool and then click OK.**

Excel displays the Correlation dialog box.

3. **Identify the range of X and Y values that you want to analyze.**

In the Input Range box, identify the worksheet range holding your data.

Excel assumes that your data is in columns, so it automatically selects the Columns radio button in the Grouped By section. If your data is in rows, select the Rows radio button instead. If the input range includes labels in the first row (or first column), select the Labels in First Row (or Labels in First Column) check box.

4. **Select an output location.**

In the Output Options radio buttons and text boxes, specify where Excel should place the results of the correlation analysis. To place the correlation results into a range in an existing worksheet, select the Output Range radio button and then identify the range address in the Output Range text box. To place the correlation results someplace else, select one of the other radio buttons.

Figure 13-11 shows a completed version of the dialog box.

5. **Click OK.**

Excel calculates the correlation coefficient for the data that you identified and places it in the specified location. Figure 13-12 shows the correlation results for list price versus units sold. The key value is shown in cell E3. The value –0.96666 suggests that a strong negative correlation exists between list price and units sold. That is, as the list price goes up, the unit sales go down.

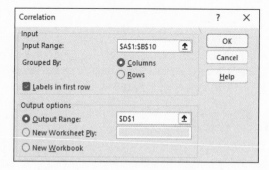

FIGURE 13-11:
The completed
Correlation
dialog box.

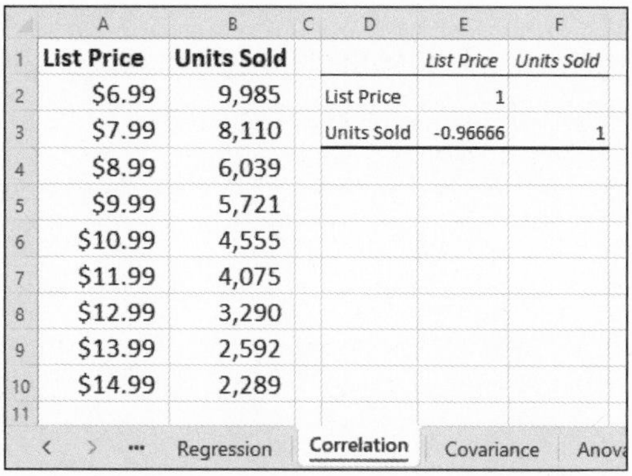

	A	B	C	D	E	F
1	**List Price**	**Units Sold**			*List Price*	*Units Sold*
2	$6.99	9,985		List Price	1	
3	$7.99	8,110		Units Sold	-0.96666	1
4	$8.99	6,039				
5	$9.99	5,721				
6	$10.99	4,555				
7	$11.99	4,075				
8	$12.99	3,290				
9	$13.99	2,592				
10	$14.99	2,289				
11						

< > ... Regression **Correlation** Covariance Anova

FIGURE 13-12: The worksheet showing the correlation results for the list price and units sold data.

Calculating the Covariance

The Covariance tool, available also through the Analysis ToolPak add-in, quantifies the relationship between two sets of values. The Covariance tool calculates the average of the product of deviations of values from the data set means.

To use this tool, follow these steps:

1. **Choose Data ⇨ Data Analysis.**

   The Data Analysis dialog box appears.

2. **In the Analysis Tools list, select the Covariance tool and then click OK.**

   Excel displays the Covariance dialog box.

3. **Identify the range of X and Y values that you want to analyze.**

   In the Input Range box, identify the worksheet range holding your data.

   Excel assumes that your data is in columns, so it automatically selects the Columns radio button in the Grouped By section. If your data is in rows, select the Rows radio button instead. If the input range includes labels in the first row (or first column), select the Labels in First Row (or Labels in First Column) check box.

4. **Select an output location.**

   Use the Output Options radio buttons and text boxes to specify where Excel should place the results of the covariance analysis. To place the results into a range in an existing worksheet, select the Output Range radio button and then identify the range address in the Output Range text box. If you want to place the results someplace else, select one of the other Output Options radio buttons.

   Figure 13-13 shows a completed version of the dialog box.

5. Click OK after you select the output options.

Excel calculates the covariance information for the data that you identified and places it in the specified location. Figure 13-14 shows the covariance results for the list price and units sold data.

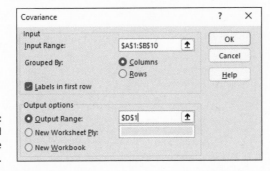

FIGURE 13-13: The completed Covariance dialog box.

	A	B	C	D	E	F
1	**List Price**	**Units Sold**			*List Price*	*Units Sold*
2	$6.99	9,985		List Price	6.666667	
3	$7.99	8,110		Units Sold	-6053.56	5882524
4	$8.99	6,039				
5	$9.99	5,721				
6	$10.99	4,555				
7	$11.99	4,075				
8	$12.99	3,290				
9	$13.99	2,592				
10	$14.99	2,289				
11						

‹ › ··· Regression | Correlation | **Covariance** | Anov

FIGURE 13-14: The worksheet showing the covariance results for the list price and units sold data.

Using the Anova Tools

The Analysis ToolPak add-in also provides three Anova (analysis of variance) tools: Anova: Single Factor, Anova: Two-Factor with Replication, and Anova: Two-Factor without Replication. With the Anova tools, you can compare sets of data by looking at the variance of values in each set.

Here are the steps to follow to use an Anova tool:

1. **Choose Data ⇨ Data Analysis.**

   The Data Analysis dialog box appears.

2. **Use the Analysis Tools list to select the Anova tool you want to work with and then click OK.**

   Excel displays the corresponding Anova dialog box.

3. **Describe the data to be analyzed.**

   In the Input Range box, identify the worksheet range holding your data.

   Excel assumes that your data is in columns, so it automatically selects the Columns radio button in the Grouped By section. If your data is in rows, select the Rows radio button instead. If the input range includes labels in the first row (or first column), select the Labels in First Row (or Labels in First Column) check box.

4. **Specify the location for the Anova results.**

   Use the Output Options buttons and boxes to specify where Excel should place the results of the analysis. If you want to place the results into a range in an existing worksheet, for example, select the Output Range radio button and then identify the range address in the Output Range text box. To place the results someplace else, select one of the other Output Options radio buttons.

   Figure 13-15 shows a completed version of the Anova: Single Factor dialog box.

5. **Click OK.**

   Excel returns the Anova calculation results, as shown in Figure 13-16.

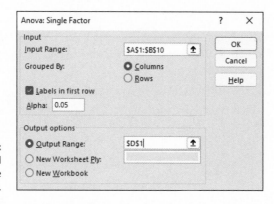

FIGURE 13-15:
The completed Anova: Single Factor dialog box.

	A	B	C	D	E	F	G	H	I	J
1	**List Price**	**Units Sold**		Anova: Single Factor						
2	$6.99	9,985								
3	$7.99	8,110		SUMMARY						
4	$8.99	6,039		*Groups*	*Count*	*Sum*	*Average*	*Variance*		
5	$9.99	5,721		List Price	9	98.91	10.99	7.5		
6	$10.99	4,555		Units Sold	9	46656	5184	6617840		
7	$11.99	4,075								
8	$12.99	3,290								
9	$13.99	2,592		ANOVA						
10	$14.99	2,289		*Source of Variation*	*SS*	*df*	*MS*	*F*	*P-value*	*F crit*
11				Between Groups	1.2E+08	1	1.2E+08	36.39254	1.74E-05	4.493998
12				Within Groups	52942778	16	3308924			
13										
14				Total	1.73E+08	17				
15										

| ‹ › ⋯ | Regression | Correlation | Covariance | **Anova** | f-test | + |

FIGURE 13-16:
The worksheet showing the Anova results for the list price and units sold data.

Performing an f-Test

The Excel Analysis ToolPak add-in also provides a tool for calculating two-sample f-test calculations. An f-test analysis enables you to compare variances from two populations.

Here are the steps to follow to use the f-Test tool:

1. Choose Data ⇨ Data Analysis.

The Data Analysis dialog box appears.

2. In the Analysis Tools list, select the F-Test Two-Sample for Variances tool and then click OK.

Excel displays the F-Test Two-Sample for Variances dialog box.

3. In the Variable 1 Range and Variable 2 Range input text boxes, identify the sample values by telling Excel in what worksheet ranges you've stored the two samples.

Enter a range address into these text boxes, or click in the text box and then select a range by clicking and dragging. If the first cell in the variable range holds a label and you want to include the label in your range selection, select the Labels check box.

4. In the Alpha text box, state the confidence level for your t-test calculation.

The confidence level is between 0 and 1. By default, the confidence level is equal to 0.05, which is equivalent to a 5-percent confidence level.

5. Describe the location for the f-test results.

Use the Output Options buttons and boxes to specify where Excel should place the results of the f-test analysis. If you want to place the results into a range in an existing worksheet, for example, select the Output Range radio button and then identify the range address in the Output Range text box. To place the results someplace else, select one of the other Output Options radio buttons.

Figure 13-17 shows a completed version of the F-Test Two-Sample for Variances dialog box.

6. Click OK.

Excel returns the f-test calculation results, as shown in Figure 13-18.

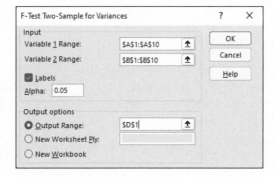

FIGURE 13-17: The completed F-Test Two-Sample for Variances dialog box.

FIGURE 13-18: The worksheet showing the F-Test Two-Sample for Variances results for the list price and units sold data.

	A	B	C	D	E	F
1	**List Price**	**Units Sold**		F-Test Two-Sample for Variances		
2	$6.99	9,985				
3	$7.99	8,110			*List Price*	*Units Sold*
4	$8.99	6,039		Mean	10.99	5184
5	$9.99	5,721		Variance	7.5	6617840
6	$10.99	4,555		Observations	9	9
7	$11.99	4,075		df	8	8
8	$12.99	3,290		F	1.13E-06	
9	$13.99	2,592		P(F<=f) one-tail	0	
10	$14.99	2,289		F Critical one-tail	0.290858	
11						

< > ⋯ Regression Correlation Covariance Anova **f-test**

An f-test analysis tests to see whether two population variances equal each other. Essentially, the analysis compares the ratio of two variances. The assumption is that if variances are equal, the ratio of the variances should equal 1.

4

The Part of Tens

IN THIS PART . . .

Buff up your basic statistics skills so that you can more easily and comfortably do data analysis with Excel.

Learn how to analyze financial data over, under, sideways, and down.

Get secrets for building better, more powerful PivotTables.

Chapter **14**

Ten Things You Ought to Know about Statistics

A big part of the "analysis" portion of "data analysis" involves things like counting, averaging, adding, and standard deviation-ing the data. In a word, much of data analysis involves statistics. Here's the thing about statistics, though: After you get beyond the basics, it's a subject that gets complicated in a hurry. Fortunately, you can leap gazelle-like over many of these early statistics hurdles by learning a few basics, and that's what this chapter is all about.

And when I say "basics," I mean *basics.* In the paragraphs that follow, you won't see any mention of statistical esoterica such as chi-squared distributions and Fourier analysis. There are no Greek letters in this chapter.

If you've never been exposed to statistics in school or a decade or two have passed since you were, you should find some useful background here to help you use some of the statistical tools that Excel provides.

Descriptive Statistics Are Straightforward

The first thing that you ought to know about statistics is that some statistical analysis and some statistical measures are pretty darn straightforward. Descriptive statistics, which include things such as the PivotTable cross-tabulations (presented in Chapters 6 through 8), as well as some of the statistical functions, make sense even to those of us who don't have a PhD in math.

For example, if you sum a set of values, you get a sum. Pretty easy, right? And finding the biggest value or the smallest value in a set of numbers is straightforward, too.

I mention this point about descriptive statistics because people often freak out when they hear the word *statistics.* That's too bad, because many of the most useful statistical tools available to you are simple, easy-to-understand descriptive statistics.

Averages Aren't So Simple Sometimes

Here's a weird thing that you might remember if you ever took a statistics class. When someone uses the term *average,* what the person usually refers to is the most common average measurement, which is a *mean.* But you should know that several other commonly accepted average measurements exist, including mode, median, and some special mean measurements such as the geometric mean and harmonic mean.

I want to quickly cover some of these, not because you need to know all this stuff, but because understanding that the term *average* is imprecise makes some of the discussions in this book and much of Excel's statistical functionality more comprehensible.

To make this discussion more concrete, assume that you're looking at a small set of values: 1, 2, 3, 4, 5. The mean in this small set of values is 3, which you calculate by adding all the numbers in the set (1+2+3+4+5) and then dividing this sum (15) by the total number of values in the set (5).

Two other common average measurements are mode and median. I start with the discussion of the median measurement because it's readily understood using the data set that I introduce in the preceding paragraph. In a sorted data set, the *median* is the middle value in the sense that there are the same number of values equal to or larger than the median as there are values equal to or smaller than the median. In the data set 1, 2, 3, 4, 5, the median is 3. Why? Because this data set has two larger values (4 and 5) and two smaller values (1 and 2). In a slightly trickier example, in the data set 1, 1, 3, 3, 3, 3, 5, the second 3 is the median because it has three equal or larger values and three equal or smaller values.

TIP

When you have an even number of values in your data set, you calculate the median by averaging the two middle values. For example, the data set 1, 2, 3, and 4 has no middle value. Add the two middle values — 2 and 3 — and then divide by 2. This calculation produces a median value of 2.5. With the median value of 2.5, half the values in the data set are equal to or larger than the median value, and half the values in the data set are equal to or smaller the median value.

The mode measurement is a third common average. The *mode* is the value that appears most often in the data set. For example, consider the data set 1, 2, 2, 2, 3, 5, 5. The values 1 and 3 occur only once, the value 5 occurs twice, but the value 2 occurs three times. That means 2 appears the most often, so the mode of this data set is 2. Note that it's possible for a data set to have no mode if all the values are unique.

REMEMBER

As I mentioned, other common statistical measures of the average exist. The mean measurement that I refer to earlier in this discussion is actually an arithmetic mean because the values in the data set get added together arithmetically as part of the calculation. You can, however, combine the values in other ways. Financial analysts and scientists sometimes use a geometric mean, for example. There's also something called a harmonic mean.

You don't need to know about (much less understand) these other average measurements, but you should remember that using the term *average* by itself is imprecise because there are so many ways to calculate an average. Make sure that people know what type of average you're using. What if someone else uses the term *average* without specifying the type? That person is probably referring to the *mean,* but you can't be certain, and a lack of certainty is dangerous when you're talking statistics.

Standard Deviations Describe Dispersion

Statistical reports usually include some vague or scary reference to either the standard deviation or its close relative, the variance. Although the formula for standard deviation is terrifying to look at — at least if you're not comfortable with the Greek alphabet — intuitively, the formula and the logic are straightforward to understand.

A *standard deviation* describes how values in a data set are dispersed around the mean. In general, if a data set has a low standard deviation, it means the values are clustered close to the mean; if the data has a high standard deviation, it means the values are spread out away from the mean.

For example, a bit later in this chapter I talk about the normal distribution, which is an arrangement of the items in a data set that, if charted (see Figure 14-1), would produce the classic bell curve: low at the beginning for the smallest values, curving up to a peak at the mean value, curving down from the mean, and then low again for the largest values. Figure 14-1 shows a graph of a standard normal distribution, which uses a mean of 0 and a standard deviation of 1. In the standard normal distribution, the values shown along the horizontal axis are the standard deviations.

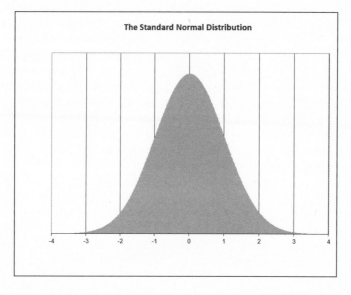

The Standard Normal Distribution

FIGURE 14-1:
A standard
normal
distribution.

That's all annoyingly vague, but you can use standard deviation to make things much more precise. That's because the standard deviation tells you something about how the items are clustered in the normal distribution (refer to Figure 14-1):

>> 68 percent of the values in the data set lie within plus or minus one standard deviation of the mean. For example, if the mean is 50 and the standard deviation is 10, then 68 percent of the values lie between 40 and 60.

>> 95 percent of the values in the data set lie within plus or minus two standard deviations of the mean. For a mean of 50 and a standard deviation of 10, 95 percent of the values lie between 30 and 70.

>> 99.7 percent of the values in the data set lie within plus or minus three standard deviations of the mean. For a mean of 50 and a standard deviation of 10, 99.7 percent of the values lie between 20 and 80.

An Observation Is an Observation

Observation is one of the terms that you'll encounter if you read anything about statistics in this book or in the Excel online Help. An observation is just an observation. That sounds circular but bear with me. Suppose that you're constructing a data set that shows daily high temperatures in your neighborhood. When you go out and observe that the temperature some fine July afternoon is 87° F, that measurement (87°) is your first observation. If you go out and observe that the high temperature the next day is 88° F, that measurement is your second observation.

Another way to define the term observation is like this: Whenever you assign a value to one of your random variables, you create an observation. For example, if you're building a data set of daily high temperatures in your neighborhood, every time that you assign a new temperature value (87° one day, 88° the next day, and so on), you're creating an observation.

A Sample Is a Subset of Values

A *sample* is a collection of observations from a population. For example, if you create a data set that records the daily high temperature in your neighborhood, your little collection of observations is a sample.

However, a sample is not a population. A *population* includes all the possible observations. In the case of collecting your neighborhood's high temperatures, the population would be the daily high temperatures for all the neighborhoods in your town.

Inferential Statistics Are Cool But Complicated

As I note earlier in this chapter, some statistics are readily understood. For example, calculating the largest value in a set of numbers is most definitely a statistical measurement, but there's no mystery behind what you're doing. Determining the largest value in a data set is an example of descriptive statistics, and for the most part, we mere mathematical mortals can wrap our heads around such statistics.

The same can't be said for the second main branch of statistics: *inferential statistics.* Inferential statistics are based on a useful but not intuitively obvious idea. If you look at a sample of values from a population and the sample is representative and large enough, you can draw conclusions about the entire population based on characteristics of the sample.

For example, for every presidential election in the United States, the major television networks (usually contrary to their earlier promises) predict the winner after only a relatively small number of votes have been calculated or counted. How do they do this? Well, they sample the population. Specifically, they stand outside polling places and ask exiting voters how they voted. If you ask a large sample of voters whether they voted for one guy or the other guy, you can make an inference about how all the voters voted. And then you can predict who has won the election.

Inferential statistics, although very powerful, possess two qualities that I need to mention:

>> **Accuracy issues:** When you make a statistical inference, you can never be 100 percent sure that your inference is correct. The possibility always exists that your sample isn't representative or that your sample doesn't return enough precision to estimate the population value.

This is partly what happened with the 2000 presidential election in the United States. Initially, some of the major news networks predicted that Al Gore had won based on exit polls. Then based on other exit polls, they predicted that George W. Bush had won. Then, perhaps finally realizing that maybe their statistics weren't good enough given the closeness of the race, or perhaps just based on their own embarrassment about bobbling the ball, they stopped predicting the race. In retrospect, their trouble with calling the race wasn't surprising because the number of votes for the two candidates was *extremely* close.

>> **Steep learning curve:** Inferential statistics quickly gets complicated. When you work with inferential statistics, you immediately start encountering terms such as *probability distribution functions,* all sorts of crazy (in some cases) parameters, and lots of Greek symbols.

WARNING

As a practical matter, if you haven't at least taken a statistics class — and probably more than one statistics class — you'll find it very hard to move into inferential statistics in a big way. You probably can, with a single statistics class and perhaps the information in this book, work with inferential statistics based on normal distributions and uniform distributions. However, working with inferential statistics and applying those inferential statistics to other probability distributions becomes very tricky. At least, that's my observation.

Probability Distributions Aren't Always Confusing

One of the statistical terms that you'll encounter a little bit in this book — and a whole bunch if you dig into the Excel Help file — is *probability distribution*. This phrase sounds tricky, and in some cases, maybe it is. But you can understand intuitively what a probability distribution is with a couple of useful examples.

One common distribution that you hear about in statistics classes, for example, is a T distribution. A *T distribution* is essentially a normal distribution except with heavier, fatter tails. There are also distributions that are skewed (have the hump tilted) one way or the other. Each of these probability distributions, however, has a probability distribution function that describes the probability distribution chart.

In the next two sections, I look at two probability distributions: uniform distribution and normal distribution.

Uniform distribution

One common probability distribution function is a uniform distribution. In a *uniform distribution*, every event has the same probability of occurrence. As a simple example, suppose that you roll a six-sided die. Assuming that the die is fair, you have an equal chance of rolling any of the values: 1, 2, 3, 4, 5, or 6. If you roll the die 60,000 times, what you would expect to see (given the large number of observations) is that you'll probably roll a 1 about 10,000 times. Similarly, you'll probably also roll a 2, 3, 4, 5, or 6 about 10,000 times each. Oh sure, you can count on some variance between what you expect (10,000 occurrences of each side of the six-sided die) and what you experience. But your actual observations would be close to your expectations.

The unique thing about this distribution is that everything is level. You could say that the probability or the chance of rolling any one of the six sides of the die is even, or *uniform*. This is how uniform distribution gets its name. Every event has the same probability of occurrence. Figure 14-2 shows a uniform distribution that I generated by simulating 60,000 dice rolls. (How did I simulate those rolls? By entering the formula =RANDBETWEEN(1,6) and then filling that formula into 60,000 cells.) As you can see, the uniform distribution is essentially a horizontal line.

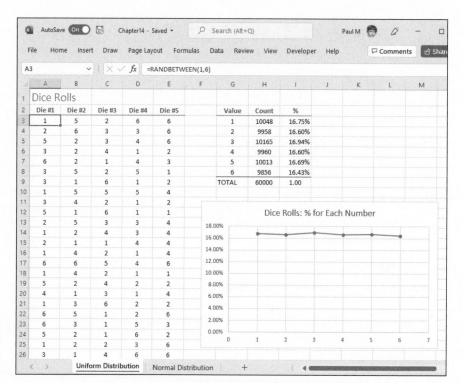

FIGURE 14-2:
A uniform
distribution
generated by
60,000 dice rolls.

Normal distribution

Another common type of probability distribution is the *normal distribution,* also
known as a *bell curve* or a *Gaussian distribution.* A normal distribution occurs natu-
rally in many situations. For example, intelligence quotients (IQs) are distributed
normally. If you take a large set of people, test their IQs, and then plot those IQs
on a chart, you get a normal distribution.

One characteristic of a normal distribution is that most of the values in the population are centered around the mean. Another characteristic of a normal distribution is that the mean, the mode, and the median all equal each other. Figure 14-1
shows a normal distribution.

Do you kind of see now where this probability distribution business is going? A
probability distribution just describes a chart that, in essence, plots probabilities.

REMEMBER

A probability distribution function is just a function, or an equation, that describes
the line of the distribution. As you might guess, not every probability distribution
looks like a normal distribution or a uniform distribution.

Parameters Aren't So Complicated

After you grasp the concept that a probability distribution is essentially an equation or formula that describes the line in a probability distribution chart, you're ready to understand that a *parameter* is an input to the probability distribution. In other words, the formula or function or equation that describes a probability distribution curve needs inputs, and those inputs are called parameters.

Some probability distribution functions need only a single parameter. For example, to work with a uniform distribution, all you need is the number of values in the data set. A six-sided die, for example, has only six possibilities. Because you know that only six possibilities exist, you can calculate that any possibility has a 1 in 6 chance of occurring.

REMEMBER

A normal distribution uses two parameters: the mean and the standard deviation.

Other probability distribution functions use other parameters.

Skewness and Kurtosis Describe a Probability Distribution's Shape

A couple of other useful statistical terms to know are skewness and kurtosis. *Skewness* quantifies the lack of symmetry in a probability distribution. In a perfectly symmetrical distribution, like the normal distribution (refer to Figure 14-1), the skewness equals zero. If a probability distribution leans to the right or the left, however, the skewness equals some value other than zero, and the value quantifies the lack of symmetry. See Figure 14-3.

Kurtosis quantifies the heaviness of the tails in a distribution. In a normal distribution, kurtosis equals zero. In other words, zero is the measurement for a tail that looks like a tail in a normal distribution. The *tail* is the thing that reaches out to the left or right. However, if a tail in a distribution is heavier than in a normal distribution, the kurtosis is a positive number. If the tails in a distribution are skinnier than in a normal distribution, the kurtosis is a negative number. See Figure 14-4.

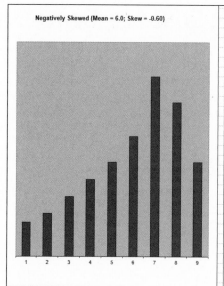

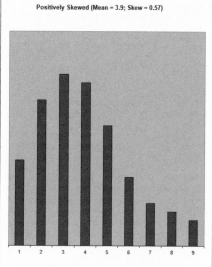

FIGURE 14-3:
Data sets that are negatively skewed (left) and positively skewed (right).

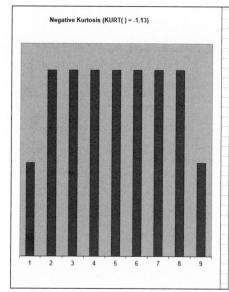

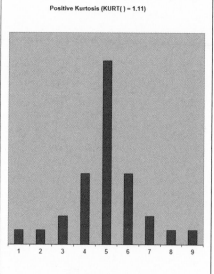

FIGURE 14-4:
Data sets that have negative kurtosis (left) and positive kurtosis (right).

Confidence Intervals Seem Complicated at First But Are Useful

Probabilities often confuse people, and perhaps this happens most during the U.S. presidential elections. Pundits talk in all sorts of confusing ways about one candidate's chances of winning (often in ways confusing to even the pundits themselves).

Say, for example, some talking head on television says, "The results of a recent poll show that candidate Stem Winder would receive 51 percent of the vote were the election held today; the margin of error was +/– 3 percent with a confidence level of 95 percent."

Okay, this sounds like a mouthful, but break it down and things get a little clearer. What the survey really means is this: The pollsters took a sample of the U.S. population and asked them whom they would vote for today, and 51 percent of the sample said they would vote for Mr. Winder.

Now here's where this gets interesting. Largely because of the size of the sample, the pollsters can do some fancy math and infer that there's sort of a 95 percent chance (more on this later) that the real percentage of people who would vote "Winder" in the entire population is between 48 and 54 percent. Note that "margin of error" is basically just another way to describe the confidence interval.

Something important to understand about confidence levels is that they're linked with the margin of error. If the pollsters in the preceding example had wanted a range of values with a confidence level of 99 percent, the margin of error they calculated would be larger.

To put it another way, perhaps a 95 percent chance (sort of) exists that the real percentage of people in the whole population who would vote "Winder" is between 48 and 54 percent, but a 99 percent chance (again, sort of) exists that the real percentage of people with that answer is between 45 and 57 percent. The wider your range of possible values, the more confidence you have that the real data point falls within your range. Conversely, the more confident you want to be that the real data point is included in your range, the wider you have to make your range.

A pet peeve of mine is when news organizations report on a poll and cite the margin of error but not the confidence level. Without knowing the confidence level that the pollster used to calculate the margin of error, the information on margin of error is meaningless.

Another important thing to understand about confidence levels is that the bigger you make your sample size, the smaller your margin of error will be using the same confidence level. If you sample two people on the sidewalk by asking them whom they plan to vote for, and one says "the challenger" and one says "the incumbent," you can't then assert with much confidence that when the whole country votes it will be a perfect 50-50 split. Data from this sample would have an enormous margin of error, unless you use an incredibly low confidence level for your calculations.

However, if you go out and randomly sample 5,000 people by asking whom they're voting for, you have some solid ground to stand on when making a prediction about who's likely to win the presidential race. Put another way, a sample of 5,000 people leads to a much smaller margin of error than a sample of two, assuming that, for both samples, you want the same level of confidence for your range.

At this point, I should make a slight correction: When I said that what the confidence interval means is that a 95 percent chance exists that the real number falls within this range, that's not quite accurate, although it was easier to use as an explanation when first describing the basic concept of a confidence interval. What an interval with 95 percent confidence really means, *technically*, is that if, hypothetically, you were to take different samples from the same population over and over and over again, and then you calculated the confidence interval for those samples in the exact same way for each new sample, about 95 percent of the time the confidence intervals you calculated from the samples would include the real number (because your data from each sample will be slightly different each time, and therefore the interval you calculate will be slightly different as well). So, when I say phrases like "95 percent chance" or "99 percent chance," that's what I really mean. (I need to include this clarification so that my old statistics professors don't start shaking their heads in shame if they read this book.)

My final point is this: Predicting election results is far from the only useful thing you can do with confidence intervals. As just one example, say that you had some Google Analytics data on two different web ads you're running to promote your small business, and you want to know which ad is more effective. You can use the confidence interval formula to figure out how long your ads need to run before Google has collected enough data for you to know which ad is better. (In other words, the formula tells you how big your sample size needs to be to overcome the margin of error.)

» Determining a loan's payments, principal, and interest

» Calculating the required interest rate for a loan

» Figuring out the internal rate of return for an investment

» Learning various ways to calculate depreciation

Chapter **15**

Ten Ways to Analyze Financial Data

All kinds of people use Excel, including scientists, engineers, mathematicians, statisticians, and pollsters. But if you could somehow survey all the world's Excel users, I bet the typical user would have something to do with the financial industry. Whether they're accountants or adjusters, bankers or borrowers, or money managers or money lenders, financial types rely on Excel every day to analyze budgets, loans, investments, and other monetary minutiae.

But it's not just the financial pros who count on Excel (sometimes literally). Financial amateurs can also use Excel to analyze mortgages, car payments, college funds, savings accounts, and other workaday finances.

Whether you make a living working with money or for money, this chapter gives you ten useful techniques for analyzing financial data using Excel.

Calculating Future Value

If you have $1,000 and plan to invest it at 5 percent interest, compounded annually for ten years, the amount you'll receive at the end of ten years is called the *future value* of $1,000. You can use the Excel FV function to calculate the amount you'll receive.

Here's the syntax of the FV function:

```
FV(rate, nper, pmt[, pv][, type])
```

The *rate* argument is the interest rate of the investment; *nper* is the term of the investment; *pmt* is the amount of each regular deposit into the investment; the optional *pv* argument is your initial investment; and the optional *type* argument is a number indicating when deposits are due (0 or blank for end of period; 1 for beginning of period).

For example, to calculate the future value of $1,000 when it's invested at 5 percent annual interest for 10 years, you use the following formula:

```
=FV(.05, 10, 0, -1000)
```

REMEMBER

When you're working with FV, cash outflows are considered negative amounts, so you need to enter the *pmt* and *pv* arguments as negative numbers.

If you plan on depositing an extra $100 per year in that same investment, the formula changes to this:

```
=FV(.05, 10, 100, -1000)
```

When calculating a future value, be careful of the values you use for the *rate* and *nper* arguments. If you're not making regular deposits or you are making a single deposit annually, you can use the annual interest rate for the *rate* argument and the number of years in the investment for the *nper* argument.

For more frequent deposits, you need to adjust the *rate* and *nper* values accordingly. As a general rule, divide the annual interest rate by the number of deposits per year, and multiply the term of the investment by the number of deposits per year. For example, with monthly deposits, divide the annual interest rate by 12 and multiply the term by 12.

For an example, suppose that with the earlier investment, you want to deposit $15 per month. Here's the revised formula to handle monthly deposits:

```
=FV(.05 / 12, 10 * 12, 15, -1000)
```

Calculating Present Value

Investors use the concept of *present value* to recognize the time value of money. Because an investor can receive interest, $1,000 today is worth less than $1,000 ten years from today. For example, $1,000 invested today at 10 percent interest per year, compounded annually, would return $2,593.74. Therefore, the present value of $2,593.74 at 10 percent, compounded annually, for 10 years is $1,000. Or, worded differently, $1,000 today is worth $2,593.74 ten years from today.

To find the present value, you can use the Excel PV function, which takes five arguments:

```
PV(rate, nper, pmt[, fv][, type])
```

The *rate* argument is the interest rate; *nper* is the number of periods in the term; *pmt* is the amount of each payment; the optional *fv* argument is the future value you're trying to find the present value of; and the optional *type* argument is a number indicating when payments are made (0 or blank for end of period; 1 for beginning of period).

For example, the following formula calculates the present value of $2,593.74, the final value of an investment that returns 10 percent interest, compounded annually, for 10 years:

```
=PV(0.1, 10, 0, 2593.74)
```

REMEMBER

When you're working with the PV function, negative numbers are cash outflows and positive numbers are cash inflows. Enter a negative number when making a payment; enter a positive number when receiving cash.

Present value also applies to loans and mortgages. The money you receive when you take out a loan is the present value of the loan. When calculating present value, be careful what you enter in the *rate* and *nper* arguments. You must divide the annual interest rate by the number of payments per year. For example, if payments are monthly, you should divide the annual interest rate by 12. You must also multiply the term by the number of payments. For example, if payments are monthly, multiply the term by 12.

For example, if you'll be making monthly $15 deposits to the preceding investment, here's the formula to calculate the revised present value of the investment:

```
=PV(0.1 / 12, 10 * 12, 15, 2593.74)
```

Determining Loan Payments

When borrowing money, whether for a mortgage, car financing, a student loan, or something else, the most basic analysis is to calculate the regular payment you must make to repay the loan. You use the Excel PMT function to determine the payment.

The PMT function takes three required arguments and two optional ones:

```
PMT(rate, nper, pv[, fv][, type])
```

The required arguments are *rate*, the fixed rate of interest over the term of the loan; *nper*, the number of payments over the term of the loan; and *pv*, the loan principal. The two optional arguments are *fv*, the future value of the loan, which is usually an end-of-loan balloon payment; and *type*, the type of payment: 0 (the default) for end-of-period payments or 1 for beginning-of-period payments.

REMEMBER

A balloon payment covers any unpaid principal that remains at the end of a loan.

The following example calculates the monthly payment on a 3 percent, 25-year $200,000 mortgage:

```
=PMT(0.03 / 12, 25 * 12, 200000)
```

Note that the result of this formula is −948.42. Why the minus sign? The PMT function returns a negative value because a loan payment is money that you pay out.

As shown in the preceding formula, if the interest rate is annual, you can divide it by 12 to get the monthly rate; if the term is expressed in years, you can multiply it by 12 to get the number of months in the term.

With many loans, the payments take care of only a portion of the principal, with the remainder due as an end-of-loan balloon payment. This payment is the future value of the loan, so you enter it into the PMT function as the *fv* argument. You might think that the *pv* argument should therefore be the partial principal — that is, the original loan principal minus the balloon amount — because the loan term is designed to pay off only the partial principal. Nope. In a balloon loan, you also pay interest on the balloon part of the principal. Therefore, the PMT function's *pv* argument must be the entire principal, with the balloon portion as the (negative) *fv* argument.

Calculating a Loan Payment's Principal and Interest

It's one thing to know the total amount for a regular loan payment, but breaking down a loan payment into its principal and interest components is often handy. The principal part is the amount of the loan payment that goes toward paying down the original loan amount, whereas the rest of the payment is the interest you're shelling out to the lender.

To calculate loan payment principal and interest, you can use the PPMT and IPMT functions, respectively. As the loan progresses, the value of PPMT increases while the value of IPMT decreases, but the sum of the two is constant in each period and is equal to the loan payment.

Both functions take the same six arguments:

```
PPMT(rate, per, nper, pv[, fv][, type])
IPMT(rate, per, nper, pv[, fv][, type])
```

The four required arguments are *rate*, the fixed rate of interest over the loan term; *per*, the number of the payment period; *nper*, the number of payments over the term of the loan; and *pv*, the loan principal. The two optional arguments are *fv*, the future value of the loan; and *type*, the type of payment: 0 for end of period or 1 for beginning of period.

For example, the following two formulas calculate the principal and interest portions of the first monthly payment on a 3 percent, 25-year, $200,000 mortgage:

```
=PPMT(0.03 / 12, 1, 25 * 12, 200000)
=IPMT(0.03 / 12, 1, 25 * 12, 200000)
```

Calculating Cumulative Loan Principal and Interest

To calculate how much principal or interest has accumulated between two periods of a loan, use the CUMPRINC or the CUMIPMT function, respectively. Both functions require the same six arguments:

```
CUMPRINC(rate, nper, pv, start_period, end_period[, type])
CUMIPMT(rate, nper, pv, start_period, end_period[, type])
```

Here, *rate* is the fixed rate of interest over the term of the loan; *nper* is the number of payments over the term of the loan; *pv* is the loan principal; *start_period* is the first period to include in the calculation; *end_period* is the last period to include in the calculation; and *type* is the type of payment: 0 for end of period or 1 for beginning of period.

For example, to find the cumulative principal or interest in the first year of a loan, set *start_period* to 1 and *end_period* to 12, as shown here:

```
CUMPRINC(0.03 / 12, 25 * 12, 200000, 1, 12, 0)
CUMIPMT(0.03 / 12, 25 * 12, 200000, 1, 12, 0)
```

For the second year, you'd set *start_period* to 13 and *end_period* to 24, and so on.

Finding the Required Interest Rate

If you know how much you want to borrow, how long a term you want, and what payments you can afford, you can calculate what interest rate will satisfy these parameters using the Excel RATE function. For example, you can use this calculation to put off borrowing money if current interest rates are higher than the value you calculate.

The RATE function takes the following arguments:

```
RATE(nper, pmt, pv[, fv][, type][, guess])
```

The three required arguments are *nper*, the number of payments over the term of the loan; *pmt*, the periodic payment; and *pv*, the loan principal. RATE can also take three optional arguments: *fv*, the future value of the loan (the end-of-loan balloon payment); *type*, the type of payment (0 for end of period or 1 for beginning of period); and *guess*, a percentage value that Excel uses as a starting point for calculating the interest rate.

TIP

If you want an annual interest rate, you must divide the term by 12 if it is currently expressed in months. Conversely, if you have a monthly payment and you want an annual interest rate, you must multiply the payment by 12.

RATE uses an iterative process in which Excel starts with an initial guess value and attempts to refine each subsequent result to obtain the answer. If you omit *guess*, Excel uses a default value of 10 percent. If after 20 tries Excel can't come up with a value, it returns a `#NUM!` error. If that happens, you should enter a *guess* value and try again.

On a related note, if you know the principal, the interest rate, and the payment, you can calculate the length of the loan by using the NPER function:

```
NPER(rate, pmt, pv[, fv][, type])
```

The NPER function's three required arguments are *rate*, the fixed rate of interest; *pmt*, the loan payment; and *pv*, the loan principal. The two optional arguments are *fv*, the future value of the loan, and *type*, the type of payment (0 or 1).

Determining the Internal Rate of Return

The *internal rate of return* is related to the net present value, which is the sum of a series of net cash flows, each of which has been discounted to the present using a fixed discount rate. The internal rate of return can be defined as the discount rate required to get a net present value of $0.

You can use the Excel IRR function to calculate the internal rate of return on an investment. The investment's cash flows don't have to be equal, but they must occur at regular intervals. IRR tells you the interest rate you receive on the investment. Here's the syntax:

```
IRR(values[, guess])
```

The *values* argument is required and represents the range of cash flows over the term of the investment. It must contain at least one positive and one negative value. The *guess* argument is optional and specifies an initial estimate for the Excel iterative calculation of the internal rate of return (the default is 0.1). If after 20 tries Excel can't calculate a value, it returns a `#NUM!` error. If you see that error, enter a value for the *guess* argument and try again.

For example, given a series of cash flows in the range B3:G3, here's a formula that returns the internal rate of return using an initial guess of `0.11`:

```
=IRR(B3:G3, 0.11)
```

TIP

You can use the NPV function to calculate the net present value of future cash flows. If all the cash flows are the same, you can use PV to calculate the present value. But when you have a series of varying cash flows, use NPV, which requires two arguments: *rate*, the discount rate over the term of the asset or investment, and *values*, the range of cash flows.

Calculating Straight-Line Depreciation

The *straight-line* method of depreciation allocates depreciation evenly over the useful life of an asset. Salvage value is the value of an asset after its useful life has expired. To calculate straight-line depreciation, you take the cost of the asset, subtract any salvage value, and then divide by the useful life of the asset. The result is the amount of depreciation allocated to each period.

To calculate straight-line depreciation, you can use the Excel SLN function:

```
SLN(cost, salvage, life)
```

SLN takes three arguments: *cost*, the initial cost of the asset; *salvage*, the salvage value of the asset; and *life*, the life of the asset in periods. If you purchase an asset mid-year, you can calculate depreciation in months instead of years.

For example, if an equipment purchase was $8,500, the equipment's salvage value is $500, and the equipment's useful life is four years, the following formula returns the annual straight-line depreciation:

```
=SLN(8500, 500, 4)
```

The *carrying value* is the cost of an asset minus the total depreciation taken to date. For example, the depreciation for an asset with a cost of $8,500, a salvage value of $500, and a useful life of four years would be allocated as follows:

Year	Annual Depreciation Expense	Accumulated Depreciation	Carrying Value
Beginning of Year 1			$8,500
End of Year 1	$2,000	$2,000	$6,500
End of Year 2	$2,000	$4,000	$4,500
End of Year 3	$2,000	$6,000	$2,500
End of Year 4	$2,000	$8,000	$500

Returning the Fixed-Declining Balance Depreciation

When calculating depreciation, accountants try to match the cost of an asset with the revenue it produces. Some assets produce more in earlier years than in later years. For those assets, accountants use accelerated methods of depreciation, which take more depreciation in the earlier years than in the later years. *Fixed-declining balance* is an accelerated method of depreciation.

To calculate fixed-declining balance depreciation, you can use the Excel DB function:

```
DB(cost, salvage, life, period[, month])
```

The DB function takes five arguments: *cost*, the cost of the asset; *salvage*, the salvage value; *life*, the useful life; *period*, the period for which you're calculating depreciation; and the optional *month*, the number of months in the first year. If you leave *month* blank, Excel uses a default value of 12.

For example, if an equipment purchase was $8,500, the equipment's salvage value is $500, and the equipment's useful life is four years, the following formula returns the depreciation amount for the first year:

```
=DB(8500, 500, 4, 1)
```

The fixed-declining balance method of depreciation depreciates an asset with a cost of $8,500, a salvage value of $500, and a useful life of four years, as follows:

Year	Annual Depreciation Expense	Accumulated Depreciation	Carrying Value
Beginning of Year 1			$8,500
End of Year 1	$4,318	$4,318	$4,182
End of Year 2	$2,124	$6,442	$2,058
End of Year 3	$1,045	$7,488	$1,012
End of Year 4	$512*	$8,000	$500

* Amount adjusted for rounding error

Determining the Double-Declining Balance Depreciation

Double-declining balance is an accelerated depreciation method that takes the rate you would apply by using straight-line depreciation, doubles it, and then applies the doubled rate to the carrying value of the asset.

To determine the double-declining balance depreciation, you can use the Excel DDB function:

```
DDB(cost, salvage, life, period[, factor])
```

The DDB function takes five arguments: *cost*, the cost of the asset; *salvage*, the salvage value; *life*, the useful life; *period*, the period for which you're calculating depreciation; and the optional *factor*, the rate at which the balance declines. The default value for *factor* is 2, but to use a value other than twice the straight-line rate, you can enter the factor you want to use, such as 1.5 for a rate of 150 percent.

For example, if an equipment purchase was $8,500, the equipment's salvage value is $500, and the equipment's useful life is four years, the following formula returns the depreciation amount for the first year:

```
=DDB(8500, 500, 4, 1, 2)
```

The double-declining balance method of depreciation depreciates an asset with a cost of $8,500, a salvage value of $1,500, and a useful life of four years, as follows:

Year	Annual Depreciation Expense	Accumulated Depreciation	Carrying Value
Beginning of Year			$8,500
End of Year 1	$4,250	$4,250	$4,250
End of Year 2	$2,125	$6,375	$2,125
End of Year 3	$625*	$7,000	$1,500
End of Year 4	$0*	$7,500	$1,500

*The DDB function does not depreciate the asset below the salvage value.

Chapter **16**

Ten Ways to Raise Your PivotTable Game

Excel comes with so many powerful data-analysis tools and features that you might be wondering why you need to learn yet another: the PivotTable. The short answer is that the PivotTable is a useful weapon to add to your data-analysis arsenal. The long answer is that PivotTables are worth learning because they come with not just one or two but a long list of benefits.

Let me count the ways: PivotTables are straightforward to build and maintain; they perform large and complex calculations amazingly fast; you can quickly update them to account for new data; PivotTables are dynamic, so components can be easily moved, filtered, and added to; and, finally, PivotTables can use most of the formatting options that you can apply to regular Excel ranges and cells.

Oh, wait, there's one more: PivotTables are fully customizable, so you can build each report the way you want. That customizability is on full display in this chapter, which covers ten techniques that will turn you into a PivotTable pro.

Turn the PivotTable Fields Task Pane On and Off

By default, when you click in the PivotTable, Excel displays the PivotTable Fields task pane and then hides the PivotTable Fields task pane again when you click outside the PivotTable report.

Nothing wrong with that on the face of it. However, if you want to work with the commands in the Ribbon's PivotTable Analyze or Design contextual tabs, you need to have at least one cell in the PivotTable report selected. But selecting any PivotTable cell means that you also have the PivotTable Fields task pane taking up precious screen real estate.

Fortunately, Excel also enables you to turn the PivotTable Fields task pane off, which gives you more room to display your PivotTable report. You can then turn the PivotTable Fields task pane back on when you need to add, move, or delete fields.

To toggle the PivotTable Fields task pane off and on, follow these steps (all two of them!):

1. **Click in the PivotTable.**

2. **Choose PivotTable Analyze ➪ Field List.**

TIP

A quick way to hide the PivotTable Fields task pane is to click the Close button in the upper-right corner of the pane.

Change the PivotTable Fields Task Pane Layout

By default, the PivotTable Fields task pane is divided into two sections: the Fields section lists the data source's available fields and appears at the top of the pane, and the Areas section contains the PivotTable areas — Filters, Columns, Rows, and Values — and appears at the bottom of the pane. You can customize this layout to suit the way you work. Here are the possibilities:

» **Fields Section and Areas Section Stacked:** The default layout.

» **Field Section and Areas Section Side-By-Side:** Puts the Fields section on the left and the Areas section on the right. Use this layout if your source data comes with a large number of fields.

>> **Fields Section Only:** Hides the Areas section. Use this layout when you add fields to the PivotTable by right-clicking the field name and then clicking the area where you want the field added (instead of dragging fields to the Areas section). By hiding the Areas section, you get more room to display the fields.

>> **Areas Section Only (2 by 2):** Hides the Fields section and arranges the areas in two rows and two columns. Use this layout if you've finished adding fields to the PivotTable and you want to concentrate on moving fields between the areas and filtering the fields.

>> **Areas Section Only (1 by 4):** Hides the Fields section and displays the areas in a single column. Use this layout if you no longer need the Fields section. Also, this layout gives each area a wider display, which is useful if some of your fields have ridiculously long names.

Here are the steps to follow to change the PivotTable Fields task pane layout:

1. **Click any cell in the PivotTable.**

2. **Click Tools.**

The Tools button is the one with the gear icon, as pointed out in Figure 16-1.

Excel displays the PivotTable Fields task pane tools.

Tools

FIGURE 16-1:
Click Tools to see
the PivotTable
Fields task pane
layout options.

3. Click the layout you want to use.

Excel changes the PivotTable Fields task pane layout based on your selection.

TIP

While you have the PivotTable Fields task pane tools displayed, note that you can also sort the field list. The default is Sort in Data Source Order, which means that Excel displays the fields in the same order as they appear in the data source. If you prefer to sort the fields alphabetically, click Sort A to Z.

Display the Details Behind PivotTable Data

The main advantage to using PivotTables is that they give you an easy method for summarizing large quantities of data into a succinct report for data analysis. In short, PivotTables show you the forest instead of the trees. However, sometimes you need to see some of those trees. For example, if you're studying the results of a marketing campaign, your PivotTable may show you the total number of ear-buds sold as a result of a 1 Free With 10 promotion (see Figure 16-2). However, what if you want to see the details underlying that number? If your source data contains hundreds or thousands of records, you need to filter the data in some way to see just the records you want.

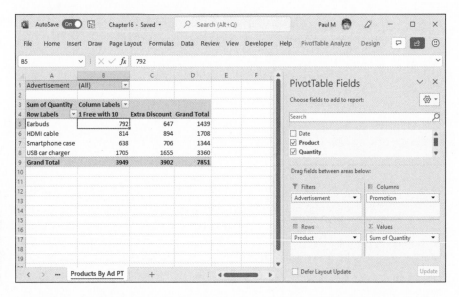

FIGURE 16-2:
You've sold 792 earbuds, but what are the details behind this number?

Fortunately, Excel gives you an easier way to see records you want by enabling you to directly view the details that underlie a specific data value. This process is called *drilling down* to the details. When you drill down into a specific data value in a PivotTable, Excel returns to the source data, extracts the records that comprise the data value, and then displays the records in a new worksheet. For a PivotTable based on a range or table, this extraction takes but a second or two, depending on how many records the source data contains.

To drill down into the details underlying a PivotTable data point, use either of the following methods:

>> Right-click the data value for which you want to view the underlying details and then click Show Details.

>> Double-click the data value.

Excel displays the underlying data in a new worksheet. For example, Figure 16-3 shows the details behind the 792 earbuds sold with the 1 Free with 10 promotion shown previously in Figure 16-2.

	A	B	C	D	E	F
1	Date	Product	Quantity	Net $	Promotion	Advertisement
2	8/21/2022	Earbuds	44	341.88	1 Free with 10	Search
3	8/20/2022	Earbuds	33	256.41	1 Free with 10	Social media
4	8/19/2022	Earbuds	77	598.29	1 Free with 10	Blog network
5	7/21/2022	Earbuds	132	1025.64	1 Free with 10	Search
6	7/20/2022	Earbuds	55	427.35	1 Free with 10	Social media
7	7/19/2022	Earbuds	99	769.23	1 Free with 10	Blog network
8	6/23/2022	Earbuds	121	940.17	1 Free with 10	Search
9	6/22/2022	Earbuds	66	512.82	1 Free with 10	Social media
10	6/21/2022	Earbuds	22	170.94	1 Free with 10	Blog network
11	6/16/2022	Earbuds	33	256.41	1 Free with 10	Blog network
12	6/15/2022	Earbuds	22	170.94	1 Free with 10	Blog network
13	6/14/2022	Earbuds	22	170.94	1 Free with 10	Blog network
14	6/5/2022	Earbuds	55	388.5	1 Free with 10	Blog network
15	6/13/2022	Earbuds	11	85.47	1 Free with 10	Blog network
16						

< >   Orders   **Sheet1**   Products By Ad PT   +

FIGURE 16-3: The details behind the earbud sales shown in Figure 16-2.

When you attempt to drill down to a data value's underlying details, Excel may display the error message *Cannot change this part of a PivotTable report.* This error means that the feature that normally enables you to drill down has been turned off. To turn this feature back on, click any cell in the PivotTable and then click PivotTable Analyze ⇨ Options to display the PivotTable Options dialog box. Click the Data tab, select the Enable Show Details check box, and then click OK.

The opposite situation occurs when you distribute the workbook containing the PivotTable and you don't want other users drilling down and cluttering the workbook with detail worksheets. In this case, click PivotTable Analyze ⇨ Options, click the Data tab, deselect Enable Show Details, and then click OK.

Sometimes you may want to see all of a PivotTable's underlying source data. If the source data is a range or table in another worksheet, you can see the underlying data by displaying that worksheet. If the source data is not so readily available, however, Excel gives you a quick way to view all the underlying data. Right-click the PivotTable's Grand Total cell (that is, the cell in the bottom-right corner of the PivotTable) and then click Show Details. (You can also double-click that cell.) Excel displays all of the PivotTable's underlying data in a new worksheet.

Apply a PivotTable Style

One of the nice things about a PivotTable is that it resides on a regular Excel worksheet, which means that you can apply formatting options such as alignments and fonts to portions of the PivotTable. This works well, particularly if you have custom formatting requirements. For example, you may have in-house style guidelines that you need to follow. Unfortunately, applying formatting can be time consuming, particularly if you're applying a number of different formatting options. And the total formatting time can become onerous if you need to apply different formatting options to different parts of the PivotTable. You can greatly reduce the time you spend formatting your PivotTables if you apply a style instead.

A *style* is a collection of formatting options — fonts, borders, and background colors — that Excel defines for different areas of a PivotTable. For example, a style might use bold, white text on a black background for labels and grand totals, and white text on a dark blue background for items and data. Defining all these formats manually might take half an hour to an hour. But with the style feature, you choose the one you want to use for the PivotTable as a whole, and Excel applies the individual formatting options automatically.

Excel defines more than 80 styles, divided into three categories: Light, Medium, and Dark. The Light category includes Pivot Style Light 16, the default formatting applied to PivotTable reports you create; and None, which removes all formatting from the PivotTable. You can also create your own style formats, as described in the next section, "Create a Custom PivotTable Style."

Here are the steps to follow to apply a style to a PivotTable:

1. **Click any cell you want to format in the PivotTable.**
2. **Click the Design tab.**

3. **In the PivotTable Styles group, click the More button.**

   The style gallery appears.

4. **Click the style you want to apply.**

   Excel applies the style.

Create a Custom PivotTable Style

You may find that none of the predefined PivotTable styles gives you the exact look that you want. In that case, you can define that look yourself by creating a custom PivotTable style from scratch.

Excel offers you tremendous flexibility when you create custom PivotTable styles. You can format 25 separate PivotTable elements. These elements include the entire table, the page field labels and values, the first column, the header row, the Grand Total row, and the Grand Total column. You can also define *stripes,* which are separate formats applied to alternating rows or columns. For example, the First Row Stripe applies formatting to rows 1, 3, 5, and so on; the Second Row Stripe applies formatting to rows 2, 4, 6, and so on. Stripes can make a long or wide report easier to read.

Having control over so many elements enables you to create a custom style to suit your needs. For example, you might need your PivotTable to match your corporate colors. Similarly, if the PivotTable will appear as part of a larger report, you might need the PivotTable formatting to match the theme used in the larger report.

The only downside to creating a custom PivotTable style is that you must do so from scratch because Excel doesn't enable you to customize an existing style. Boo, Excel! So, if you need to define formatting for all 25 PivotTable elements, creating a custom style can be time consuming.

If you're still up for it, however, here are the steps to plow through to create your very own PivotTable style:

1. **Click the Design tab.**

2. **In the PivotTable Styles group, click More.**

   The style gallery appears.

3. **Click New PivotTable Style.**

   The New PivotTable style dialog box appears, as shown in Figure 16-4.

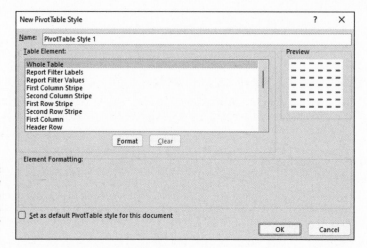

FIGURE 16-4:
Use the New
PivotTable Style
dialog box to
define your
custom style.

4. **Type a name for your custom style.**

5. **In the Table Element list, select the PivotTable feature you want to format.**

6. **Click Format.**

The Format Cells dialog box appears.

7. **Use the options in the Font tab to format the element's text.**

You can choose a font, a font style (such as bold or italic), and a font size. You can also choose an underline, a color, and a strikethrough effect.

8. **Use the options in the Border tab to format the element's border.**

You can choose a border style, color, and location (such as the left edge, top edge, or both).

9. **Use the options in the Fill tab to format the element's background color.**

You can choose a solid color or a pattern. You can also click the Fill Effects buttons to specify a gradient that changes from one color to another.

10. **Click OK.**

Excel returns you to the New PivotTable Style dialog box.

11. **Repeat Steps 5 through 10 to format other table elements.**

Handily, the New PivotTable Style dialog box includes a Preview section that shows you what the style will look like when it's applied to a PivotTable. If you're particularly proud of your new style, you might want to use it for all your PivotTables. Why not? To tell Excel to use your new style as the default for any future PivotTable you forge, select the Set as Default PivotTable Style for This Document check box.

12. **When you're all done at last, click OK.**

Excel saves the custom PivotTable style.

Weirdly, after you close the New PivotTable Style dialog box, Excel doesn't apply the new style to the current PivotTable. Dumb! To apply the style yourself, select any cell in the PivotTable, click Design, click the More button in the PivotTable Styles group to open the style gallery, and then click your style in the Custom section that now appears at the top of the gallery.

If you need to make changes to your custom style, open the style gallery, right-click your custom style, and then click Modify. Use the Modify PivotTable style dialog box to make your changes, and then click OK.

If you find that you need to create another custom style that's similar to an existing custom style, don't bother creating the new style from scratch. Instead, open the style gallery, right-click the existing custom style, and then click Duplicate. In the Modify PivotTable Style dialog box, adjust the style name and formatting, and then click OK.

If you no longer need a custom style, you should delete it to reduce clutter in the style gallery. Click the Design tab, open the PivotTable Styles gallery, right-click the custom style you no longer need, and then click Delete. When Excel asks you to confirm, click OK.

Preserve PivotTable Formatting

Excel has a nasty habit of sometimes not preserving your custom formatting when you refresh or rebuild the PivotTable. For example, if you applied a bold font to some labels, those labels might revert to regular text after a refresh. Excel has a feature called Preserve Formatting that enables you to preserve such formatting during a refresh; you can retain your custom formatting by activating it.

The Preserve Formatting feature is always activated in default PivotTables. However, another user could have deactivated this feature. For example, you may be working with a PivotTable created by another person and that person may have deactivated the Preserve Formatting feature.

Note, however, that when you refresh or rebuild a PivotTable, Excel reapplies the report's current style formatting. If you haven't specified a style, Excel reapplies the default PivotTable style (named Pivot Style Light 16); if you have specified a style — as described in the previous section "Apply a PivotTable Style" — Excel reapplies that style.

Here are the steps to follow to configure a PivotTable to preserve formatting:

1. **Click any cell you want to work with in the PivotTable.**

2. **Choose PivotTable Analyze ⇨ Options.**

   The PivotTable Options dialog box appears with the Layout & Format tab displayed.

3. **Deselect the Autofit Column Widths on Update check box.**

   Deselecting this option prevents Excel from automatically formatting things such as column widths when you pivot fields.

4. **Select the Preserve Cell Formatting on Update check box.**

5. **Click OK.**

   Excel preserves your custom formatting each time you refresh the PivotTable.

Rename the PivotTable

When you create the first PivotTable in a workbook, Excel gives it the uninspiring name PivotTable1. Subsequent PivotTables are named sequentially (and just as uninspiringly): PivotTable2, PivotTable3, and so on. However, Excel also repeats these names when you build new PivotTables based on different data sources. If your workbook contains a number of PivotTables, you can make them easier to distinguish by giving each one a unique and descriptive name. Here's how:

1. **Click any cell you want to work with in the PivotTable.**

2. **In the PivotTable Analyze tab's PivotTable group, use the PivotTable Name text box to type the new name for the PivotTable.**

   The maximum length for a PivotTable name is 255 characters.

3. **Click outside the text box.**

   Excel renames the PivotTable.

Turn Off Grand Totals

A default PivotTable that has at least one row field contains an extra row at the bottom of the table. This row is labeled Grand Total and includes the total of the values associated with the row field items. However, the value in the Grand Total row may not actually be a sum. For example, if the summary calculation is Average, the Grand Total row includes the average of the values associated with the row field items.

Similarly, a PivotTable that has at least one column field contains an extra column at the far right of the table. This column is also labeled "Grand Total" and includes the total of the values associated with the column field items. If the PivotTable contains both a row and a column field, the Grand Total row also has the sums for each column item, and the Grand Total column also has the sums for each row item.

Besides taking up space in the PivotTable, these grand totals are often not necessary for data analysis. For example, suppose you want to examine quarterly sales for your salespeople to see which amounts are over a certain value for bonus purposes. Because your only concern is the individual summary values for each employee, the grand totals are useless. In such a case, you can tell Excel not to display the grand totals by following these steps:

1. Click any cell you want to work with in the PivotTable.

2. Click Design ⇨ Grand Totals.

Excel displays a menu of options for displaying the grand totals.

3. Click the option you prefer.

The menu contains four items:

- **Off for Rows and Columns:** Turns off the grand totals for both the rows and the columns

- **On for Rows and Columns:** Turns on the grand totals for both the rows and the columns

- **On for Rows Only:** Turns off the grand totals for just the columns

- **On for Columns Only:** Turns off the grand totals for just the rows

Excel puts the selected grand total option into effect.

TIP

The field headers that appear in the report are another often-bothersome PivotTable feature. These headers include Sort & Filter buttons, but if you don't use those buttons, the field headers just clutter the PivotTable. To turn off the field headers, click in the PivotTable and then choose PivotTable Analyze⇨ Field Headers.

Reduce the Size of PivotTable Workbooks

PivotTables often result in large workbooks because Excel must keep track of a great deal of extra information to keep the PivotTable performance acceptable. For example, to ensure that the recalculation involved in pivoting happens quickly and efficiently, Excel maintains a copy of the source data in a special memory area called the *pivot cache*.

If you build a PivotTable from data that resides in a different workbook or in an external data source, Excel stores the source data in the pivot cache. This greatly reduces the time Excel takes to refresh and recalculate the PivotTable. The downside is that it can increase both the size of the workbook and the amount of time Excel takes to save the workbook. If your workbook has become too large or it takes too long to save, follow these steps to tell Excel not to save the source data in the pivot cache:

1. **Click any cell in the PivotTable.**
2. **Click PivotTable Analyze ⇨ Options.**

   The PivotTable Options dialog box appears.
3. **Click the Data tab.**
4. **Deselect the Save Source Data with File check box.**
5. **Click OK.**

   Excel no longer saves the external source data in the pivot cache.

Use a PivotTable Value in a Formula

You might need to use a PivotTable value in a worksheet formula. You normally reference a cell in a formula by using the cell's address. However, this won't work with PivotTables because the addresses of the report values change as you pivot, filter, group, and refresh the PivotTable.

To ensure accurate PivotTable references, use Excel's GETPIVOTDATA function. This function uses the data field, PivotTable location, and one or more (row or column) field/item pairs that specify the exact value you want to use. This way, no matter what the PivotTable layout is, as long as the value remains visible in the report, your formula reference remains accurate.

Here's the syntax of the GETPIVOTDATA function:

```
GETPIVOTDATA(data_field, pivot_table, [, field1, item1][, ...]
```

The two required fields are *data_field*, which is the name of the field you're using in the PivotTable's Values area, and *pivot_table*, which specifies the cell address of the upper-left corner of the PivotTable. The rest of the arguments come in pairs: a field name and an item in that field.

For example, here's a GETPIVOTDATA formula that returns the PivotTable value where the Product field item is Earbuds and the Promotion field item is 1 Free with 10:

```
=GETPIVOTDATA("Quantity", $A$3, "Product", "Earbuds",
    "Promotion", "1 Free with 10")
```

Figure 16-5 shows this formula in action.

GETPIVOTDATA is a bit complicated, so let me put your mind at ease right away by saying you'll almost never have to peck out this function and all its arguments by hand. Instead, Excel conveniently handles everything for you when you click the PivotTable value you want to use in your formula. Phew!

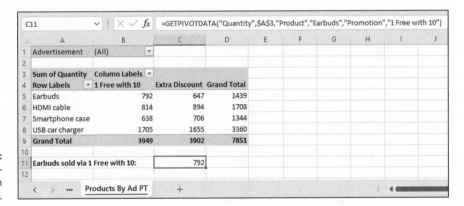

FIGURE 16-5:
The GETPIVOT-
DATA function
doing its thing.

Appendix

Glossary of Data Analysis and Excel Terms

absolute reference: A cell address used in a formula that Excel doesn't adjust if you copy the formula to some new location. To create an absolute cell reference, you precede the column letter and row number with a dollar sign ($).

Access: A database program developed and sold by Microsoft. Use Access to build and work with large, sophisticated, relational databases; you can export information from an Access database to Excel by opening the resource (such as a table) and then choosing External Data ⇨ Excel.

add-in: Software that adds one or more features to Excel. ***See also*** *Analysis ToolPak; Solver*.

Analysis ToolPak: An add-in that provides Excel with extra functions and tools for statistical analysis.

arithmetic operators: The standard operators that you use in Excel formulas. To add numbers, use the addition (+) operator. To subtract numbers, use the subtraction (–) operator. To multiply numbers, use the multiplication (*) operator. To divide numbers, use the division (/) operator. You can also perform exponential operations by using the exponential operator (^). ***See*** *operator precedence*.

ascending order: A sorting option that arranges text in A-to-Z order and arranges values in smallest-to-largest order. ***See also*** *chronological order; descending order*.

AutoFilter: An Excel tool (available from the Data tab's Filter command) that enables you to view a subset of your original table. For example, in the case of a grocery list table, you could use AutoFilter to create a subset that shows only those items that you'll purchase at a particular store, in specified quantities, or that exceed a certain price.

automatic subtotals: Formulas that Excel adds to a worksheet automatically. Excel sets up automatic subtotals based on data groupings in a selected field.

average: Typically, the arithmetic mean for a set of values. Excel offers several averaging functions. ***See also*** *median; mode*.

best-fit trend line: A straight line through a chart's data points where the differences between the chart points that reside above the line and those that reside below the line cancel each other out. **See also** *trend analysis*.

binomial distributions: Used to calculate probabilities in situations in which you have a limited number of independent trials, or tests, that can either succeed or fail. Success or failure of any one trial is independent of other trials.

Boolean expression: **See** *logical expression*.

break-even analysis: A worksheet model that calculates the number of units a product or business must sell to recoup all costs (or, to put it another way, to reach a profit of $0).

calculated field: Used to insert a new row or column into a PivotTable and then fill the new row or column with a formula.

calculated item: An amount shown in a PivotTable that you create by calculating a formula. Frankly, adding a calculated item usually doesn't make any sense. But, hey, strange things happen all the time, right?

changing cell: A worksheet cell that Excel modifies in an attempt to find a solution to a problem. Also called a *variable cell*.

chart legend: Identifies the data series that you plot in your chart.

chart type: Includes column, bar, line, pie, XY, surface, and so on.

chronological order: A sorting option that arranges labels or values in chronological order such as Monday, Tuesday, Wednesday, and so on. **See also** *ascending order; descending order*.

coefficient of determination: A measure of how well a trend line fits the data.

color scales: A data visualization feature that compares the relative values in a range by applying shading to each cell, where the color reflects each cell's value.

combinations: Given a data set, the number of ways that a subset of that data can be grouped, without repeats, where the order isn't important (that is, each subset is unique). **See also** *permutations*.

comma-separated values: A type of delimited text file in which each record appears on a line of text and each field is separated by a comma.

comparison operator: A mathematical operator used in a logical expression. For example, the > comparison operator makes *greater than* comparisons, and the = operator makes *equal to* comparisons. **See also** *logical expressions*.

conditional formatting: A special format that Excel applies only to cells that satisfy one or more criteria.

consolidating: Combining the data from multiple worksheets — called the *source ranges* — into a single summary report — the *destination range*.

constraint: A condition that a cell in a data model must satisfy before Solver accepts a solution.

correlation: A measure of the relationship between two sets of data.

counting: Used for useful statistical functions for counting cells in a worksheet or table. Excel provides four counting functions: COUNT, COUNTA, COUNTBLANK, and COUNTIF. Excel also provides two useful functions for counting permutations and combinations: PERMUT and COMBIN.

covariance: Calculates the average of the product of deviations of values from the means of the data set.

criteria: Conditions that specify which subset of data you want to extract from a table or database.

criteria range: A worksheet range that contains copies of a table's header as well as one or more logical expressions that define a filter for the table.

cross-tabulation: An analysis technique that summarizes data in two or more ways. For example, if you run a business and summarize sales information both by customer and by product, that's a cross-tabulation because you tabulate the information in two ways. *See also PivotTable*.

CSV: *See comma-separated values.*

custom calculation: A formula that you define yourself to produce PivotTable values that wouldn't otherwise appear in the report if you used only the source data and Excel's predefined summary calculations.

data analysis: The application of tools and techniques to organize, study, reach conclusions and sometimes also make predictions about a specific collection of information.

database functions: A special set of functions for quick statistical analysis of information stored in Excel tables.

database query: *See query.*

delimited text file: A type of text file. Delimited text files use special characters, called *delimiters,* to separate fields of information in the report. For example, such files commonly use the Tab character to delimit. *See also importing*.

dependent variable: In regression analysis, the variable that changes with respect to the independent variable.

descending order: A sorting order that arranges labels in reverse alphabetical order and values in largest-value-to-smallest-value order. *See also ascending order; chronological order*.

descriptive statistics: Describe the values in a set. For example, if you sum a set of values, that sum is a descriptive statistic. If you find the largest value or the smallest value in a set of numbers, that's also a descriptive statistic.

dirty: Describes data that's disorganized, inconsistent, or incorrect.

drilling down: In a PivotTable, displaying the data source details behind a calculated value.

exponential trend: A trend that rises or falls at an increasing rate.

exporting: In the context of databases, moving information to another application. If you tell your accounting system to export a list of vendors that Excel can later read, for example, you're exporting. Many business applications, by the way, do easily export data to Excel. *See also* importing.

external data: Data that resides outside the active Excel workbook in another workbook, a file, a database, a server, or a website.

field: In a table or database, a category or type of information. In an Excel table, each column represents a field.

field settings: Determine what Excel does with a field when it's cross-tabulated in the PivotTable. *See also* cross-tabulation; PivotTable.

filter: A condition that Excel applies to a table that defines a subset of the table's records.

fixed-width: A type of text file in which each item uses a set amount of space.

formulas: Calculation instructions entered into worksheet cells. Essentially, this business about formulas going into workbook cells is the heart of Excel. Even if an Excel workbook did nothing else, it would still be an extremely valuable tool. In fact, the first spreadsheet programs did little more than calculate cell formulas. *See also* text labels; value.

frequency distribution: Organizes the values in a data set into numeric ranges called *bins* and then tells you the number of observations that fall in each bin.

function: A prebuilt formula that you can use instead of constructing a custom formula to perform standard calculations such as the average or the standard deviation.

function arguments: Needed in most functions; also called *inputs* or *parameters*. All database functions need arguments, which you include inside parentheses. If a function needs more than one argument, you separate arguments by using commas. *See also* database functions.

future value: The amount that money invested now will be worth at a specified time in the future given an interest rate and regular deposits.

header row: A top row of field names in your table range.

histogram: A chart that shows a frequency distribution.

icon set: A data visualization feature that adds a particular icon to each cell in the range, with that icon telling you something about the cell's value relative to the rest of the range.

importing: In the context of databases, grabbing information from some other application. Excel can import information from popular databases (such as Microsoft Access), from web page tables, and from text files. ***See also*** *exporting.*

independent variable: In regression analysis, the variable based on which the dependent variable changes.

inferential statistics: Based on a very useful, intuitively obvious idea that if you look at a sample of values from a population, and if the sample is representative and large enough, you can draw conclusions about the population based on characteristics of the sample.

iteration: A formula optimization technique that tries multiple interim solutions in an attempt to converge on the true solution.

kurtosis: A measure that indicates whether the curve formed by some sample data is peaked (positive kurtosis) or flat (negative kurtosis). ***See also*** *skewness.*

linear trend: A trend in which the dependent variable is related to the independent variable by some constant amount.

linear regression: Regression analysis in which the best-fit trend line is a straight line.

list: ***See*** *table.*

logarithmic trend: A trend in which the data rises or falls very quickly at the beginning, but then slows down and levels off over time.

logical expression: Describe a comparison that you want to make. To construct a logical expression, you use a comparison operator and then a value used for the comparison.

mean: ***See*** *average.*

median: The middle value in a set of values. Half the values fall below the median, and half the values fall above the median. ***See also*** *average; mode.*

Microsoft Access: ***See*** *Access.*

Microsoft Query: ***See*** *Query.*

mode: The most common value in a set. ***See also*** *average; median.*

moving average: Smooths a data series by averaging the series values over a specified number of preceding periods.

nonlinear regression: Regression analysis in which the best-fit trend line is a curve.

normal distribution: The infamous bell curve. Also known as a *Gaussian distribution.*

objective cell: In an optimization process, the cell that contains the formula you want to optimize. Also called the *target cell.* ***See also*** *changing cell; constraint.*

observation: An item from a data set. Suppose that you're constructing a data set that shows daily high temperatures in your neighborhood. When you go out and *observe* that the temperature some fine July afternoon is 87°F, that measurement is your observation.

Open Database Connectivity (ODBC): A database standard that enables a program to connect to and manipulate a data source.

one-input data table: A data table that varies only one of the formula's input cells.

operator precedence: Standard rules that determine the order of arithmetic operations in a formula. For example, exponential operations are performed first. Multiplication and division operations are performed second. Addition and subtraction operations are performed third. To override these standard rules, use parentheses. ***See also*** *formulas.*

optimization modeling: A problem-solving technique in which you look for the optimum value of an objective function while explicitly recognizing constraints.

outer field: In a PivotTable, the field "farthest" from the value area: the leftmost field if you have two fields in the row area; the topmost field if you have two fields in the column area. The other field is called the *inner field* because it's "closest" to the value area.

outlier: A value that's much higher or lower than the other values in the same data set.

parameter: An input to a probability distribution function.

percentile: The percentage of items in a sample that are at the same level or a lower level than a given value. ***See also*** *rank.*

permutations: Given a data set, the number of ways that a subset of that data can be grouped, in any order, without repeats. ***See also*** *combinations.*

pivot cache: An area of memory that Excel uses to store a PivotTable's source data.

PivotChart: A cross-tabulation that appears in a chart. ***See also*** *cross-tabulation.*

pivoting: Moving a field from one area to another in a PivotTable.

PivotTable: Perhaps the most powerful analytical tool that Excel provides. Use the PivotTable command to cross-tabulate data stored in Excel tables. ***See also*** *cross-tabulation.*

polynomial trend: A trend with a best-fit line of multiple curves derived using an equation that uses multiple powers of x.

population: The complete set of observations for some phenomenon. ***See also*** *sample.*

power trend: A trend in which the data increases or decreases steadily.

present value: The amount that some future value is worth now given an investment's interest rate and regular deposits.

primary key: In sorting, the field first used to sort records. ***See also*** *secondary key; sort;* and, if you're really interested, *tertiary key.*

probability distribution: A chart that plots probabilities. *See also normal distribution; uniform distribution.*

probability distribution function: An equation that describes the line of the probability distribution. *See also probability distribution.*

query: A database feature that specifies how you want to extract, sort, and filter data to use in a worksheet.

Query Wizard: A tool that comes with Excel and enables you to query a database and then place the results into an Excel workbook.

R^2: *See coefficient of determination.*

rank: The position of an item in a data set relative to the other items. *See also percentile.*

raw data: Data that has not been manipulated or analyzed in any way.

record: A collection of related fields in a table. In Excel, each record goes into a separate row.

refreshing pivot data: Updating the information shown in a PivotTable or pivot chart to reflect changes in the underlying data. You can click the Refresh data tool provided by the PivotTable toolbar button to refresh.

regression analysis: Plotting pairs of independent and dependent variables in an XY chart and then finding a linear or exponential equation that best describes the plotted data.

regression equation: A mathematical equation that specifies the exact relationship between the dependent variable and the independent variable.

relational database: Essentially, a collection of tables. *See also table.*

relative reference: A cell reference used in a formula that Excel adjusts if you copy the formula to a new cell location. *See also absolute reference.*

running total: The cumulative sum of the values that appear in a given set of data.

sample: A collection of observations from a population.

scatter plot: An XY chart that visually compares pairs of values. A scatter plot is often a good first step when you want to perform regression analysis. *See also regression analysis.*

scenario: A data-analysis technique that stores multiple input values for a worksheet model and enables you to apply those values quickly.

secondary key: In sorting, the second field used to sort records. The secondary key comes into play only when the primary keys of records have the same value. *See also primary key; sort.*

skewness: A measure of the symmetry of a distribution of values. *See also kurtosis.*

solve order: The order in which calculated item formulas should be solved. ***See also*** *calculated item.*

Solver: An Excel add-in with which you perform optimization modeling. ***See also*** *optimization modeling.*

Solver variables: The variables in an optimization modeling problem. ***See*** *optimization modeling.*

sort: To arrange table records in some order, such as alphabetically by last name. Excel includes easy-to-use tools for doing this, by the way.

standard deviation: Describes dispersion about the data set's mean. You can think of a standard deviation as an average deviation from the mean. ***See also*** *average; variance.*

summary calculation: The calculation that Excel uses to populate the PivotTable data area.

table: A collection of related data stored in a row-and-column format, where each row represents a single item of data and each column represents a single type or category of data.

tertiary key: In sorting, the third field used to sort records. The tertiary key comes into play only when multiple records have not only primary keys that match but also secondary keys that match. ***See also*** *primary key; secondary key; sort.*

text file: A file that's all text. Many programs export text files, by the way, because other programs (including Excel) often easily import text files.

text functions: Used to manipulate text strings in ways that enable you to easily rearrange and manipulate the data that you import into an Excel workbook. Typically, these babies are extremely useful tools for scrubbing or cleaning the data that you want to analyze later.

text labels: Includes letters and numbers that you enter into worksheet cells but that you don't want to use in calculations. For example, your name, a budget expense description, and a telephone number are all examples of text labels. None of these pieces of information gets used in calculations.

top/bottom rule: A conditional formatting rule in which Excel applies a conditional format to those items that are at the top or bottom of a range of values.

trend analysis: Data analysis that identifies the overall direction over time of the values in a data set.

trend line: A line through a chart's data points that visualizes the overall trend of the data.

two-input data table: A data table that varies two of the formula's input cells.

uniform distribution: Having the same probability of occurrence in every event. One common probability distribution function is a uniform distribution.

value: Some bit of data that you enter into a workbook cell and may want to later use in a calculation. For example, the actual amount that you budget for some expense would always be a number or value. *See also* formulas; text labels.

variance: Describes dispersion about the data set's mean. The variance is the square of the standard deviation. *See also* average; standard deviation.

web query: Grabbing data from a table that's stored in a web page. Excel provides a very slick tool for doing this, by the way.

weighted average: A version of the average calculation that takes into account the relative importance of each value in a data set.

what-if analysis: A worksheet data model designed to help you analyze hypothetical scenarios.

x-values: The independent values in a regression analysis.

XML: Extensible Markup Language, a standard that enables the management and sharing of structured data using simple text files.

y-intercept: In a trend line, the value of *y* at the point where the trend line crosses the y-axis.

y-values: The dependent values in a regression analysis.

z-value: In statistics, describes the distance between a value and the mean in terms of standard deviations. (How often does one get to include a legitimate *Z* entry in a glossary! Not often, but here I do.) *See also* average; standard deviation.

Index

Symbols

+ (addition), 81–82, 151
{} (braces), 36
, (comma), 83
/ (division), 151
= (equal to), 50, 72
= (equals sign), 151
> (greater than), 50, 72, 81–82, 151
>= (greater than or equal to), 72
< (less than), 72, 151
<= (less than or equal to), 72
* (multiplication), 81–82, 151
<> (not equal to), 72
- (subtraction), 151

A

absolute reference, 317
Access, 56, 78, 317
Access tables
  as external data, 78
  importing data from, 80–81
Access Web Content dialog box, 86–87
Add Constraint dialog box, 51
Add Scenario dialog box, 40–41
add-in. *See also* Analysis ToolPak; Solver
  defined, 317
  Power Pivot, 192
  Solver, 46–47
adding
  column subtotals in Excel tables, 63–64
  constraints to Solver, 50–52
  data labels to PivotCharts, 173
  fields in PivotCharts, 126–127, 164
  fields to PivotTables areas, 126–127
  PivotChart titles, 175–177
  running total summary calculations, 144–146
  tables to data models, 193

Add-Ins dialog box, 46–47, 247
addition (+), 81–82, 151
adjusting
  PivotChart type, 172–173
  PivotTables Fields Task pane layout, 304–306
  PivotTables summary calculations, 138–140
Advanced Filter dialog box, 74
analysis, trend
  about, 203
  calculating best-fit values, 206–208
  calculating exponential trend values, 216–218
  calculating forecasted linear values, 212–214
  defined, 324
  extending linear trends, 210–212
  extending linear trends using fill handle, 211
  extending linear trends using Series command, 211–212
  LINEST function, 208
  LOGEST function, 218
  plotting best-fit trend lines, 204–206
  plotting exponential trend lines, 214–216
  plotting forecasted values, 208–210
  plotting logarithmic trend lines, 218–220
  plotting polynomial trend lines, 222–223
  plotting power trend lines, 220–221
analysis of variance (ANOVA), 271
Analysis ToolPak
  defined, 317
  loading, 246–247
analyzing
  cell values with color scales, 15–16
  cell values with data bars, 14–15
  cell values with icon sets, 16–17
AND function, 19
ANOVA (analysis of variance), 271
Anova: Single Factor dialog box, 275
ANOVA tools, 274–276

VARPA, 111
VAR.S, 241–242
future value
 calculating, 37, 294
 defined, 320
FV function, 294

G

generating
 custom conditional formatting rules, 17–18
 custom PivotTable styles, 309–311
 data models, 9
 data tables, 32–36
 descriptive statistics, 247–250
 Excel tables, 57–61
 frequency distributions, 258–260
 grouped frequency distributions, 240–241
 index summary calculations, 147–148
 one-input data tables, 32–34
 PivotCharts, 165–169
 PivotCharts from Excel tables, 166–169
 PivotTables from Excel tables, 119–121
 PivotTables from external data, 122–124
 random numbers, 255–257
 scenarios, 40–42
 two-input data tables, 34–36
GETPIVOTDATA function, 315
Goal Seek, data analysis with, 37–39
Goal Seek dialog box, 37–39
gradient fill, 15
Grand Totals, turning off in PivotTables, 312–313
greater than (>), 50, 72, 81–82, 151
Greater Than dialog box, 11
greater than or equal to (>=), 72
GRG Nonlinear, 49
grouped frequency distributions, creating, 240–241
grouping
 date values, 128–129
 numeric values, 128–129
 PivotTable values, 128–130

related data, 24–26
text values, 130
time values, 128–129
Grouping dialog box, 128–129
GROWTH function, 216–218

H

header row, 320
headers, 57
highlighting
 cells, 10–11
 cells based on formulas, 19–20
 top/bottom values in ranges, 13–14
histogram, 258, 320
Histogram dialog box, 259

I

icon sets
 analyzing cell values with, 16–17
 defined, 320
icons, explained, 3
IF function, 19
Import Data dialog box, 80, 83–84, 84–85, 89–90, 97, 187–188
importing. *See also* exporting
 data from Access tables, 80–81
 data from web pages, 86–88
 data from Word tables, 81–82
 defined, 321
 delimited text files, 83–84
 external data, 80–90
 external data tables, 187–189
 fixed-width text files, 84–86
 related tables from external data sources, 193–194
 text files, 82–83
 XML files, 88–90
independent variable, 321
Index calculation, 147–148
index summary calculations, 147–148
indicators icon sets, 17

creating relationships between tables with, 197–199

managing data models with, 192–199

power trend, 322

power trend lines, plotting, 220–221

PPMT function, 297

present value

calculating, 295

defined, 322

preserving PivotTable formatting, 311–312

primary key, 322. *See also* secondary key; sort; tertiary key

principal, calculating, 297

probability distribution, 323

probability distribution function, 323. *See also* probability distribution

probability distributions, 287–288. *See also* normal distributions; uniform distributions

Product calculation, 138

programs, data from other, 79–80

PV function, 295

Q

Query Wizard, 91, 94–97, 323

Query Wizard-Choose Columns dialog box, 94–95

Query Wizard-Filter Data dialog box, 95–96

Query Wizard-Finish dialog box, 96–97, 122

Query Wizard-Sort Order dialog box, 96

query/querying

building PivotTables from, 122–123

data sources, 94–97

defined, 323

external databases, 90–97

R

R². *See* coefficient of determination

RAND function, 255

RANDBETWEEN function, 255

Random Number Generation dialog box, 256–257

Random Number Generator tool, 256–257

random numbers, generating, 255–257

Range measure, 248

ranges

converting Excel tables to, 61

converting to Excel tables, 58–60

highlighting top/bottom values in, 13–14

rank, 253–254, 323. *See also* percentile

Rank and Percentile dialog box, 253–254

RANK.AVG function, 236–238, 246, 253

RANK.EQ function, 236–238, 246, 253

RATE function, 298–299

ratings icon sets, 17

raw data, 8, 323

RDBMS (relational database management system), 122

recalculating data tables, 37

records

defined, 323

filtering in Excel tables, 67–68

sorting in Excel tables, 64–67

refreshing

data models, 198–199

pivot data, 323

PivotTable data, 125–126

regression, determining, 269–271

regression analysis, 323

Regression dialog box, 269–271

regression equation, 205, 323

relational database, 323. *See also* table

relational database management system (RDBMS), 122

relationships

creating between tables, 186–187

creating between tables with Power Pivot, 197–199

types, 186

viewing details, 196–197

relative reference, 323. *See also* absolute reference

Remember icon, 3

removing

conditional formatting rules, 21–22

fields in PivotCharts, 164

renaming PivotTables, 312

report filters, 131–132, 132–133

TABLE function, 36

Table Import Wizard dialog box, 193–194

table row, 57

tables, 324

tables, data

about, 32

adding top data models, 193

basing PivotTables on multiple, 189–192

compared with Excel tables, 32

creating, 32–36

creating relationships between, with Power Pivot, 197–199

importing external, 187–189

importing from external data sources, 193–194

recalculating, 37

skipping, 37

viewing table relationships, 195–196

tables, Excel

about, 55

adding column subtotals in, 63–64

analyzing information in, 61–76

applying advanced filters in, 72–76

applying multiple filters, 71

applying predefined AutoFilters, 69–71

building, 57–61

building PivotCharts from, 166–169

building PivotTables from, 119–121

clearing filters, 68

compared with data tables, 32

converting ranges to, 58–60

converting to ranges, 61

creating relationships between, 186–187

filtering records, 67–68

maintenance of, 60–61

resizing, 61

retrieving values from, 101–102

sorting records, 64–67

turning off AutoFilter, 68–69

uses for, 55–57

tags, 88–90

target cell, 44

Technical Stuff icon, 3

techniques

about, 7

conditional formatting, 9–22

consolidating data from multiple worksheets, 26–29

grouping related data, 24–26

summarizing data with subtotals, 22–24

tertiary key, 324. *See also* primary key; secondary key; sort

text files

defined, 324

as external data, 78

importing, 82–83

text labels, 324

Text Options tab (PivotCharts), 177

text values, grouping, 130

three-color scales, 16

time values, grouping, 128–129

Tip icon, 3

Title Options tab (PivotCharts), 177

titles, PivotChart, 175–177

tools

ANOVA, 274–276

t-test, 264–267

tools, data-analysis

about, 31

data tables, 32–37

Goal Seek, 37–39

Scenarios, 39–43

Solver, 43–53

Top 10 Filter dialog box, 133–134

Top 10 Items dialog box, 13–14

top values, highlighting in ranges, 13–14

top/bottom rule, 13–14, 324

transforming data, 199–200

trend analysis

about, 203

calculating best-fit values, 206–208

calculating exponential trend values, 216–218

calculating forecasted linear values, 212–214

defined, 324

extending linear trends, 210–212

extending linear trends using fill handle, 211

extending linear trends using Series command, 211–212

LINEST, 208

LINEST function, 208

LOGEST, 218

LOGEST function, 218

plotting best-fit trend lines, 204–206

plotting exponential trend lines, 214–216

plotting forecasted values, 208–210

plotting logarithmic trend lines, 218–220

plotting polynomial trend lines, 222–223

plotting power trend lines, 220–221

TREND function, 206–208, 212–214

trendline, 324

t-test tools, 264–267

t-Test: Two-Sample Assuming Equal Variances dialog box, 265–266

turning off

AutoFilter, 68–69

Grand Totals in PivotTables, 312–313

PivotTable Fields Task pane, 304

subtotals for fields in PivotTables, 149

turning on PivotTable Fields Task pane, 304

two-color scales, 16

two-input data tables, 34–36, 325

U

uniform distributions, 255, 287–288, 325

unknowns, 44

updates, for this book, 4

V

Value area

adding fields to, 127

PivotCharts, 163

in PivotTables, 118

value field header, in PivotTables, 118

Value Field Settings dialog box, 139, 141–142, 144, 145–146, 148

value filters, 133–134

values. *See also* formulas; text labels; workbooks

defined, 325

duplicate, 11–12

filtering in PivotTables, 131–135

grouping in PivotTables, 128–130

PivotTable, 314–315

retrieving from tables, 101–102

samples as subsets of, 285

Var calculation, 139

VAR function, 111

VARA function, 111

variable cells, 44

variance. *See also* average; standard deviation

calculating, 241–242

defined, 325

Varp calculation, 139

VARP function, 111

VAR.P function, 241–242

VARPA function, 111

VAR.S function, 241–242

viewing

relationships details, 196–197

table relationships, 195–196

W

Warning icon, 3

Web API, 87

web pages

as external data, 78

importing data from, 86–88

web query, 325

websites

book updates, 4

Cheat Sheet, 3–4

sample workbooks, 3

weighted average, 147, 325

what-if analysis. *See also* data tables

defined, 325

performing, 9

Author Bio

Paul McFedries has been a technical writer for 30 years (no, that is not a typo). He has been messing around with spreadsheet software since installing Lotus 1-2-3 on an IBM PC clone in 1986. He has written more than 100 books (nope, not a typo) that have sold more than four million copies worldwide (again, not a typo). Paul's books include the Wiley titles *Excel All-in-One For Dummies*, *Excel Data Analysis For Dummies*, *Teach Yourself VISUALLY Excel*, and *Teach Yourself VISUALLY Windows 11*. Paul invites everyone to drop by his personal website (`https://paulmcfedries.com`) and to follow him on Twitter (`@paulmcf`) and Facebook (`www.facebook.com/PaulMcFedries/`).

Dedication

To Karen and Chase, who make life fun.

Acknowledgments

If we're ever at the same cocktail party and you overhear me saying something like "I wrote a book," I hereby give you permission to wag your finger at me and say "Tsk, tsk." Why the scolding? Because although I did write this book's text and take its screenshots, those represent only a part of what constitutes a book. The rest of it is brought to you by the dedication and professionalism of Wiley's editing, graphics, and production teams, who toiled long and hard to turn my text and images into an actual book.

I offer my heartfelt thanks to everyone at Wiley who made this book possible, but I'd like to extend some special thank-yous to the folks I worked with directly: Executive Editor Steve Hayes, Project Manager and Copy Editor Susan Pink, and Technical Editor Guy Hart-Davis.

Publisher's Acknowledgments

Executive Editor: Steve Hayes
Project Manager and Copy Editor: Susan Pink
Technical Editor: Guy Hart-Davis
Proofreader: Debbye Butler

Production Editor: Tamilmani Varadharaj
Cover Image: © Pixels Hunter/Shutterstock

Dummies is the global leader in the reference category and one of the most trusted and highly regarded brands in the world. No longer just focused on books, customers now have access to the dummies content they need in the format they want. Together we'll craft a solution that engages your customers, stands out from the competition, and helps you meet your goals.

Advertising & Sponsorships

Connect with an engaged audience on a powerful multimedia site, and position your message alongside expert how-to content. Dummies.com is a one-stop shop for free, online information and know-how curated by a team of experts.

- Targeted ads
- Video
- Email Marketing
- Microsites
- Sweepstakes sponsorship

20 MILLION PAGE VIEWS
EVERY SINGLE MONTH

15 MILLION UNIQUE
VISITORS PER MONTH

43%
OF ALL VISITORS ACCESS THE SITE
VIA THEIR MOBILE DEVICES

700,000 NEWSLETTER SUBSCRIPTIONS
TO THE INBOXES OF

300,000 UNIQUE INDIVIDUALS EVERY WEEK

# of dummies

Custom Publishing

Reach a global audience in any language by creating a solution that will differentiate you from competitors, amplify your message, and encourage customers to make a buying decision.

- Apps
- Books
- eBooks
- Video
- Audio
- Webinars

Brand Licensing & Content

Leverage the strength of the world's most popular reference brand to reach new audiences and channels of distribution.

For more information, visit dummies.com/biz

PERSONAL ENRICHMENT

Staying Sharp

9781119187790
USA $26.00
CAN $31.99
UK £19.99

Facebook

Carolyn Abram

9781119179030
USA $21.99
CAN $25.99
UK £16.99

Guitar

Mark Phillips
Jon Chappell

9781119293354
USA $24.99
CAN $29.99
UK £17.99

Investing

Eric Tyson, MBA

9781119293347
USA $22.99
CAN $27.99
UK £16.99

Beekeeping

Howland Blackiston

9781119310068
USA $22.99
CAN $27.99
UK £16.99

Digital Photography

Julie Adair King

9781119235606
USA $24.99
CAN $29.99
UK £17.99

Meditation

Stephan Bodian

9781119251163
USA $24.99
CAN $29.99
UK £17.99

Pregnancy

9781119235491
USA $26.99
CAN $31.99
UK £19.99

Samsung Galaxy S7

Bill Hughes

9781119279952
USA $24.99
CAN $29.99
UK £17.99

iPhone

Edward C. Baig
Bob "Dr. Mac" LeVitus

9781119283133
USA $24.99
CAN $29.99
UK £17.99

Crocheting

Karen Manthey
Susan Brittain

9781119287117
USA $24.99
CAN $29.99
UK £16.99

Nutrition

Carol Ann Rinzler

9781119130246
USA $22.99
CAN $27.99
UK £16.99

PROFESSIONAL DEVELOPMENT

Windows 10

Andy Rathbone

9781119311041
USA $24.99
CAN $29.99
UK £17.99

AutoCAD

Bill Fane

9781119255796
USA $39.99
CAN $47.99
UK £27.99

Excel 2016

Greg Harvey, PhD

9781119293439
USA $26.99
CAN $31.99
UK £19.99

QuickBooks 2017

9781119281467
USA $26.99
CAN $31.99
UK £19.99

macOS Sierra

Bob "Dr. Mac" LeVitus

9781119280651
USA $29.99
CAN $35.99
UK £21.99

LinkedIn

Joel Elad, MBAs

9781119251132
USA $24.99
CAN $29.99
UK £17.99

Windows 10

Woody Leonhard

9781119310563
USA $34.00
CAN $41.99
UK £24.99

SharePoint 2016

Rosemarie Withee
Ken Withee

9781119181705
USA $29.99
CAN $35.99
UK £21.99

Fundamental Analysis

Matt Krantz

9781119263593
USA $26.99
CAN $31.99
UK £19.99

Networking

Doug Lowe

9781119257769
USA $29.99
CAN $35.99
UK £21.99

Office 2016

Wallace Wang

9781119293477
USA $26.99
CAN $31.99
UK £19.99

Office 365

Rosemarie Withee
Ken Withee
Jennifer Reed

9781119265313
USA $24.99
CAN $29.99
UK £17.99

Salesforce.com

Liz Kao
Jon Paz

9781119239314
USA $29.99
CAN $35.99
UK £21.99

Coding

Nikhil Abraham

9781119293323
USA $29.99
CAN $35.99
UK £21.99

dummies.com

dummies®
A Wiley Brand

Learning Made Easy

ACADEMIC

9781119293576
USA $19.99
CAN $23.99
UK £15.99

9781119293637
USA $19.99
CAN $23.99
UK £15.99

9781119293491
USA $19.99
CAN $23.99
UK £15.99

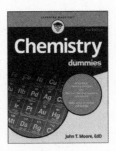

9781119293460
USA $19.99
CAN $23.99
UK £15.99

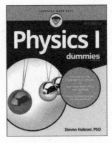

9781119293590
USA $19.99
CAN $23.99
UK £15.99

9781119215844
USA $26.99
CAN $31.99
UK £19.99

9781119293378
USA $22.99
CAN $27.99
UK £16.99

9781119293521
USA $19.99
CAN $23.99
UK £15.99

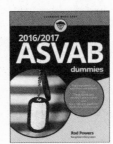

9781119239178
USA $18.99
CAN $22.99
UK £14.99

9781119263883
USA $26.99
CAN $31.99
UK £19.99

Available Everywhere Books Are Sold

dummies.com

Small books for big imaginations

GETTING STARTED WITH Coding
Get Creative with Code!
Camille McCue, PhD

9781119177173
USA $9.99
CAN $9.99
UK £8.99

MODDING Minecraft™
Build Your Own Minecraft Mods!
Sarah Guthals, PhD
Stephen Foster, PhD
Lindsey Handley, PhD

9781119177272
USA $9.99
CAN $9.99
UK £8.99

MAKING YouTube® VIDEOS
Star in Your Own Video!
Nick Willoughby

9781119177241
USA $9.99
CAN $9.99
UK £8.99

DESIGNING Digital Games
Create Games with Scratch™!
Derek Breen

9781119177210
USA $9.99
CAN $9.99
UK £8.99

GETTING STARTED WITH Raspberry Pi™
Program Your Raspberry Pi!
Richard Wentk

9781119262657
USA $9.99
CAN $9.99
UK £6.99

EXPERIMENTING WITH Science
Think, Test, and Learn!
Chris J. Mullins, PhD

9781119291336
USA $9.99
CAN $9.99
UK £6.99

CREATING Digital Animations
Animate Stories with Scratch™!
Derek Breen

9781119233527
USA $9.99
CAN $9.99
UK £6.99

GETTING STARTED WITH Engineering
Think Like an Engineer!
Camille McCue, PhD

9781119291220
USA $9.99
CAN $9.99
UK £6.99

WRITING Computer Code
Learn the Language of Computers!
Chris Minnick and Eva Holland

9781119177302
USA $9.99
CAN $9.99
UK £8.99

Unleash Their Creativity

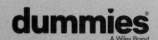